The Complete Guide to

REAL ESTATE
FINANCE for
INVESTMENT
PROPERTIES

The Complete Guide to
REAL ESTATE
FINANCE for
INVESTMENT
PROPERTIES

How to Analyze Any
Single-Family, Multifamily,
or Commercial Property

STEVE BERGES

WILEY

John Wiley & Sons, Inc.

Published by John Wiley & Sons, Inc., Hoboken, New Jersey.

Published simultaneously in Canada.

For general information on our other products and services please contact our Customer Care Department within the United States at (800) 762-2974, outside the United States at (317) 572-3993 or fax (317) 572-4002.

Wiley publishes in a variety of print and electronic formats and by print-on-demand. Some material included with standard print versions of this book may not be included in e-books or in print-on-demand. If this book refers to media such as a CD or DVD that is not included in the version you purchased, you may download this material at http://booksupport.wiley.com. For more information about Wiley products, visit www.wiley.com.

Library of Congress Cataloging-in-Publication Data:

Berges, Steve, 1959–
    The complete guide to real estate finance for investment properties : how to analyze any single-family, multifamily, or commercial property/Steve Berges.
      p. cm.
    Includes index.
    ISBN 0-471-64712-8 (cloth)
    1. Real property—Valuation. 2. Real estate investment—Rate of return. 3. Real property—Finance. 4. Residential real estate—Finance. 5. Apartment houses—Finance. 6. Commercial real estate—Finance. I. Title: Real estate finance for investment properties. II. Title.

HD1387.B397 2004
332.63'24—dc22

10 9 8 7 6 5 4 3 2 1

It has been said that there are angels here among us. This book is dedicated to my sister, Melanie, who is one of them. Angels are special messengers of God who have come to minister to the needs of His children here upon the earth. I have observed my sister's unwavering devotion to her family, friends, and faith throughout her entire life. Not once have I ever heard her complain of the heavy burdens she bears. She has instead chosen to take the high road by walking in faith and humility. She always has a smile on her face and uplifting words of encouragement for my family. I know that the light and joy that radiate from her countenance are truly that of an angel. My heart cries out in gratitude to her. My lips praise her name. My spirit is uplifted because of her. Thank you, Melanie, for your example of love and charity for all of us who are privileged to be a part of your life. Thank you for being an angel here among us.

CONTENTS

▪ Contents ▪

■ Contents ■

The Complete Guide to

REAL ESTATE FINANCE for INVESTMENT PROPERTIES

Part 1

Real Estate Finance

Chapter 1

Introduction to
Real Estate Finance

$\mathbb{A}$s investors continue to migrate from the stock market to the real estate market, the need for sound financial analysis of income-producing properties is greater than ever. Just as buying high-flying stocks with no regard to intrinsic values resulted in hundreds of thousands of investors losing their life savings, so will buying real estate with reckless disregard to property values result in a similar outcome. While an abundance of books have been written on how to buy and sell houses, the market is virtually devoid of any works that specifically address the topic of the principles of valuation as they apply to real estate. Notable exceptions include more expensive titles such as *Real Estate Finance and Investments* by Brueggeman and Fisher, with a list price of $125, and *Commercial Real Estate Analysis and Investments* by Geltner, boasting a list price of $114.

The Complete Guide to Real Estate Finance for Investment Properties: How to Analyze Any Single Family, Multifamily, or Commercial Property focuses on the concepts of financial analysis as they pertain to real estate and is intended to help fill the void that currently exists regarding this subject. This represents a marked contrast from the works previously referred to in three primary ways. First of all, the other works are much more expensive. Second, they have been written to appeal to a different audience in that they are written in a textbook format with both the student and the professional in mind. Finally, the other works deal with advanced theoretical principles of finance, which are of little value to the investor who most likely has no background in finance.

The Complete Guide to Real Estate Finance for Investment Properties, on the other hand, is designed to appeal to those individuals who are actively investing in income-producing properties, as well as to those who desire to invest in them. Furthermore, those same individuals who are now investors will at some point have a need to divest themselves of their holdings. Whether an investor is buying or selling, the basis for all decisions must be founded on the fundamental principles of finance as they apply to real estate valuations. The failure to understand these key principles will almost certainly result in the failure of the individual investor. At a minimum, it will place him or her at a competitive disadvantage among those who do understand them. Recall the myriad of investors who bought stocks for no other reason than that they received a so-called hot tip from a friend or coworker—and who later collectively lost billions of dollars. A similar outcome is almost certain for those individuals investing in real estate who fail to exercise sound valuation principles and act on nothing more than the advice of someone who has no business giving advice, such as a broker with a supposedly hot tip.

The Complete Guide to Real Estate Finance for Investment Properties is further intended to take the theories of real estate finance discussed in other books and demonstrate how they can be used in real-world situations. In other words, it is the practical application of these theories that really matters to investors. An in-depth examination of several case studies will provide the learning platform necessary for investors to make the transition from the theory of real estate finance to its practical application. Investor comprehension will be further augmented through the use of several proprietary financial models developed by me for the sole purpose of making sound investment decisions.

Now that I have established what this book *is* about, I'll take a brief moment to establish what it *is not* about. The term *finance* as used throughout this book is generally intended to refer to principles of financial analysis and not to debt instruments such as loans or mortgages that are used for *financing* real estate. This is not a book about creative methods of borrowing money or structuring nothing-down deals. Hundreds of those types of books are already available, including a few of my own. My purpose in specifically defining what this book is *not* about stems from the misleading titles of some currently very popular real estate books that contain the word *finance* in their titles. Perhaps the phrase "real estate finance" means creative borrowing techniques to the authors who wrote them, but to professionals schooled in the principles of finance, the phrase encompasses a completely different body of knowledge. This is not to say, however, that financing mechanisms are not discussed in this book, for they certainly are. Debt and equity instruments are discussed out of necessity, as their respective costs must be properly understood for the purpose of measuring returns and values, as well as evaluating the implications of using different types of financial instruments for different types of transactions.

This book is organized into three parts, beginning with Part 1, which examines the principles of real estate finance. Chapter 1 introduces the world of financial analysis as it applies to real estate investments. Chapter 2 focuses on primary investment elements and their effect on financing. Chapter 3 then centers on secondary investment elements, and Chapter 4 focuses on still other investment elements and their impact on financing. Chapter 5 shifts to an examination of the various types of debt and equity instruments available and their impact on returns. Chapter 6 includes a discussion on various investment performance measurements and ratios, including return on investment, capitalization ratio, and debt service coverage ratio. Chapter 7 is devoted to a more advanced analysis of real estate investments and includes topics such as understanding present value and future value concepts, internal rate of return (IRR), calculations, and modern real estate portfolio theory. Chapter 8 explores the realm of the three most commonly used valuation methods for the different classes of real estate. Chapter 9 provides a discussion on financial statements, including how to more fully understand them and how you can use them to make prudent buy-and-sell decisions.

Part 2 takes most of the information discussed in Part 1 and uses it in a case study format. Chapter 10 examines real estate finance as it applies to the valuation of single-family houses. Chapter 11 provides an in-depth look at converting property from one use to another. Chapter 12 is a case study that examines a multifamily apartment complex and walks the reader through a comprehensive analysis. Finally, Chapter 13 demonstrates how understanding finance and the different valuation methods can provide significant opportunities to create value for the astute investor by converting a single-family property into a commercial office building.

Part 3 consists of an epilogue containing words of inspiration and several motivating ideas, appendixes, and an extensive glossary.

FINANCE AS A DISCIPLINE

If you are a business student, the first two years of college for both accounting and finance majors are nearly identical. Each requires the basic English, history, math, and general business studies. By the third year of college, however, the two disciplines begin to chart separate courses. While both subjects deal with numbers and money, they are quite different in the way they do so.

The accounting discipline, for example, centers on principles used primarily for bookkeeping purposes and is based on a body of rules referred to as the *generally accepted accounting principles* (GAAP). Although there is some disagreement by scholars of many of the more advanced rulings, the principles established in GAAP are nevertheless to be firmly applied and adhered to when recording entries. As a general rule, the accounting principles are rigid rules that must be applied for bookkeeping and tax purposes.

The discipline of finance, on the other hand, centers more on the valuation and use of money than on record keeping. Finance is an exploration into the world of micro- and macroeconomic conditions that impact the value of a business's assets, liabilities, and investments. While there are certainly rules and laws that govern the principles of finance, it is a subject that remains fluid and dynamic. The expansion and contraction of businesses live and die by those who understand these laws and their effect on value.

Professors Lawrence Schall and Charles Haley, authors of *Intro-duction to Financial Management* (New York: McGraw-Hill, 1988, p. 10), further expound on the discipline of finance by asserting that "Finance is a body of facts, principles, and theories dealing with the raising (for example, by borrowing) and using of money by individuals, businesses, and governments." In part, finance deals with the raising of funds to be used for investment purposes to help these various types of entities generate a return on their capital. In addition, the authors state (ibid., pp. 10–11):

The individual's financial problem is to maximize his or her well-being by appropriately using the resources avail-able. Finance deals with how individuals divide their income between consumption (food, clothes, etc.) and investment (stocks, bonds, real estate, etc.), how they choose from among available investment opportunities, and how they raise money to provide for increased con-sumption or investment.

Firms also have the problem of allocating resources and raising money. Management must determine which invest-ments to make and how to finance those investments. Just as the individual seeks to maximize his or her happiness, the firm seeks to maximize the wealth of its owners (stock-holders).

Finance also encompasses the study of financial markets and institutions, and the activities of governments, with stress on those aspects relating to the financial decisions of individuals and companies. A familiarity with the limita-tions and opportunities provided by the institutional envi-ronment is crucial to the decision-making process of individuals and firms. In addition, financial institutions and governments have financial problems comparable to those of individuals and firms. The study of these problems is an important part of the field of finance.

There you have it. Professors Schall and Haley have outlined some of the fundamental issues that financial managers in both private and public sectors deal with on an ongoing basis. Raising capital, whether debt or equity, is essential to the successful operation of a firm. What is even more essential is the proper management of that capital.

I recall very distinctly during my sophomore year of college being faced with the decision of choosing the accounting or finance discipline. At the time, I didn't know any accountants and I didn't know any financial analysts, so I wasn't quite sure whom to turn to. What I did know, however, was that most of my colleagues were choosing the accounting route and encouraged me to do so as well. After all, that's where all the jobs were, according to them. I didn't really care if that's where all the jobs were. All I cared about was becoming fully engrossed in a field in which I would be the happiest.

My assessment of accounting was that it was rather dry and boring. Accounting represented mundane and repetitive tasks governed by a rigid set of principles. It was the recording of a company's income and assets that reflected its value at that specific moment in time. This is typically referred to in accounting circles as a "snapshot in time." Quite frankly, snapshots bored me. I was more interested in making movies than in taking pictures. Finance opens up an entire world of possibilities that accounting can't even dream of. It takes the snapshot made by accountants and brings it to life by exploring the vast universe not of what a company is, but rather, that of what it can become. Finance scrutinizes every strength and weakness of the photograph to measure its true potential. It exhausts every possibility to breathe the breath of life into it. Finance is an exciting field that allows individuals to use all of the creative faculties inherent within them to grow in ways limited only by one's imagination.

I can only wonder whether my colleagues who chose the accounting field are happy in their profession. As for me, I chose the road less traveled and haven't looked back since. Some 20 years or so later, I can say with all the sincerity of my heart that for me it was the right choice. I should add that it is not my intent to offend those of you who may be accountants or to demean your role as a professional in any way, as reports generated by accountants provide valuable information for both internal and external users of financial statements. My assessment of the accounting profession represents exactly that—my assessment.

THE RELEVANCE OF FINANCE AS IT APPLIES TO VALUE

In Chapter 4 of *The Complete Guide to Investing in Rental Properties* (New York: McGraw-Hill, 2004), I described my zeal for finance, along with a portion of my background, as follows:

> Let me begin this chapter by emphatically stating that I thoroughly enjoy the subject of finance, and in particular as it applies to real estate. Finance and real estate are the two greatest passions of my professional life. For as long as I can remember, I have always been fascinated with money. This fascination eventually helped shape my course in life as I later majored in finance in both my undergraduate and graduate studies.
>
> After graduating, I had the opportunity to work as a financial analyst at one of the largest banks in Texas. As part of the mergers and acquisitions group, my work there centered around analyzing potential acquisition targets for the bank. One way companies grow is by acquiring smaller companies that do the same thing they do. This is especially true of banks. Big banks merge with other big banks, and they buy, or acquire, other banks that are usually, but not always, smaller than they are. I believe our bank was at the time about $11 billion strong in total assets. It was my job to analyze banks which typically ranged in size from about $25 million up to as much as about $2 billion. I used a fairly complex and sophisticated model to properly assess the value of the banks. This experience provided me with a comprehensive understanding of cash flow analysis which I later applied to real estate.

Like many of you, in my earlier years, I owned and managed rental properties and read just about every new real estate book that came out. They all seemed to be saying the same thing, with only slight variations in theme, some delving into nothing-down techniques while others focused on slowly accumulating a portfolio of properties, gradually building a level of cash flow sufficient to provide a living, otherwise known as the *buy-and-hold approach.*

The more I read, the more I discovered that none of these books focused on what matters most in real estate, that being the accumulation of properties that are properly valued, as well as their subsequent disposition, with the difference being sufficient enough to allow investors the opportunity to profit. Proponents of the buy-and-hold strategy would argue that because the holding period extends over many years, price doesn't matter as long as an investor can purchase real estate with favorable enough terms. Nothing could be further from the truth. It is precisely this kind of misinformation that led thousands, if not millions, of investors over the cliff in the collapse of the stock market in the three-year period that began in the year 2000.

Price didn't matter as long as it was going up and the terms were good. Since value is a function of the price paid, and price didn't matter, value didn't matter, either. Investors overextended themselves buying on margin and otherwise using borrowed funds with absolutely no regard for an asset's value. Most of these investors probably had no conceptual basis for their purchase decisions to begin with. In the end, many of those same investors watched in horror as their life savings evaporated right before their very eyes.

Although I had bought and sold real estate for a number of years prior to my experience at the bank, it wasn't until I gained a more complete understanding of the principles of finance learned during my graduate studies and my tenure at the bank that I was able to significantly accelerate my investment goals. I developed my own proprietary financial models, which enabled me to more fully analyze an asset's value based on its cash flows and price relationship to similar assets. The combination of these financial analysis tools and a sound understanding of valuation principles has allowed me to increase my personal real estate investment activities from a meager $25,000 a year in volume to a projected $8 to $10 million this year alone. Through duplication and expansion, which are part of a well-defined plan, I fully expect to increase these projections to buy and sell over $100 million in real estate annually within the next three to five years. This may be a bit aggressive for most investors, but I can see this level of activity in my mind's eye just as clearly and vividly as the sun shining in all its glory on a midsummer's day. The pieces are already being put into place to help me achieve this not-too-distant objective.

Achieving goals of this magnitude exemplifies the difference between the finance and accounting disciplines. The world of finance can unlock the doors of commerce in a way that most accounting professionals can only dream of. A working knowledge of the principles of cash flow analysis coupled with a comprehension of valuation analysis will allow investors to chart their own course in the real estate industry—or any other industry for that matter.

Chapter 2

Primary Investment Elements and Their Effect on Financing Strategies

To achieve the magnitude of investment activity referred to in my own personal example in Chapter 1, an investor must have clearly defined goals. The goals you establish will directly impact your financing strategies. Three primary financing elements around which all real estate investment activity centers are time, volume, and the type of property (see Exhibit 2.1). Once you have determined your time horizon, the rate at which you intend to buy and sell, along with the type of real estate you will invest in, the proper financial instruments may then be put in place.

TIME HORIZON

Most real estate professionals incorporate the element of *time* into their investment strategy. The element of time refers to the duration of the holding period. In other words, it is the length of time a particular piece of investment property is intended to be held. While some investors, for example, prefer to adopt a short-term approach by "flipping" or "rehabbing" houses, other investors prefer to adopt an intermediate-term approach, which includes buying, managing,

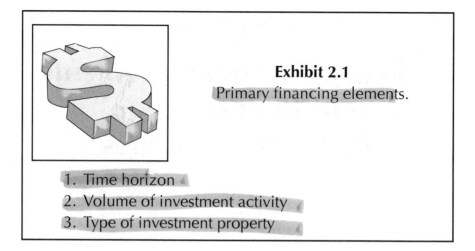

Exhibit 2.1
Primary financing elements.

1. Time horizon
2. Volume of investment activity
3. Type of investment property

and holding rental property for three to five years. Still others prefer to purchase office or industrial buildings and hold them for periods as long as 10, 20, or even 30 years. Establishing your investment horizon before obtaining financing is crucial to developing a sound strategy. You must know beforehand if you are going to hold the property for just a short time, for many years, or for somewhere in between, since the variable of time is used to calculate interest rates. Time will also have an impact on whether you obtain a floating rate or a fixed-rate loan, as well as any prepayment penalties that may be associated with the loan.

In *The Complete Guide to Flipping Properties* (New Jersey: John Wiley & Sons, 2004), I elaborated on the element of time as follows:

Time can have a significant impact on the growth rate of your real estate portfolio. Time affects such things as the tax rate applied to your gain or loss. The long term capital gains tax rate has historically been more favorable than the short term tax rate. Time is also the variable in the rate of inventory turnover. Large retailers are willing to accept lower profit margins on items they merchandise in exchange for a higher inventory turnover rate. Would you rather earn twenty percent on each item, or house, you sell and have a turnover rate of one, or would you rather earn eight percent on each item you sell and have a turnover rate of three? Let's do the math.

$$\text{Turnover ratio} = \frac{\text{turnover}}{\text{years}} = \frac{1}{1} \times 20\% = 20\% = \text{total return}$$

or

$$\text{Turnover ratio} = \frac{\text{turnover}}{\text{years}} = \frac{3}{1} \times 8\% = 24\% = \text{total return}$$

This simple example clearly illustrates that an investor can accept a lower rate of return on each property bought and sold and earn a higher overall rate of return, provided that the frequency, or turnover rate, is increased. I should mention that this example does not, of course, take into consideration transaction costs. These costs may or may not be significant depending on your specific situation, but they must be factored in when analyzing a potential purchase.

Investment time horizons typically fall into one of three categories: *short term, intermediate term,* and *long term.* Short-term investors are defined as those individuals who buy and sell real estate with a shorter duration. They typically hold their investments less than one to two years. This class of investor most often seeks gains by adding value through making improvements to the property, or by taking advantage of market price inefficiencies, which may be caused by any number of factors, including distress sales from the loss of a job, a family crisis such as divorce, or perhaps a death in the family. The shorter holding period does not allow enough time for gains through natural price appreciation caused by supply and demand issues or inflationary pressures.

The short-term investor may furthermore seek to profit by using the higher-inventory-turnover strategy and, as a result, may be willing to accept smaller returns, but with greater frequency, thus realizing an overall rate of return considerably higher than the long-term approach, as demonstrated previously. Since current tax codes penalize short-term investors by imposing higher tax rates on short-term capital gains, they must factor this into their analysis before ever purchasing a property.

The proper financing mechanism is also a key part of an investor's analysis. In a short-term strategy, an investor can often take advantage of a loan with a more favorable floating or adjustable rate as opposed to a longer-term fixed-rate loan. In addition, depending on the type of financial instrument procured, principal payments may not be required. This provision allows an investor to minimize his or her outgoing cash flow by making interest-only payments. Cash flow is the name of the game in real estate. Learn to use it to your benefit. Finally, you should be aware of any prepayment penalties that may be imposed on short-term financing. Banks are especially notorious for assessing this additional type of fee income on a loan. Their decision to do so is based on the premise that since the loan is short term in nature, they must charge additional fees to offset their other costs associated with making the loan, such as administrative costs. That argument, however, is the same one lenders use to justify charging a loan-origination fee, which is typically one point, or 1 percent. If you have a good track record and are an established investment professional, prepayment penalties can usually be negotiated down to a minimum, and oftentimes will be waived all together.

Intermediate-term investors most often hold their properties for at least two years but no more than five years. This class of investor typically seeks gains through a combination of increases in property values, resulting from price appreciation due to supply and demand constraints in the local market, and by making modest improvements to the property. Reducing debt to increase cash flow is not as high a priority for intermediate-term investors as it is for their long-term counterparts. This class of investor also tends to be more highly leveraged than do long-term investors. Finally, since intermediate-term investors hold their investment properties for a minimum of two years, they are able to take advantage of the lower and more favorable long-term capital gains tax rate. As the tax laws are currently written, income derived from the sale of assets with a holding period shorter than 18 months will be treated as ordinary income and therefore subject to a higher tax rate.

Once again, the proper financing mechanism is a key part of an investor's analysis. In an intermediate-term strategy, an individual can, like the short-term investor, take advantage of a more favorable floating-rate loan. If the time horizon is firmly established as one that will not exceed five years, I recommend using floating-rate instruments in most cases, since they almost always carry lower interest rates than do fixed-rate loans. The exception to this recommendation is, however, that if rates are forecast to rise in the near future, it may be better to lock in a fixed rate now than to run the risk of rapidly increasing rates. Similarly to short-term financial instruments, you may be able to obtain a loan in which principal payments are not required.

Depending on the needs of the seller, you may even be able to negotiate a deal in which no periodic payments whatsoever are required. This includes both principal and interest. I've used this technique myself; as a matter of fact, I very recently closed on a land deal valued at $3.3 million that will not require any periodic principal or interest payments. The seller agreed to carry the note and allow the interest to accrue. The interest will become payable at the time individual lots from the land are released, which occurs when my company, Symphony Homes, builds a house on it (see Appendix B). At that time, a construction loan is obtained to pay both the accrued interest and the principal balance to the seller. Interest-only payments are then made to the bank over the next four months or so until the house is completed and sold.

Long-term investors may purchase real estate properties and keep them in the family for generations. They will typically hold them for a minimum of five years, but oftentimes much longer. Long-term investors seek gains through capital appreciation by simply holding and maintaining their investments while making improvements on an as-needed basis. They sometimes seek to minimize the associated debt and maximize the cash flow generated by the property through an acceleration of both interest and principal payments. Although in the short term, investors adopting this strategy will decrease the property's cash flow by making larger monthly payments, they will eventually increase its cash flow by eliminating the debt altogether. As a result, long-term investors are usually not fully leveraged. They generally prefer the positive cash flow to being excessively leveraged. Long-term investors are able to take advantage of the more favorable long-term capital gains tax rates when they do eventually decide to sell. In addition, long-term investors may elect to take advantage of deferring the tax liability indefinitely through a provision outlined in the Internal Revenue Code referred to as a 1031 exchange.

Investors adopting a long-term strategy will most likely desire to insulate themselves from variations that occur in a sometimes volatile interest rate environment by locking in fixed-rate loans at the time of purchase. However, like short-term investors, they can take advantage of more favorable floating-rate loans. Depending on the type of financing instrument used, long-term investors may or may not be subject to prepayment penalties. Some debt instruments, such as conduit loans, carry heavy prepayment penalties in the early years. Conduit loans are reserved for larger income-producing properties and usually have a minimum loan amount of $1 million, although smaller loans are available. A complex prepayment penalty is almost always imposed on these types of loans, since the loans are securitized and then sold to investors. The prepayment penalties are used to ensure that investors who buy the loans are guaranteed a minimum yield on their related investment.

VOLUME OF INVESTMENT ACTIVITY

The element of *volume* is the second significant factor that affects an investor's strategy and the type of financing to be used. For example, increasing the volume of units bought and sold, or *flipped,* increases the investor's opportunity to generate profits. By the same token, increasing the volume of units bought, managed, and held in a portfolio increases the investor's opportunity to generate income.

Increasing the volume, however, can significantly increase your transaction costs, especially if you're a short-term investor. If, for example, the lender charges you one or two points every time you obtain a loan for a house you're going to flip, the costs for financing can add up quickly and will significantly increase the annualized rate of interest. Let's look at an example. Assume you are purchasing a house for $100,000 to rehab and then flip. Let's also assume that you're pretty good at doing this and that the average time it takes you to buy, rehab, and sell a property is three months.

Purchase price = $100,000
Interest rate = 6.0%
Loan-origination fee = 1.0%
Turnaround time = 3 months
Interest paid = $100,000 × 6.0% ÷ 12 × 3 = $1,500
Loan-origination fee = $100,000 × 1.0% = $1,000
Total interest and fees = $1,500 + $1,000 = $2,500
Effective interest rate = ($2,500 ÷ $100,000) ÷ 3 × 12 = 10.0%

As illustrated in this example, although the stated interest rate of 6.0 percent would be considered a very competitive rate for most investors, the effective rate of 10.0 percent is not nearly as competitive. In fact, in a 6.0 percent interest rate environment, many investors would not walk, but would instead *run* out of the bank if the lender told them the interest rate would be 10.0 percent.

Okay, so maybe $1,000 isn't a deal killer for this particular investment, but now let's factor in volume. Instead of buying just one house per year, assume you have assembled a team of individuals to work with you and have increased your volume to 100 houses per year. The $1,000 in additional fees has now become $100,000. Who wants to leave $100,000 on the table for the lender? Nobody, that's who (besides the lender).

The best way to eliminate fees of this type is by negotiating with your lender for a line of credit. A line of credit will provide you with a predetermined amount of money to draw against to finance not only the purchase of the houses, but also the repair work that will be needed as well. A line of credit is just like a credit card, but with a much higher limit. An investor can borrow as much as needed up to the predetermined credit limit. Since funds are borrowed only as they are needed, this helps to reduce the overall carrying costs the investor otherwise might incur.

I should add that, as a general rule, lenders will not extend a line of credit to anyone who does not have a solid financial statement, which includes strong cash reserves. Lines of credit are most often unsecured, which means the lender has no collateral. The terms *lender* and *no collateral* mix together about as well as water mixes with oil. One could arguably draw the conclusion that lenders must be insecure, since they always want some type of security. I suppose that might be stretching it a bit, though. In reality, lenders just want to protect their interests. When they loan money, they like to get something of value in return to hold as collateral just in case the borrower defaults. With an unsecured line of credit, the lender has no such protection, and that is exactly why it is difficult to get unsecured loans.

Although you may not be able to get an unsecured line of credit, you may be able to start with a secured line of credit by offering the lender some type of collateral. Forms of collateral you may be able to offer include equity in any type of asset you own, such as the following:

- Your personal residence
- Investment property you may own and have equity in
- Business property such as an office building or equipment
- Notes payable to you that are secured by an asset (for instance, from owner-financed sales)
- Financial instruments such as stocks, bonds, certificates of deposit, and annuities
- Retirement accounts (only if the lender can secure an interest in them, though)
- Precious metals such as gold, silver, and platinum
- Personal assets such as boats, automobiles, jewelry, and furnishings

Once investors have proven to a lender that they are capable of repaying loans on a timely basis, the lender may gradually become more comfortable with extending larger lines of credit. This will depend in large part on an investor's own personal financial strength.

If lenders determine that particular investors are tapped out and have depleted their cash reserves, those lenders may not be willing to lend them anything. It's all about building relationships and trust over an extended period of time. It doesn't happen overnight, but it will happen as long as an investor is able to prove that he or she is responsible and trustworthy.

TYPE OF PROPERTY

The *type of property* an investor purchases is the third primary element that affects an investor's strategy and the type of financing to be used. Property types that produce income are most commonly classified as single-family, multifamily, or commercial. The type of loan obtained for any real estate property will largely be determined by the type of property being purchased. Financial institutions provide an array of products that are suited for particular investment types.

The term *single-family property* is a bit misleading, as it actually encompasses all real estate with at least one living unit and not more than four living units. In other words, a house, as well as a duplex, triplex, and fourplex, are all classified as single-family properties as far as lenders are concerned. Because single-family properties are by far the most common of the three types, mortgages are readily available for them from most financial institutions.

Loan provisions for single-family properties will of course vary from lender to lender. By either shopping around yourself or using the services of a mortgage broker, you can easily compare the alternatives available among conventional lenders and select the one that best meets your needs. In *The Complete Guide to Investing in Rental Properties* (New York: McGraw-Hill, 2004), I elaborated in considerable detail on the intricacies of financing for single-family properties. Following is an excerpt taken from Chapter 5.

Conventional bank financing is often available through small local banks. These types of banks may operate with just one or two branches and have a small deposit base of only $15 to $20 million, or they may be somewhat larger with as many as five to ten branches and $200 million in deposits. One primary advantage to using a local bank is that they can often provide borrowers with more flexibility than more conventional sources such as a mortgage company. Local banks may, for example, loan money to purchase a rental property as well as to make improvements to it.

Small local banks are also much more likely to be familiar with the local area and would therefore have a greater degree of confidence in the specific market than a larger regional or national lender would. A personal relationship with a local banker is much easier to establish also than with other types of lenders such as conventional mortgage companies. In a local bank where decisions are made in part based upon these relationships, an investor can go into a bank, introduce himself, and speak directly with the lender. This affords investors with an opportunity to sell themselves as well as their project. Once a relationship has been established and the banker gets to know you and is comfortable with you, future loan requests will be much easier and will likely require less documentation, possibly as little as updating your personal financial statement.

Local banks are one of many sources available to finance single-family properties. Additional alternatives you may wish to consider include obtaining a mortgage, using an existing line of credit, or having the seller carry all or part of the note. You may also want to consider using an option agreement, which is more fully explained in Chapter 5.

Financing for multifamily properties typically involves using a network of institutional lenders or investors different from those mortgage companies that provide financing for single-family properties. Remember, the primary criterion that separates the two property types is the number of units. Single-family housing is considered to be anything from one to four units, whereas multifamily properties are those with five or more units. In *The Complete Guide to Buying and Selling Apartments* (New Jersey: John Wiley & Sons, 2004), I described several of the lending programs available to multifamily investors. Following is an excerpt from Chapter 7.

Specialty apartment lending programs are designed specifically with the small multifamily investor in mind. They are the product of listening to feedback from investors such as yourself and have been streamlined and tailored especially for borrowers in the apartment business. In addition, since many lenders focus on the larger-sized loans, these programs were devised to serve a once overlooked segment of the apartment lending business. Interest rates for this type of loan are usually very competitive and typically below prime. Loan amounts vary according to the underwriting guidelines established by each lender, but generally range from approximately $100,000 to $2,000,000.

A variety of terms are offered, including one, three, five, seven, and ten years. Amortization periods are commonly 20 or 25 years, with some lenders offering 30-year periods. Other advantages of this type of loan include lender fees, which are kept to a minimum, and third-party report requirements, which are often not as stringent. A primary disadvantage of the specialty apartment lending programs is that the maximum loan amount is usually around $2 million. Since this type of loan was designed with the smaller investor in mind, the maximum loan amounts are capped at lower levels.

This excerpt was written when the prime lending rate hovered around 7½ percent, which, believe it or not, was not that long ago. Since the current prime lending rate is a historically low 4 percent, specialty apartment programs are no longer priced below prime. They do, however, remain at very competitive rates and provide attractive terms and conditions designed specifically to meet the needs of the small multifamily investor.

For larger real estate investments such as office buildings, retail strip centers, or large-scale apartment complexes, the financial instruments used become more sophisticated and complex. One commonly used financing mechanism is referred to as a *conduit loan.* Conduit loans are typically originated by large institutional firms, such as insurance companies, which usually have hundreds of millions, or even billions, of dollars in investment capital. Once again, referring to *The Complete Guide to Buying and Selling Apartments,* I described in part the nature of conduit loans as they apply to multifamily unit financing:

> Conduit financing differs from conventional bank loans in several ways. First, conduit loans are pooled together when a certain dollar amount is reached, say $500 million. They are then "securitized" or packaged together and sold to investors who seek to maintain a specific yield or return on their capital. Since the loans are pooled together, it is very difficult to pay off a single loan out of the pool prior to the end of the term, and in many cases, the borrower is "locked out" or prohibited from prepaying the loan. Conventional bank loans, on the other hand, are not securitized but are instead treated as individual loans and maintained and serviced directly by the issuing bank.
>
> Another key difference is that unlike conventional bank loans, which are priced off of the prime lending rate, conduit loans are generally priced off of an index such as Treasury notes, which correspond to the term of the loan. A loan with a 10-year term, for example, may use the 10-year Treasury as its benchmark. A spread is then factored into the rate by adding the spread to the 10-year Treasury. Spreads are stated in "basis points," so a spread of 215 basis points is equivalent to 2.15 percent. If the 10-year Treasury is currently priced at 5.30 and the spread is 215 basis points (or "bips" as lenders like to call them), then the interest rate applied to the loan would be 7.45 percent. Conduit loans also differ from conventional bank loans in the degree of personal liability associated with each type. With conduit loans, there is usually no personal liability while there is almost always full personal liability for conventional bank financing.

After completing two or three smaller-scale commercial or multi-family purchases using a more traditional financing mechanism such as a conventional bank loan, you should be ready to accept the challenge of the more sophisticated conduit loans. Remember, too, that conduit loans are designed for investments with a longer holding period and therefore would not be suitable for a fix and flip type of application.

In summary, the three elements of time, volume, and property type must all be considered collectively rather than individually. For example, the financing instrument used for an Investor A, who acquires single-family property to hold on a long-term basis, is very different than that for Investor B, who purchases single-family property to buy and sell on a short-term basis. While Investor A purchases one property each year to hold for many years, Investor B purchases 50 properties each year and holds them just long enough to rehab and flip them. Although both investors are purchasing similar types of properties, the financing mechanisms for each investor are very different. Investor A will most likely get a 30-year conventional mortgage to finance his property, and Investor B will most likely use a line of credit to finance her activities. The same principles hold true for investors purchasing multifamily and commercial property. In fact, a change in any one of the three variables will have a direct effect on the financial instrument used in your investment activities. The more familiar you become with the interaction that occurs among these three variables, the better able you will be to use them to your advantage.

Chapter 3

Secondary Investment Elements and Their Effect on Financing Strategies

In Chapter 2, we examined the three primary financing elements around which all real estate investment activity centers. They are the elements of time, volume, and property type. In this chapter, we discuss the three secondary investment elements that affect real estate financing activities. They are the cost of funds, the amortization period, and the amount of funds borrowed (see Exhibit 3.1). It is essential for individuals to understand how each of these three variables affects the profitability of the various types of real estate investments. A material change of any one of the three elements would change the cash flow of the property. For income-producing properties, asset value is derived directly from the net income of the property, so a change in any one of the three secondary elements may have an impact on its value, whether negative or positive. With the proper financial model, an investor can easily assess the impact of changes in value by experimenting with these three elements, or variables.

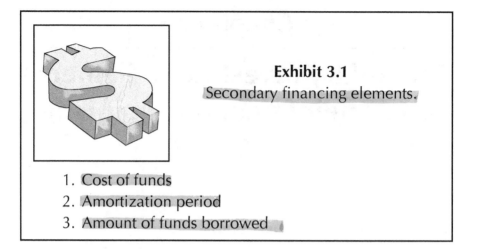

Exhibit 3.1
Secondary financing elements.

1. Cost of funds
2. Amortization period
3. Amount of funds borrowed

COST OF FUNDS

The *cost of funds* is the first of the three secondary financing elements that affect real estate financing and, consequently, real estate value. The cost to borrow funds is expressed in terms of an *interest rate* and represents the portion of the loan payment that the lender charges for loaning money. Changes in the interest rate charged to purchase income-producing property have a direct effect on the property's value. In Chapter 8, we explore in great detail the three primary appraisal methods, one of which is the *income capitalization method.* This appraisal method rests on the premise that a stream of income can be converted into a single capital value. If there is a reduction in the stream of income, the capital value must likewise be reduced. An increase to any degree in the cost of funds borrowed would have a negative effect on an investment property's income stream and would subsequently reduce its capital value.

The cost of funds, or interest rate, varies widely among lenders. Both banks and mortgage companies tend to be fairly competitive, as do conduit lenders. Banks typically offer loans for shorter durations and price their loans using the prime lending rate as the benchmark. Mortgage companies, on the other hand, often offer loans for longer durations and price them using an index such as Treasury bills or the London Interbank Offered Rate (LIBOR). Likewise, conduit loans are also benchmarked off Treasury bills. The loan is priced according to a spread, which is added to the term of a Treasury note and which corresponds to the term of the loan. In other words, a loan with a 10-year term is priced by adding a spread to a 10-year Treasury note. Spreads are stated in what is referred to as *basis points.* A spread of 185 basis points is equivalent to 1.85 percent. If the 10-year Treasury is currently priced at 4.30 and the spread is 185 basis points, then the interest rate applied to the loan would be 6.15 percent.

The interest paid on borrowed money represents the cost of funds, so the higher the rate, the greater the amount paid. On a smaller loan of, let's say, $100,000, a difference of 0.5 percent in the interest rate will have only minimal impact on the viability of an investment opportunity. On a larger loan of $1 million, however, the difference of 0.5 percent is much greater. When applying for a loan, you should make every effort to negotiate the best possible rate, especially on larger loans. I recently met with one of the lenders with whom my company, Symphony Homes, does business to review our financial statements from the previous fiscal year and to plan for the coming year. Since I do several million dollars' worth of business with this lender each year, I don't hesitate to ask for better pricing. I reminded him that our company works with several other lenders who are eager to earn more of our business. My expectation is that he will soon be giving me a call with more favorable pricing.

To help better understand the impact of various differences in changes in the interest rate, take a moment to review Table 3.1. Using a real estate loan calculator developed for Symphony Homes, the effect of changes in interest rates can be examined on a base loan of $2.5 million. The loan spread matrix illustrates how changes in the rate affect changes in the monthly payments. With a loan amount of $2.5 million and a rate of 6.25 percent, the monthly payment would be $15,392.93. By reducing the rate by 0.5 percent, the payment is reduced to $14,589.32, which represents a monthly savings of $803.61 and an annual savings of $9,643.32 to the investor. The matrix allows you to quickly and easily examine the effect of changes in rate applied to different loan amounts at different rates.

Table 3.1 Chart of Monthly Payments

Symphony Homes, Inc. www.symphony-homes.com
The Value Play www.thevalueplay.com

Loan Amount: $2,500,000.00
Interest Rate: 6.25%
Term: 360 months

Total Interest Paid: $3,041,454.80
Total Amount Paid: $5,541,454.80

Loan / Rate	Loan Amounts Incremented by $5000			Interest Rates Incremented by $^{1}/_{2}$%			
	4.75%	5.25%	5.75%	6.25%	6.75%	7.25%	7.75%
$2,475,000	$12,910.77	$13,667.04	$14,443.43	$15,239.00	$16,052.80	$16,883.86	$17,731.20
$2,480,000	$12,936.85	$13,694.65	$14,472.61	$15,269.79	$16,085.23	$16,917.97	$17,767.02
$2,485,000	$12,962.94	$13,722.26	$14,501.79	$15,300.57	$16,117.66	$16,952.08	$17,802.84
$2,490,000	$12,989.02	$13,749.87	$14,530.96	$15,331.36	$16,150.09	$16,986.19	$17,838.66
$2,495,000	$13,015.10	$13,777.48	$14,560.14	$15,362.14	$16,182.52	$17,020.30	$17,874.49
$2,500,000	$13,041.18	$13,805.09	$14,589.32	$15,392.93	$16,214.95	$17,054.41	$17,910.31
$2,505,000	$13,067.27	$13,832.70	$14,618.50	$15,423.72	$16,247.38	$17,088.52	$17,946.13
$2,510,000	$13,093.35	$13,860.31	$14,647.68	$15,454.50	$16,279.81	$17,122.62	$17,981.95
$2,515,000	$13,119.43	$13,887.92	$14,676.86	$15,485.29	$16,312.24	$17,156.73	$18,017.77
$2,520,000	$13,145.51	$13,915.53	$14,706.04	$15,516.07	$16,344.67	$17,190.84	$18,053.59
$2,525,000	$13,171.60	$13,943.14	$14,735.21	$15,546.86	$16,377.10	$17,224.95	$18,089.41

Value Play Real Estate Software, 3.0.01

www.thevalueplay.com

Now let's take a look at how the reduction in the cost of funds by 0.5 percent has affected the value of the property. We have already established the owner would save an additional $9,643.32 each year. This means that the income stream from the property will increase by that same amount. To capitalize the value of the increase in the income stream, we simply convert the cash flow to a single capital value, as follows:

Present value of income stream

$$= \frac{\text{income}}{\text{capitalization rate}} = \frac{\$9,643.32}{.08} = \$120,541.50$$

In this example, a capitalization rate, or cap rate, of 8.0 percent was assumed. Converting the additional income in this example gives us a single capital value of $120,541.50, which is a direct result of the reduction in the cost of funds by only 0.5 percent. Although it may initially seem that this would increase the value of the property, because interest payments do not affect NOI, the value of the property does not change. It does, however, affect the return on investment (ROI), since the added cash flow represents a savings to the investor, which in turn increases the rate of return. When you begin to understand the relationship between the cost of funds and its effect on value and returns, you can then begin to take full advantage of its powerful and dynamic force. Remember that all it takes is a small change in the interest rate to have a dramatic impact on the rate of return.

AMORTIZATION PERIOD

The *amortization period* is the second of the three secondary financing elements that affect real estate financing. While the interest paid on a loan refers to the cost of borrowing funds, the amortization period refers to the length of time used to calculate loan payments if the loan were fully amortized, or repaid, over the stated loan period.

An amortization schedule provides a list, or schedule, of the payments to be made over the life of the loan. This schedule shows the portion of each payment that is applied to principal and the portion of each payment that is applied to interest. This information is useful because it allows investors to see at a glance how much of the payment is being applied to reduce the balance of the loan at any given point over the period the loan is amortized. The shorter the amortization period, the higher the payment; conversely, the longer the amortization period, the lower the payment. Let's look at a simple example.

Loan amount = PV = $500,000
Interest rate = i = 6.50%
Amortization period = n = 180; payment = pmt = $4,355.54
Amortization period = n = 360; payment = pmt = $3,160.34

In this example, the difference between a 15-year loan period and a 30-year loan period is $1,195.20 per month. The question becomes, is it better to get a 15-year loan with a higher monthly payment or a 30-year loan with a lower monthly payment? I recommend using the 30-year amortization period because it provides greater flexibility. For example, if a person then wanted to apply more to the loan each month, let's say the equivalent difference of the 15-year payment, he or she would be able to do so, but would not be obligated to do so. Since cash flow is so important in the real estate business, investors should do everything possible to minimize the monthly cash outflows. This includes the portion paid out each month for principal and interest.

I've known other investors, however, whose intentions were to buy an investment property and hold it for the long term. Many of these investors preferred shorter amortization periods so they could repay an investment property's loan more quickly. Doing so would enable them to enjoy a higher cash flow from the property once the loan was repaid. Even in situations such as this, I recommend building flexibility into the loan by using a 30-year amortization period. The investor can then pay off the loan over a shorter period of time if desired. This way the investor has the option to pay a little extra each month, but doesn't have to. This option is especially important when a unit is vacant and no income is being generated.

Table 3.2 illustrates a monthly loan amortization schedule using $500,000 as the amount borrowed, an interest rate of 6.5 percent, a 30-year period, and a monthly prepayment of $217. Only the first 39 months are shown for the sake of brevity. Now let's examine Table 3.3. This schedule illustrates the total amount applied to both interest and principal. Note how paying an additional $217 per month reduced the repayment period from 30 years to about 25 years. As has already been established, there is a trade-off when prepaying the loan since the monthly cash flow from the property is reduced by exactly the amount of additional principal paid. In this example, five years is shaved off of the total repayment schedule, but $217 per month is sacrificed in the process.

Another reason to use a longer amortization period is because, by doing so, the debt service coverage ratio (DSCR) improves. This is especially important to lenders. They want to make sure that the real estate being considered for investment purposes will generate enough cash to service the debt. In other words, lenders want and need to be assured that the real estate is throwing off enough cash on its own to repay the loan. Using a longer amortization period reduces the monthly cash outflow, which in turn leaves more cash available for the loan payment. The ratio is calculated as follows:

$$\text{Debt service coverage ratio} = \frac{\text{net operating income}}{\text{principal} + \text{interest}} = \text{DSCR}$$

The ratio is a simple measure of the relationship of cash generated from an investment to the debt required to pay for that investment. The minimum DSCR varies from lender to lender, but in general it can be as low as 0.75 or as high as 1.40. Most lenders look for a minimum DSCR of 1.00 to 1.20. This concept is more fully explored in Chapter 6.

Table 3.2 Loan Amortization Schedule—Monthly

				Loan Amount: $500,000.00 Number of Payments: 360		Interest Rate: 6.500% Payment Amount: $3,160.34	
PMT	Month	Principal	Interest	Total Principal	Total Interest	Prepayment	BALANCE
PMT	Month	Principal	Interest	Total Principal	Total Interest	Prepayment	Balance
1	Jan 2005	$669.01	$2,708.33	$669.01	$2,708.33	$217.00	$499,330.99
2	Feb 2005	$672.63	$2,704.71	$1,341.64	$5,413.04	$217.00	$498,658.36
3	Mar 2005	$676.27	$2,701.07	$2,017.91	$8,114.11	$217.00	$497,982.09
4	Apr 2005	$679.94	$2,697.40	$2,697.85	$10,811.51	$217.00	$497,302.15
5	May 2005	$683.62	$2,693.72	$3,381.47	$13,505.23	$217.00	$496,618.53
6	Jun 2005	$687.32	$2,690.02	$4,068.79	$16,195.25	$217.00	$495,931.21
7	Jul 2005	$691.05	$2,686.29	$4,759.84	$18,881.54	$217.00	$495,240.16
8	Aug 2005	$694.79	$2,682.55	$5,454.63	$21,564.09	$217.00	$494,545.37
9	Sep 2005	$698.55	$2,678.79	$6,153.18	$24,242.88	$217.00	$493,846.82
10	Oct 2005	$702.34	$2,675.00	$6,855.52	$26,917.88	$217.00	$493,144.48
11	Nov 2005	$706.14	$2,671.20	$7,561.66	$29,589.08	$217.00	$492,438.34
12	Dec 2005	$709.97	$2,667.37	$8,271.63	$32,256.45	$217.00	$491,728.37
13	Jan 2006	$713.81	$2,663.53	$8,985.44	$34,919.98	$217.00	$491,014.56
14	Feb 2006	$717.68	$2,659.66	$9,703.12	$37,579.64	$217.00	$490,296.88
15	Mar 2006	$721.57	$2,655.77	$10,424.69	$40,235.41	$217.00	$489,575.31
16	Apr 2006	$725.47	$2,651.87	$11,150.16	$42,887.28	$217.00	$488,849.84
17	May 2006	$729.40	$2,647.94	$11,879.56	$45,535.22	$217.00	$488,120.44
18	Jun 2006	$733.35	$2,643.99	$12,612.91	$48,179.21	$217.00	$487,387.09
19	Jul 2006	$737.33	$2,640.01	$13,350.24	$50,819.22	$217.00	$486,649.76
20	Aug 2006	$741.32	$2,636.02	$14,091.56	$53,455.24	$217.00	$485,908.44
21	Sep 2006	$745.34	$2,632.00	$14,836.90	$56,087.24	$217.00	$485,163.10
22	Oct 2006	$749.37	$2,627.97	$15,586.27	$58,715.21	$217.00	$484,413.73
23	Nov 2006	$753.43	$2,623.91	$16,339.70	$61,339.12	$217.00	$483,660.30
24	Dec 2006	$757.51	$2,619.83	$17,097.21	$63,958.95	$217.00	$482,902.79
25	Jan 2007	$761.62	$2,615.72	$17,858.83	$66,574.67	$217.00	$482,141.17
26	Feb 2007	$765.74	$2,611.60	$18,624.57	$69,186.27	$217.00	$481,375.43
27	Mar 2007	$769.89	$2,607.45	$19,394.46	$71,793.72	$217.00	$480,605.54
28	Apr 2007	$774.06	$2,603.28	$20,168.52	$74,397.00	$217.00	$479,831.48
29	May 2007	$778.25	$2,599.09	$20,946.77	$76,996.09	$217.00	$479,053.23
30	Jun 2007	$782.47	$2,594.87	$21,729.24	$79,590.96	$217.00	$478,270.76
31	Jul 2007	$786.71	$2,590.63	$22,515.95	$82,181.59	$217.00	$477,484.05
32	Aug 2007	$790.97	$2,586.37	$23,306.92	$84,767.96	$217.00	$476,693.08
33	Sep 2007	$795.25	$2,582.09	$24,102.17	$87,350.05	$217.00	$475,897.83
34	Oct 2007	$799.56	$2,577.78	$24,901.73	$89,927.83	$217.00	$475,098.27
35	Nov 2007	$803.89	$2,573.45	$25,705.62	$92,501.28	$217.00	$474,294.38
36	Dec 2007	$808.25	$2,569.09	$26,513.87	$95,070.37	$217.00	$473,486.13
37	Jan 2008	$812.62	$2,564.72	$27,326.49	$97,635.09	$217.00	$472,673.51
38	Feb 2008	$817.03	$2,560.31	$28,143.52	$100,195.40	$217.00	$471,856.48
39	Mar 2008	$821.45	$2,555.89	$28,964.97	$102,751.29	$217.00	$471,035.03

Table 3.3 Loan Amortization Schedule—Annual

	Loan Amount: $500,000.00		Interest Rate: 6.500%	
	Number of Payments: 360		Payment Amount: $3,160.34	
Year	Period	Principal Paid During Period	Interest Paid During Period	Total Paid During Period
Year	Period	Total Annual Principal	Total Annual Interest	Total Annual Payment
1	Jan–Dec 2005	$8,271.63	$32,256.45	$40,528.08
2	Jan–Dec 2006	$8,825.58	$31,702.50	$40,528.08
3	Jan–Dec 2007	$9,416.66	$31,111.42	$40,528.08
4	Jan–Dec 2008	$10,047.30	$30,480.78	$40,528.08
5	Jan–Dec 2009	$10,720.18	$29,807.90	$40,528.08
6	Jan–Dec 2010	$11,438.12	$29,089.96	$40,528.08
7	Jan–Dec 2011	$12,204.17	$28,323.91	$40,528.08
8	Jan–Dec 2012	$13,021.51	$27,506.57	$40,528.08
9	Jan–Dec 2013	$13,893.60	$26,634.48	$40,528.08
10	Jan–Dec 2014	$14,824.07	$25,704.01	$40,528.08
11	Jan–Dec 2015	$15,816.85	$24,711.23	$40,528.08
12	Jan–Dec 2016	$16,876.14	$23,651.94	$40,528.08
13	Jan–Dec 2017	$18,006.37	$22,521.71	$40,528.08
14	Jan–Dec 2018	$19,212.30	$21,315.78	$40,528.08
15	Jan–Dec 2019	$20,498.97	$20,029.11	$40,528.08
16	Jan–Dec 2020	$21,871.82	$18,656.26	$40,528.08
17	Jan–Dec 2021	$23,336.63	$17,191.45	$40,528.08
18	Jan–Dec 2022	$24,899.53	$15,628.55	$40,528.08
19	Jan–Dec 2023	$26,567.11	$13,960.97	$40,528.08
20	Jan–Dec 2024	$28,346.32	$12,181.76	$40,528.08
21	Jan–Dec 2025	$30,244.75	$10,283.33	$40,528.08
22	Jan–Dec 2026	$32,270.28	$8,257.80	$40,528.08
23	Jan–Dec 2027	$34,431.48	$6,096.60	$40,528.08
24	Jan–Dec 2028	$36,737.42	$3,790.66	$40,528.08
25	Jan–Dec 2029	$38,221.21	$1,330.26	$39,551.47

Value Play Real Estate Software, 3.0.01   www.thevalueplay.com

AMOUNT OF FUNDS BORROWED

The *amount of funds borrowed* is the last of the three secondary financing elements that affect real estate financing. The amount of funds borrowed, or loan amount, is the amount of money being borrowed to finance an investment. The relationship between the loan amount and the down payment is an inverse relationship. As the amount of money being borrowed for an investment property increases, the amount applied toward the down payment decreases;

Table 3.4 Scenario I: 5 Year Pro Forma Income Statement As of January 1st

Cost and Revenue Assumptions

Land	350,000
Building	3,000,000
Improvements	0
Closing Costs	25,000
Total	3,375,000
Number of Units	75
Average Monthly Rent	600
Gross Monthly Revenues	45,000

Financing Assumptions

Total Purchase	3,375,000	100.00%
Owner's Equity	843,750	25.00%
Balance to Finc	2,531,250	75.00%
	Annual	Monthly
Interest Rate	6.500%	0.542%
Amort Period	25	300
Payment	205,094	17,091

Key Ratios

Total Square Feet	64,500.00
Avg Sq Ft/Unit	860.00
Avg Rent/Sq Ft	0.70
Avg Cost/Sq Ft	52.33
Avg Unit Cost	45,000.00
Capitalization Rate	9.45%
Gross Rent Multiplier	6.25
Expense/Unit	3,417.92
Expense/Foot	3.97

Rental Increase Projections
Average Monthly Rent
Operating Expense Projections

	Year 1	Year 2	Year 3	Year 4	Year 5
Rental Increase Projections	0.00%	3.50%	4.00%	3.00%	3.00%
Average Monthly Rent	600	621	646	665	685
Operating Expense Projections	0.00%	-2.50%	0.00%	2.50%	2.50%

Operating Revenues

		Actual Monthly	Year 1	Year 2	Year 3	Year 4	Year 5
Gross Scheduled Income		45,000	540,000	558,900	581,256	598,694	616,654
Vacancy Rate	5.0%	2,250	27,000	27,945	29,063	29,935	30,833
Net Rental Income		42,750	513,000	530,955	552,193	568,759	585,822
Other Income		5,200	62,400	64,584	67,167	69,182	71,258
Gross Income	100.0%	47,950	575,400	595,539	619,361	637,941	657,080

Operating Expenses

		Actual Monthly	Year 1	Year 2	Year 3	Year 4	Year 5
Repairs and Maintenance	12.2%	5,850	70,200	68,445	68,445	70,156	71,910
Property Management Fees	3.8%	1,845	22,140	21,587	21,587	22,126	22,679
Taxes	7.3%	3,477	41,724	40,681	40,681	41,698	42,740
Insurance	2.6%	1,250	15,000	14,625	14,625	14,991	15,365
Salaries and Wages	5.8%	2,780	33,360	32,526	32,526	33,339	34,173
Utilities	8.8%	4,230	50,760	49,491	49,491	50,728	51,996
Trash Removal	0.8%	400	4,800	4,680	4,680	4,797	4,917
Professional Fees	0.5%	250	3,000	2,925	2,925	2,998	3,073
Advertising	1.0%	500	6,000	5,850	5,850	5,996	6,146
Other	1.6%	780	9,360	9,126	9,126	9,354	9,588
Total Op. Exp.	44.6%	21,362	256,344	249,935	249,935	256,184	262,588

Net Operating Income

	Rate						
Net Operating Income	55.4%	26,588	319,056	345,604	369,425	381,758	394,491
Interest on Loan	28.6%	13,711	163,301	160,502	157,515	154,329	150,929
Dep. Exp. - Building		9,091	109,091	109,091	109,091	109,091	109,091
Dep. Exp. - Equip.		0	0	0	0	0	0
Net Income Before Taxes		3,786	46,664	76,011	102,819	118,338	134,471
Income Tax Rate	0.0%	0	0	0	0	0	0
Net Income After Taxes		3,786	46,664	76,011	102,819	118,338	134,471

Cash Flow From Operations

Net Income After Taxes	3,786	46,664	76,011	102,819	118,338	134,471
Dep. Exp.	9,091	109,091	109,091	109,091	109,091	109,091
Total CF From Ops.	12,877	155,755	185,102	211,910	227,429	243,562
Interest on Loan	13,711	163,301	160,502	157,515	154,329	150,929
Total Cash Available for Loan Servicing	26,588	319,056	345,604	369,425	381,758	394,491
Debt Service	17,091	205,094	205,094	205,094	205,094	205,094
Remaining After Tax CF From Ops	9,497	113,962	140,509	164,331	176,663	189,397
Plus Principal Reduction	3,483	41,793	44,592	47,579	50,765	54,165
Total Return	12,980	155,755	185,102	211,910	227,429	243,562

CF/Debt Servicing Ratio	155.57%	155.57%	168.51%	180.12%	186.14%	192.35%

Net Income ROI		5.53%	9.01%	12.19%	14.03%	15.94%
Cash ROI		13.51%	16.65%	19.48%	20.94%	22.45%
Total ROI		18.46%	21.94%	25.12%	26.95%	28.87%

Net CFs From Investment - 1 Yr Exit	(843,750)	1,124,505				
Net CFs From Investment - 3 Yr Exit	(843,750)	113,962	140,509	1,667,046		
Net CFs From Investment - 5 Yr Exit	(843,750)	113,962	140,509	164,331	176,663	2,097,042

Annualized IRR - 1 Yr	15.94%	
Annualized IRR - 3 Yr	22.45%	
Annualized IRR - 5 Yr	28.87%	

	Exit Price	Gain on Sale	Cap Rate	IRR
Estimated Exit Price/Gain On Sale - 1 Yr	3,500,000	125,000	9.12%	33.27%
Estimated Exit Price/Gain On Sale - 3 Yr	3,900,000	525,000	9.47%	34.72%
Estimated Exit Price/Gain On Sale - 5 Yr	4,200,000	825,000	9.39%	31.07%

Table 3.5   Scenario II: 5 Year Pro Forma Income Statement As of January 1st

Cost and Revenue Assumptions

Land	350,000
Building	3,000,000
Improvements	0
Closing Costs	25,000
Total	3,375,000

Number of Units	75
Average Monthly Rent	600
Gross Monthly Revenues	45,000

Rental Increase Projections

Average Monthly Rent	5.0%
Operating Expense Projections	100.0%

Financing Assumptions

Total Purchase	100.00%	3,375,000
Owner's Equity	10.00%	337,500
Balance to Finc	90.00%	3,037,500

	Annual	Monthly
Interest Rate	6.500%	0.542%
Amort Period	25	300
Payment	246,113	20,509

	0.00%	3.50%
	600	621
	0.00%	-2.50%

Key Ratios

Total Square Feet	64,500.00
Avg Sq Ft/Unit	860.00
Avg Rent/Sq Ft	0.70
Avg Cost/Sq Ft	52.33
Avg Unit Cost	45,000.00
Capitalization Rate	9.45%
Gross Rent Multiplier	6.25
Expense/Unit	3,417.92
Expense/Foot	3.97

	4.00%	3.00%	3.00%
	646	665	685
	0.00%	2.50%	2.50%

	Actual			Projected		
	Monthly	Year 1	Year 2	Year 3	Year 4	Year 5
Operating Revenues						
Gross Scheduled Income	45,000	540,000	558,900	581,256	598,694	616,654
Vacancy Rate	2,250	27,000	27,945	29,063	29,935	30,833
Net Rental Income	42,750	513,000	530,955	552,193	568,759	585,822
Other Income	5,200	62,400	64,584	67,167	69,182	71,258
Gross Income	47,950	575,400	595,539	619,361	637,941	657,080
Operating Expenses						
Repairs and Maintenance	5,850	70,200	68,445	68,445	70,156	71,910
Property Management Fees	1,845	22,140	21,587	21,587	22,126	22,679
Taxes	3,477	41,724	40,681	40,681	41,698	42,740
Insurance	1,250	15,000	14,625	14,625	14,991	15,365
Salaries and Wages	2,780	33,360	32,526	32,526	33,339	34,173
Utilities	4,230	50,760	49,491	49,491	50,728	51,996
Trash Removal	400	4,800	4,680	4,680	4,797	4,917
Professional Fees	250	3,000	2,925	2,925	2,998	3,073
Advertising	500	6,000	5,850	5,850	5,996	6,146
Other	780	9,360	9,126	9,126	9,354	9,588
Total Op. Exp.	21,362	256,344	249,935	249,935	256,184	262,588

Percentage column (Actual): Vacancy Rate 5.0%; Gross Income 100.0%; Repairs and Maintenance 12.2%; Property Management Fees 3.8%; Taxes 7.3%; Insurance 2.6%; Salaries and Wages 5.8%; Utilities 8.8%; Trash Removal 0.8%; Professional Fees 0.5%; Advertising 1.0%; Other 1.6%; Total Op. Exp. 44.6%

Net Operating Income

Net Operating Income	55.4%	26,588	319,056	345,604	369,425	381,758	394,491
Interest on Loan	34.3%	16,453	195,961	192,602	189,018	185,195	181,115
Dep. Exp. - Building		9,091	109,091	109,091	109,091	109,091	109,091
Dep. Exp. - Equip.		0	0	0	0	0	0
Net Income Before Taxes		1,044	14,004	43,911	71,316	87,472	104,286
Income Tax Rate	0.0%	0	0	0	0	0	0
Net Income After Taxes		1,044	14,004	43,911	71,316	87,472	104,286

Cash Flow From Operations

Net Income After Taxes	1,044	14,004	43,911	71,316	87,472	104,286
Dep. Exp.	9,091	109,091	109,091	109,091	109,091	109,091
Total CF From Ops.	10,135	123,095	153,002	180,407	196,563	213,376
Interest on Loan	16,453	195,961	192,602	189,018	185,195	181,115
Total Cash Available for Loan Servicing	26,588	319,056	345,604	369,425	381,758	394,491
Debt Service	20,509	246,113	246,113	246,113	246,113	246,113
Remaining After Tax CF From Ops	6,079	72,943	99,491	123,312	135,645	148,378
Plus Principal Reduction	4,179	50,152	53,511	57,095	60,918	64,998
Total Return	10,258	123,095	153,002	180,407	196,563	213,376

CF/Debt Servicing Ratio	129.64%	129.64%	140.42%	150.10%	155.11%	160.29%

Net Income ROI		4.15%	13.01%	21.13%	25.92%	30.90%
Cash ROI		21.61%	29.48%	36.54%	40.19%	43.96%
Total ROI		36.47%	45.33%	53.45%	58.24%	63.22%

Net CFs From Investment - 1 Yr Exit	(337,500)	585,595				
Net CFs From Investment - 3 Yr Exit	(337,500)	72,943	99,491	1,146,570		
Net CFs From Investment - 5 Yr Exit	(337,500)	72,943	99,491	123,312	135,645	1,597,553

	Exit Price	Gain on Sale	Cap Rate		IRR
Estimated Exit Price/Gain On Sale - 1 Yr	3,500,000	125,000	9.12%	Annualized IRR - 1 Yr	73.51%
Estimated Exit Price/Gain On Sale - 3 Yr	3,900,000	525,000	9.47%	Annualized IRR - 3 Yr	64.72%
Estimated Exit Price/Gain On Sale - 5 Yr	4,200,000	825,000	9.39%	Annualized IRR - 5 Yr	53.29%

conversely, as the loan amount decreases, the down payment increases. It is logical to assume that the more money borrowed, the greater the monthly payment will be, and the less money borrowed, the smaller the monthly payment will be. Although an investor might conclude from this reasoning that it makes sense to put down as much money as possible to decrease the monthly payment and thereby increase the property's cash flow, that conclusion would be wrong. According to the *other people's money* (OPM) principle, which deals with the concept of leverage, the greater the percentage of money borrowed the greater the return on equity will be. Even though the monthly payment will increase by borrowing more, since the returns are measured as a ratio of the income generated by the property to the amount of one's capital invested in it, the rate of return is greater due to the increase in leverage. The OPM principle, along with the principle of leverage, is discussed in greater detail in the next chapter.

Several years ago, I developed a financial model I use extensively to analyze and evaluate investment properties, which I call *The Value Play Income Analyzer.* In Part 2, "Case Study Review, The Practical Application of Valuation Analysis," the model is explained in much greater detail. For now, however, I'd like to focus on three key measurements in the model. They are net income return on investment (net income ROI), cash ROI, and total ROI. Let's take a moment to examine the effect of changes in the amount of funds borrowed on these three ratios by looking at two different scenarios.

In Table 3.4 (Scenario I), Investor A has used the Income Analyzer to evaluate an apartment building available for sale with a total purchase price of $3,375,000. Under this scenario, the total amount of funds borrowed by Investor A is $2,531,250. This leaves a balance of $843,750, or 25 percent, required for the down payment. In this scenario, Investor A will realize a net income ROI of 5.53 percent, a cash ROI of 13.51 percent, and a total ROI of 18.46 percent in Year 1 on the invested capital, or cash down payment. Although many investors would be satisfied with these returns, let's see if there is a way for us to improve them.

In Table 3.5 (Scenario II), all variables within the model are held constant and are exactly the same as in Table 3.4 with the exception of two—the amount of funds borrowed and the down payment, or owner's equity. In Scenario II, the down payment has been decreased to $337,500, which is a 10 percent investment, and the amount of funds borrowed has been increased to $3,037,500. The monthly payment required to service the debt in this scenario is $20,509. This compares unfavorably to the monthly payment of $17,091 in Scenario I and results in a net decrease of remaining after tax cash flow (CF) of $3,418 per month.

At first glance, you may be inclined to believe that Investor A in Scenario I is better off than Investor B in Scenario II, since Investor A pockets an additional $3,418 per month. In Scenario II, Investor B will realize a net income ROI of 4.15 percent, a cash ROI of 21.61 percent, and a total ROI of 36.47 percent in Year 1 on the invested capital. According to our analysis, Investor B will earn almost twice as much as Investor A. By increasing the amount of funds borrowed and decreasing the amount of funds invested, you can actually earn a higher rate of return on your invested capital. While it is true that there is less cash remaining at the end of each period, the investor in Scenario II fares much better than the investor in Scenario I. This is because the returns are measured as a ratio of the remaining cash to the investor's equity or invested capital. Once again, by investing less of your own money, you actually earn a higher rate of return than you otherwise would, in spite of the fact that the remaining cash has decreased.

In summary, the three secondary investment elements that affect real estate financing activities are the cost of funds, the amortization period, and the amount of funds borrowed. Understanding the interaction among these three variables and their relationship to one another is essential for assessing how changes in any one of the three can affect the profitability of the various types of real estate investments. The better you understand these principles, the greater will be your chances for success in the real estate business.

Chapter 4

Additional Investment Elements and Their Effect on Financing Strategies

In Chapter 2, we examined the three primary financing elements around which real estate investment activity centers—time, volume, and property type. In Chapter 3 we learned about the three secondary financing elements that affect real estate financing activities—cost of funds, amortization period, and amount of funds borrowed. Three additional elements have an effect on real estate financing: loan duration, lender fees, and prepayment penalties (see Exhibit 4.1). Duration must be considered before obtaining a loan to ensure the life of it is best suited to an investor's needs. It is also important to be familiar with the many types of fees charged by lenders and to know their effect on the overall cost of an investment. Finally, investors should also be aware of any type of prepayment penalty that may be imposed by the lender.

LOAN DURATION

The first additional element that has an effect on real estate financing is *loan duration*. Loan duration refers to a loan's life, or term. For instance, a loan duration of 10 years means that it will expire at

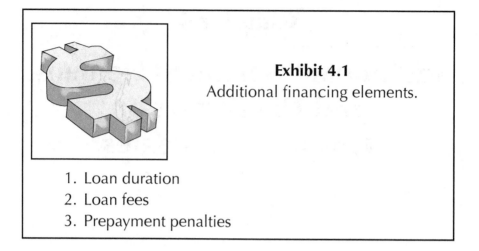

Exhibit 4.1
Additional financing elements.

1. Loan duration
2. Loan fees
3. Prepayment penalties

the end of the 10-year period and must at its expiration either be renewed or paid in full. A loan with a duration of 10 years may or may not have an amortization period equal to its duration period. Whereas *amortization* refers to the length of time used to calculate the amount of payment to be made each period, *duration* refers to the length of time the loan will exist. For example, a loan with a 10-year duration, or term, can have a 15-, 20-, or 30-year amortization period. At the end of its term, any remaining loan balance will have to be repaid in full if the lender chooses not to renew or extend it.

Regardless of what type of financing is obtained for an investment property, investors should be familiar with loan terms and the impact they will have on their financing of real estate. Using the most appropriate term is best determined by the estimated length of time an investment is intended to be held. For example, investors who intend to hold a property for a period of 10 or more years would most likely want to obtain a fixed-rate loan with a term that matches the full amortization period, which is typically 30 years. Financing the property with a shorter term, say five years, would force an investor to refinance the property at the end of the term, or in five years.

Depending on the current interest rate environment, it may be better to lock in a lower rate at the time of initial financing, since rates can change suddenly and without notice. Investors who plan to hold a property for 10 years or more will need to procure a loan with a corresponding time frame. If a decline in market interest rates occurs at some point in the future, an investor always has the option to refinance. If prepayment penalties exist, however, they, too, must be factored into the refinance decision. An increase in market interest rates will not affect the mortgage, because a measure of protection has been built in to insulate the investment from a higher-rate environment by choosing the most appropriate financing term to begin with.

Loans having longer durations can sometimes work to an investor's disadvantage, especially if the property being purchased is intended to be held for only a short while. If, for instance, a rehab property has been identified and the property will be held for one year or less before disposing of it, then a loan with a shorter duration is preferable, because such loans typically have lower rates than those with longer durations. This is because lenders can more accurately predict interest rates over a shorter time frame than they can over a longer time frame.

A one-year adjustable rate mortgage, or ARM, is almost certain to have an interest rate ranging from ½ to 1 percent lower than a loan with a 30-year term. A one-year ARM typically has a fixed rate for the first six months or one year, and then adjusts either annually or semiannually thereafter. A comparable loan from a bank may carry a rate to match a one-year ARM, but may also have a one-year term, meaning that instead of adjusting, the loan will expire and have to be satisfied by either renewing it or repaying it.

When selecting the duration or term that best meets an investor's financing needs, the investment objectives must first be determined. Investors must establish beforehand how long a property is to be held before committing themselves to a particular debt instrument. Will the property be purchased and added to a portfolio containing other rental properties and subsequently held for many years, or will it instead be held for only a short period of time to capture a gain created by making improvements to it? Investors should establish their investment objectives prior to making a commitment to the lender and then choose a loan with a duration best suited to the desired opportunity.

LOAN FEES

The second additional element that has an effect on real estate financing is the *loan fee* assessed by the lender. Loan fees come in all shapes and sizes and in all kinds of disguises. They are masked by using terms such as *application fees, review fees, underwriting fees, loan-origination fees, mortgage broker fees,* and *points charged at closing.* Since some lenders are overly aggressive and assess a fee or charge for just about everything, I suggest asking for a list of all costs that will be charged by both the lender and the mortgage broker (if applicable). Although by law lenders and brokers are required to disclose all costs, these issues should be addressed up front. Even after receiving the schedule of costs, it pays to be careful, since some charges may show up on the settlement statement at the last moment just prior to the loan closing. This is especially true when using a mortgage broker.

Lenders are required by the federal Real Estate Settlement Procedures Act to provide borrowers with a good faith estimate (GFE) of the fees due at closing, and they must do so within three days of the loan application. These mortgage fees, also called *settlement costs,* cover the various expenses associated with mortgage financing. Since closing costs usually range from between 3 and 5 percent of the sale price, it's best to wait until receiving a good faith estimate before signing any loan. In fact, it's a good idea to obtain good faith estimates from several lenders and compare their respective costs. Take just a moment to review the good faith estimate in Exhibit 4.2. The form lists 15 different lender fees alone, as well as a number of additional fees by parties that may have an interest in the transaction.

Although the broker is legally obligated to disclose all reasonable and customary fees, the broker doesn't always know what fees the lender will charge. The broker and the lender are not one and the same. The broker acts as a third party to assist the purchaser in obtaining the most appropriate type of financing. If brokers use lenders they have not used before, they may not be aware of the lender's complete fee structure. I myself have been surprised on more than one occasion by unexpected charges that show up at the time of closing. I was especially surprised on a new build-to-suit

Exhibit 4.2 Good Faith Estimate
(not a loan commitment).

This Good Faith Estimate is being provided by a mortgage broker, and no lender has yet been obtained.

The information provided below reflects estimates of the charges which you are likely to incur at the settlement of your loan. The fees listed are estimates - actual charges may be more or less. Your transaction may not involve a fee for every item listed. The numbers listed beside the estimates generally correspond to the numbered lines contained in the HUD-1 or HUD-1A settlement statement which you will be receiving at settlement. The HUD-1 or HUD-1A settlement statement will show you the actual cost for items paid at settlement.

HUD-1	DESCRIPTION OF CHARGES	AMOUNT
801	Loan Origination Fee @ % + $	
802	Loan Discount Fee @ % + $	
803	Appraisal Fee	
804	Credit Report	
805	Inspection Fee	
806	Mortgage Insurance Application Fee	
807	Assumption Fee	
808	Mortgage Broker Fee @ % + $	
809	Tax Related Service Fee	
810	Processing Fee	
811	Underwriting Fee	
812	Wire Transfer Fee	
813	Application Fee	
814	Commitment Fee	
815	Lender's Rate Lock-In Fee	
901	Interest @ /day for days	
902	Mortgage Insurance Premium	
903	Hazard Insurance Premium	
904	County Property Taxes	
906	Flood Insurance	
1001	Hazard Ins. @ /mo. for months	
1002	Mortgage Ins. @ /mo. for months	
1004	Tax & Assmt. @ /mo. for months	
1006	Flood Insurance @ /mo. for months	
1008	Aggregate Escrow Adjustment	
1101	Settlement or Closing/Escrow Fee	
1102	Abstract or Title Search	
1103	Title Examination	
1105	Document Preparation Fee	
1106	Notary Fee	
1107	Attorney's Fee	
1108	Title Insurance	
1201	Recording Fee	
1202	City/County Tax/Stamps	
1203	State Tax/Stamps	
1204	Intangible Tax	
1301	Survey	
1302	Pest Inspection	

"S"/"B" designates those costs to be paid by Seller/Broker. "A" designates those costs affecting APR. "F" designates financed costs.

These estimates are provided pursuant to the Real Estate Settlement Procedures Act of 1974, as amended (RESPA). Additional information can be found in the HUD Special Information Booklet, which is to be provided to you by your mortgage broker or lender, if your application is to purchase residential property and the Lender will take a first lien on the property.

Mailing Address

Property Address

Proposed Loan Amount	Loan Type		Estimated Interest Rate
Preparation Date	☐ FHA ☐ VA	☐ Conventional	Loan Number

_____   Date

_____   Date

_____   Date

_____   Date

home we sold several months ago that closed just recently. The mortgage broker charged its client over $6,000 in broker fees for a loan amount of only a little more than $200,000! That's equivalent to about 3 percent of the loan amount. What surprised me even more, however, was that the homeowner had not even received a good faith estimate until the day before the closing.

The loan application fee is a charge that some lenders assess at the time formal application is made. Application fees range anywhere from no charge at all to as much as $500 on single-family residential properties. On larger commercial or multifamily loans, the initial application fee can be as high as $2,500 to $5,000. The fee is charged to offset costs incurred by the lender or broker for items such as administrative costs and credit reports. Justification for the charges results from a need to recover costs as well as the inability of some applicants to qualify for loans. Charging an application fee serves to filter out those individuals who may not be capable of qualifying for a loan. If, for example, the applicant believes he may not be able to qualify for a loan and knows an application fee of $250 will be charged regardless of whether he qualifies, chances are he will not bother with the application. Although lenders who charge an application fee will most likely have fewer applicants, the quality of those applicants is likely to be higher.

Application fees are oftentimes negotiable. If you know you have good credit and will have no problem qualifying for a loan, be sure to tell the lender or broker and ask for the application fee to be waived. Many times the answer will be yes. The party taking the application, however, may elect to charge the fee up front and agree to credit it back to you at the time of closing. This helps reduce the risk to the lender that the borrower will switch to another mortgage company or bank at some point in the process. If the borrower has paid a $500 application fee, for example, on a single-family investment property, or perhaps a $5,000 fee on a multifamily property, and knows she will receive a credit for it at the time of closing, there's a very good chance she will stay with the lender to see the loan through to the closing.

Underwriting fees have come about over the past few years as yet another way to tack on additional charges. The justification for this charge is similar to that of the application fee in that, similarly to personnel who are paid for processing the loan application, the underwriting department must be paid for its job of underwriting the loan. Using that logic, it seems reasonable to expect that at some point in the future, we might begin seeing other types of fees show up, such as a "loan committee fee" for reviewing the loan, or perhaps a "human resources fee" to cover the cost of hiring all the other departments that are charging us fees. The list is limited only by one's imagination.

Loan-origination fees, still another way of charging the borrower, are usually equivalent to one point, or 1 percent, of the total amount of the loan. On a $100,000 loan, for example, the fee would be $1,000. Justification for this fee is supposedly based on the costs incurred by the lender to actually make the loan once it has been approved. Legal documents must be drawn up and processed, the loan must be funded, and everything must be properly recorded. Some lenders will waive the loan-origination fee altogether or roll it into the interest rate on the loan by increasing the rate by 25 basis points, which is the equivalent of one-fourth of a point.

Mortgage brokers earn the majority of their income from the fees generated by placing loans. Since they are not direct lenders, brokers do not earn anything from the interest being charged. Interest is paid to the lender and not to the broker. A mortgage broker is similar to a real estate broker in that they are both compensated only when they sell something. Both types of brokers are paid on a percentage basis. While the real estate agent is paid a *commission,* the mortgage broker is paid *points.* Brokers typically charge between 1 and 2 percent of the loan amount, sometimes more and sometimes less. Factors that may affect the fees they charge are items such as the borrower's creditworthiness, the size of the loan, and their ability to receive back-end fees from the lender. Don't be fooled by brokers who charge 1 percent on a $100,000 loan amount and tell you they are making only $1,000 on the transaction. Brokers are almost always compensated by the lender for differences in the spread of the rate charged. For example, if the base rate a lender charges is 6.00 percent with zero points to the borrower, the broker will likely be paid a back-end fee of 1 percent by the lender. If the broker is able to sell the same loan to you at, let's say 6.25 percent, the broker can double his or her income on the loan and receive 2 percent from the lender. Both front-end and back-end fees are legally required to be disclosed on the good faith estimate. Borrowers have a right to know how much they are being charged for the lender's services. If you're an investor with good credit and have a strong personal financial statement, mortgage brokers are less likely to play such games with you. You're probably familiar with the term *caveat emptor,* but just in case you're not, the literal translation means "buyer beware" or "let the buyer beware." In the case of loan fees, however, I suppose we could say "let the borrower beware."

Points are often made available to borrowers to buy down the interest rate applied to a loan. Since one point is equivalent to 1 percent, an investor paying one point on a $100,000 loan would pay $1,000 in additional up-front fees. For every point paid, the interest rate on the loan is decreased by approximately ⅛ to ¼ of a percent. This is only a general guideline, as rate spreads vary widely among lenders, but the lender you are working with can usually provide an exact quote by looking at rate sheets. Since rate spreads are dynamic and change with minor fluctuations in the market, the rate quoted may be good for just that particular moment, or it may be good for the remainder of the day.

Take a moment to review Table 4.1. In this example, six different rate scenarios are compared. The loan amount of $1 million and the term of 240 months are held constant, while the interest rate and the points are changed in each scenario. A base interest rate of 7.00 percent with zero points is applied on the first line. In each subsequent rate scenario, the interest rate is decreased in quarter-point increments while simultaneously increasing the amount of discount points paid by the borrower. In the first example, an investor who borrows $1 million and pays no points and holds the loan throughout the duration of its 20-year life would pay a total of $1,860,717.45, with a monthly payment of $7,752.99. In the last example, the investor borrows the same $1 million for the same 20-year period, but instead elects to pay five discount points to buy the rate down from 7.00 percent to 5.75 percent. The investor in this scenario would pay a total of $1,735,000.42, which includes the $50,000 for points paid, and would have a monthly payment of $7,020.84. Buying down the rate in this example would save the investor $732.15 per month and $125,717.03

Table 4.1 Loan Comparisons

Symphony Homes, Inc. www.symphony-homes.com
The Value Play www.thevalueplay.com

Loan Amount	Interest Rate	Payments	Points	Payment	Total Paid	Cost of Loan	Cost of Points
$1,000,000.00	0.07%	240	0%	$7,752.99	$1,860,717.45	$860,717.45	$0.00
$1,000,000.00	0.0675%	240	1%	$7,603.64	$1,834,873.62	$824,873.62	$10,000.00
$1,000,000.00	0.065%	240	2%	$7,455.73	$1,809,375.53	$789,375.53	$20,000.00
$1,000,000.00	0.0625%	240	3%	$7,309.28	$1,784,227.69	$754,227.69	$30,000.00
$1,000,000.00	0.06%	240	4%	$7,164.31	$1,759,434.54	$719,434.54	$40,000.00
$1,000,000.00	0.0575%	240	5%	$7,020.84	$1,735,000.42	$685,000.42	$50,000.00

Value Play Real Estate Software, 3.0.01

www.thevalueplay.com

over the life of the loan. What this example assumes, however, is that the investor will hold the property for the full twenty-year period. If an investor determines ahead of time that a property is going to be maintained in her portfolio for the long term, then it makes sense to pay the additional points up front. On the other hand, if the property is going to be held for only five years, then it is better to pay the higher interest rate with zero points. In this example, an investor would need to hold the property for five years and nine months to realize any benefit of paying the additional points. The break-even point can be calculated by dividing the cost of points over the savings per month. In this example, the break-even point is calculated as follows:

$$\text{Breakeven} = \frac{\text{cost of points}}{\text{monthly savings}}$$

$$= \frac{\$50,000}{(\$7,752.99 - \$7,020.84)} = 68.29 \text{ months}$$

One additional factor to consider is what the future value of the $50,000 applied toward the discount points would be if it were instead used to purchase another investment property. We have already established that over a 20-year investment horizon, buying the interest rate down by applying the $50,000 would save $125,717.03 over and above all other costs. The question becomes, can the $50,000 be used to invest in another asset over a 20-year period to achieve an even greater return? To determine this, we must solve for i, which is the rate required to earn a return on the investment of $125,717.03. To set the problem up correctly, we know that $50,000 is the total amount invested, and $125,717.03 is the total amount returned. Using a financial calculator, the answer can easily be solved as follows:

Initial investment = present value = PV = $50,000 (cash flow out)
Total amount returned = future value = FV = $125,717.03 (cash flow in)
Number of years = n = 20

To solve for the total return, solve for i
Interest rate $= i = 4.72\%$

By solving for i, we discover that an investor would have to earn a return of 4.72% or greater to come out ahead. If the investor could not earn at least a 4.72% return, he would be better off paying down the interest rate with the $50,000, assuming, of course, that the property will be held for the 20-year duration.

Now let's assume the investor has an alternative choice, which is to invest the $50,000 in a small multifamily apartment building. Let's also keep the math very simple by assuming he is able to purchase a building with only 10 percent down, which is not at all an unreasonable assumption. Using this kind of leverage, the investor is able to purchase a building valued at $500,000 ($50,000 ÷ 0.10 = $500,000). Let's also assume the investor purchased the property at a 10 cap, which means the capitalization rate is 10 percent. An apartment building with a cost of $500,000 and a cap rate of 10 will yield a net operating income (NOI) of $50,000, which is the amount of money left over after vacancy losses and operating expenses have been deducted from gross revenues. It is the portion of income available to service, or pay, the debt used to finance an investment. Take a moment to review the following equations.

$$\text{Price} = \frac{\text{net operating income}}{\text{capitalization rate}} = \frac{\$50,000}{0.10} = \$500,000$$

$$PV \text{ of apartment building} = \frac{\text{NOI}}{\text{cap rate}} = \frac{\$50,000}{.10} = \$500,000$$

$$\text{Cap rate} = \frac{\text{net operating income}}{\text{price}} = \frac{\$50,000}{\$500,000} = 10.0\%$$

Now let's take the analysis a step further by calculating the required debt service on the $450,000 loan that was required to finance the building. We'll also assume the investor will use the same loan program as he did with the first investment, as follows:

Loan amount = PV = \$450,000
Number of years = n = 20
Interest rate = i = 7.0%
Annual debt service = pmt = \$42,476.82

Let's take a moment to recap. We have established that the investment of \$50,000 in a \$500,000 apartment building will yield \$50,000 of NOI and will be used to pay the annual debt service of \$42,476.82. Where does that leave us? Let's take a look.

$$\$50,000.00 - \$42,476.82 = \$7,523.18 = \text{remaining cash}$$
$$= \text{cash return on investment}$$
$$\$7,523.18/\$50,000.00 = 15.05\% \text{ cash ROI}$$

In this example, the investor would earn a cash ROI of about 15 percent, which compares favorably to the 4.72 percent return if the same \$50,000 were used to buy down the interest rate. It is important to note also that the cash ROI does not reflect the added value of the tax savings resulting from depreciation, nor does it reflect the added value of a reduction in the principal balance, or loan balance, that occurs over the life of the loan. In summary, it appears that our investor will fare much better by investing the \$50,000 in an apartment building than by buying down the interest rate on the purchase of his first investment property.

PREPAYMENT PENALTIES

The third additional element that has an effect on real estate financing is known as a *prepayment penalty.* Although you would think a bank or other lending institution would be happy to have its loan repaid, believe it or not, many financial institutions charge their customers a substantial fee for repaying a loan prematurely. This is especially true on larger commercial and multifamily loans. You may think, "Why would anyone want to pay off a loan early?" There are two primary reasons loans are prepaid. The first is due to changes in interest rates. If, for example, an investor obtained a large loan with a fixed rate of 7 percent, and rates then declined to 6 percent, the investor would most likely want to take advantage of the favorable change by refinancing. When people refinance, it is oftentimes through another institution. This means the existing lender loses a good loan to a competitor and, as a result, loses the income associated with that loan. To discourage customers from refinancing early in the life of the loan, lenders build in a prepayment penalty. See Exhibit 4.3 for a sample of prepayment penalty disclosures.

The second primary reason loans are prepaid results from a change in ownership. If, for example, an investor obtained a loan with a five-year term that had a provision for a prepayment penalty and decided to sell the property after just one year, the lender would charge a fee, or penalty, for prepaying the loan. Up until the mid-1980s or so, most loans were *assumable,* which meant the buyer could assume, or transfer, the note into her name without having to get a new loan. If the loan could be assumed by another party, then it would not have to be prepaid and no penalty would be assessed. Although assumable loans still exist, they are not nearly as common as they used to be. In fact, most single-family mortgage notes have a "due on sale" clause, which means that the note must be repaid in full if a sale or transfer in ownership occurs.

Prepayment penalty fees are structured in numerous ways and can sometimes be substantial. Prepayment fee structures range from a simple declining penalty structure to a quite complex fee structure for commercially oriented conduit loans. For example, a loan with a simple declining prepayment penalty structure having a three-year term may have a fee structure as follows:

Prepay Loan in Year	Prepayment Penalty Fee
1	5%
2	4%
3	3%
4	0%

In this example, if an investor borrowed money and then decided to repay the loan in Year 1, a penalty of 5 percent of the outstanding loan balance would be imposed on her. If she repaid the loan in full in Year

---

Exhibit 4.3

Prepayment penalty disclosure (2% penalty—Missouri).

YOU MAY HAVE TO PAY A PENALTY IF YOU SIGN A PREPAYMENT PENALTY RIDER TO NOTE AND YOU PREPAY ALL OR A PORTION OF YOUR LOAN AHEAD OF SCHEDULE SET FORTH IN YOUR NOTE.

WHAT IS A PREPAYMENT?
"Prepay" means to pay more than your scheduled principal and interest payment. Anything you pay in excess of your scheduled monthly payment amount of principal and interest, provided you have no outstanding late charges or other fees due, will be applied to reduce, or prepay, your outstanding loan balance ahead of the schedule contemplated in your Note. The most common form of "prepayment" occurs when you payoff your loan in its entirety by either refinancing or selling your property and using the sale proceeds to payoff the loan.

WHAT IS A PREPAYMENT PENALTY AND WHY SHOULD I ACCEPT IT?
A prepayment penalty is a penalty you must pay if you prepay your loan. It is your choice whether or not your loan has a prepayment penalty. Generally speaking, your acceptance of a prepayment penalty has value to your lender and to you. The lender benefits because the risk of losing the investment in your loan is diminished in the early years. You benefit because you are able to get a lower interest rate and margin, and/or reduce your out-of-pocket closing costs. In other words, if you want to waive the prepayment penalty, your rate and margin may be higher, and/or your closing costs may be increased. Ask us how your rate and margin and/or closing costs would change without the Prepayment Penalty Rider to Note.

CAN YOU MAKE PREPAYMENTS WITHOUT PAYING A PENALTY?
Yes. In any 12-month period during the term of the prepayment penalty, you can prepay up to 20% of your original loan balance

---

without penalty. After the term of the prepayment penalty, you can prepay your loan without penalty.

DOES A PREPAYMENT PENALTY LAST FOR THE LIFE OF THE LOAN?

No. The prepayment penalty applies only during the early term of the loan. The most common "Prepayment Penalty Term is three years, although your prepayment penalty term may be different (see your prepayment penalty rider to note for your actual prepayment penalty term). Once this term has expired, you will no longer have to pay a prepayment penalty if you prepay your loan.

HOW IS THE PREPAYMENT PENALTY CALCULATED?

Your prepayment penalty is equal to 2 percent of the balance of the Note. Any prepayment is payable at the time of the loan payoff or upon request from the note holder.

PREPAYMENT PENALTY TERM

I have discussed my prepayment options with my loan officer and have decided to obtain the following prepayment penalty term:

[   ] First five (5) years of the loan   _____ _____ Initials

[   ] First four (4) years of the loan   _____ _____ Initials

[   ] First three (3) years of the loan   _____ _____ Initials

[   ] First two (2) years of the loan   _____ _____ Initials

[   ] First one (1) year of the loan   _____ _____ Initials

[   ] No prepayment penalty   _____ _____ Initials

Acknowledged by:

_____   _____

Borrower   Date   Borrower   Date

CS-004 09/99
Missouri

2, she would incur a prepayment penalty of 4 percent of the remaining loan balance. If the loan were repaid in Year 3, a 3 percent penalty would be imposed. Finally, if she prepaid the loan at any time during Year 4 or thereafter, there would be no prepayment penalty.

Let's look at an example to determine how prepayment penalties affect a loan transaction. In this example, Investor Green has just acquired a small multifamily apartment building with a purchase price of $800,000. While Investor Green has bought and sold many single-family houses over the years, this transaction represents his very first apartment deal. Since the loan amount is substantially more than he is used to borrowing through his traditional financing sources, Investor Green is forced to locate a new source of funding. Investor Green is new to the world of high finance and agrees to a loan with prepayment penalty fees structured as follows:

Prepay Loan in Year	Prepayment Penalty Fee
1	4%
2	3%
3	0%

Investor Green closes on the property and is now the proud owner of his first apartment building. Shortly after purchasing it, Green happens to come across a book titled *The Complete Guide to Buying and Selling Apartments* (New Jersey: John Wiley & Sons, 2004), and discovers a technique that author Steve Berges refers to as the *value play.* The value play strategy advocates a buy-and-sell philosophy rather than a buy-and-hold approach. The idea is to purchase a property that has upside potential, create value in it by making property improvements, increasing revenues, and decreasing expenses, and subsequently sell it to capture the gain, then move on to the next deal and start the process over. Investor Green decides to implement the value play strategy with his recent purchase and, after improving the property and discovering ways to enhance its revenues, decides to sell in Year 2. Let's now take a look at how the prepayment penalties affected his transaction. To keep the calculations simple, we'll also assume this is an interest-only loan with no payments made to the principal balance.

Purchase price = $800,000
Loan amount = $680,000
Interest rate = 6.25%
Loan origination Fee = 0.0%
Turnaround time = 18 months
Interest paid = $680,000 × 6.25% ÷ 12 × 18 = $63,750
Year 2 prepayment penalty = $680,000 × 3.0% = $20,400
Total interest and fees = $63,750 + $20,400 = $84,150
Effective interest rate = ($84,150 ÷ $680,000) ÷ 18 × 12 = 8.25%

As illustrated in this example, although the stated interest rate of 6.25 percent would be considered a competitive rate for most investors, the effective rate of 8.25 percent is not nearly as attractive. If our good friend Investor Green had been told up front that his interest rate would be 8.25 percent, he probably would have politely told the lender, "No thank you," and moved on to the next lender. Although he left an extra $20,400 on the table, because Green adopted the value play strategy and applied it to this transaction, he was able to walk away with a handsome profit. Next time around, however, he'll be a little wiser by negotiating with the lender in advance for the best possible terms, which includes the elimination of prepayment penalties.

As an investor, you should define your objectives with each and every property you buy *before* you buy it. This includes defining your time investment time horizon as well. If, for example, you intend to purchase a property and implement the value play strategy, you know you're going to be holding the note for only a short period of time. If, for instance, you obtained a $1 million loan with a 5 percent penalty in Year 1 and prepaid it in that same year, you would be subject to paying a penalty of $50,000. Ouch! No one wants to leave that much money on the table. You can easily avoid getting into a situation like this by knowing what your investment time horizon is ahead of time. Understanding the nature of prepayment penalties and how they are applied can potentially save you tens of thousands of dollars. Minimize your exposure by obtaining a loan that doesn't have a prepayment penalty to begin with. Then you don't have to worry about it.

In summary, three additional financing considerations investors need to be mindful of are a loan's duration, any collateral fees that may be charged by the lender or mortgage broker upon the origination of the loan, and any penalties which may be imposed as a result of paying off the loan early. The prudent investor should obtain financing with shorter durations to take advantage of more favorable rates and also to lock in rates for longer durations for those investment opportunities that may have longer life cycles. The careful investor should also use a cost-benefit analysis to determine whether it makes sense to buy down the interest rate by paying additional points up front. Finally, the careful investor will become familiar with the specifics of any prepayment penalty clauses should they exist.

Chapter 5

Structuring Financial Instruments

In Chapters 2, 3, and 4, we learned about the many different elements that directly impact financing for investment properties. Factors such as the time horizon, the volume of transactions, and the type of property being purchased all influence an investor's decision-making process. Furthermore, financing elements such as the cost of funds, the amortization period, and the amount of funds being borrowed affect the viability and profitability of a potential investment opportunity. Finally, elements such as loan duration, lender fees, and prepayment penalties will also have an impact on whether an income-producing property can meet an investor's return criteria. In this chapter, we not only explore the different ways investors can structure purchases, but also the advantages and disadvantages of each (see Exhibit 5.1). We also analyze the effect these various financing mechanisms have on returns.

LEVERAGE

A lever is a tool supported by a fulcrum that can be used to lift heavy objects. Archimedes, an ancient Greek mathematician and physicist, calculated the law of the lever. He is reported to have said that if he had a lever long enough and a fulcrum large enough, he could lift the world. When applied to real estate, the principle of *leverage* enables

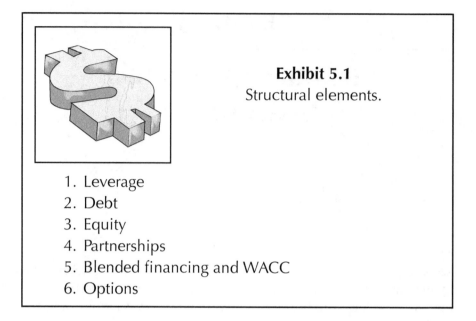

Exhibit 5.1
Structural elements.

1. Leverage
2. Debt
3. Equity
4. Partnerships
5. Blended financing and WACC
6. Options

investors to purchase properties they would otherwise not be capable of purchasing. Applying the law of leverage to the various financing mechanisms that are available can potentially allow individuals to greatly magnify the return on their investments. In fact, without leverage, many people would not even be able to purchase real estate since they can barely save enough money to make even a small down payment.

Investors use the law of leverage to help them *lever up* the returns on their holdings. The application of this law suggests that investors will use a *lever* to lift something that they would otherwise not be able to lift. The lever is supported by a *fulcrum,* which is defined as the support on which the lever turns. In the case of real estate, the fulcrum represents the use of other people's money, commonly referred to as the *OPM principle.* On one end of the lever is an investor's initial capital outlay, however small it may be, and on the other end of the lever is the real estate being levered. The fulcrum enables investors to apply the law of leverage.

The law of leverage as it applies to real estate rests on the premise that the cost of other people's money must be less than the return on the asset being invested in. For example, if an investor borrows funds from a financial institution in the form of debt, the cost of that debt must be less than the expected return on the assets it is invested in. If it is not, then it makes no sense to borrow those funds, because the investor will lose money.

Let's look at a simple example. If the interest rate on a loan is 6.0 percent and the expected return on assets (ROA) is 10 percent, then the leverage is said to be *positive* and would represent a viable investment opportunity. On the other hand, if the cost of funds is 8.5 percent and the expected ROA is 5.75 percent, the leverage is said to be *negative* and would not represent a viable investment opportunity. The difference between the cost of funds and the ROA is referred to as the *spread.* One of the most common mistakes novice investors make is based on the false assumption that any property purchased with nothing down must be a good investment since they didn't have to put any money down. What they fail to realize, however, is that if the property has a negative spread and a negative monthly cash flow because it is highly leveraged, the investment will not generate a positive return. On the contrary, it will generate a negative return requiring monthly cash injections that can literally destroy investors if they have no reserves.

Take a moment to review Table 5.1. It illustrates the effect of price appreciation using no leverage and an initial investment of $500,000, which represents 100 percent of the purchase price. The table applies 5, 10, and 20 percent growth rates over a period of 25 years. An investor in this scenario using an annual growth rate of 5 percent will enjoy a total return of 238.6 percent over the 25-year period. Not bad.

Now let's compare the returns in Table 5.1 to those in Table 5.2, which illustrates the effect of price appreciation on leverage using an initial investment of $75,000, or 15 percent of the purchase price. This table also applies 5, 10, and 20 percent growth rates over a period of 25 years. An investor in this scenario using an annual growth rate of 5 percent will enjoy a total return of a remarkable 1,590.9 percent over the same 25-year period! The use of leverage has allowed the investor in the second scenario to enjoy a return almost seven times greater than the investor in the first scenario.

Table 5.1 Effect of Leverage on Invested Capital Applying Annual Appreciation Only

Purchase Price:	$500,000
Percent Down:	100.0%
Down Payment:	$500,000

Number of Years	Annual Appreciation Rate					
	5.0%	Ret on Inv	10.0%	Ret on Inv	20.0%	Ret on Inv
1	525,000	5.0%	550,000	10.0%	600,000	20.0%
2	551,250	10.3%	605,000	21.0%	720,000	44.0%
3	578,813	15.8%	665,500	33.1%	864,000	72.8%
4	607,753	21.6%	732,050	46.4%	1,036,800	107.4%
5	638,141	27.6%	805,255	61.1%	1,244,160	148.8%
6	670,048	34.0%	885,781	77.2%	1,492,992	198.6%
7	703,550	40.7%	974,359	94.9%	1,791,590	258.3%
8	738,728	47.7%	1,071,794	114.4%	2,149,908	330.0%
9	775,664	55.1%	1,178,974	135.8%	2,579,890	416.0%
10	814,447	62.9%	1,296,871	159.4%	3,095,868	519.2%
11	855,170	71.0%	1,426,558	185.3%	3,715,042	643.0%
12	897,928	79.6%	1,569,214	213.8%	4,458,050	791.6%
13	942,825	88.6%	1,726,136	245.2%	5,349,660	969.9%
14	989,966	98.0%	1,898,749	279.7%	6,419,592	1183.9%
15	1,039,464	107.9%	2,088,624	317.7%	7,703,511	1440.7%
16	1,091,437	118.3%	2,297,486	359.5%	9,244,213	1748.8%
17	1,146,009	129.2%	2,527,235	405.4%	11,093,056	2118.6%
18	1,203,310	140.7%	2,779,959	456.0%	13,311,667	2562.3%
19	1,263,475	152.7%	3,057,955	511.6%	15,974,000	3094.8%
20	1,326,649	165.3%	3,363,750	572.7%	19,168,800	3733.8%
21	1,392,981	178.6%	3,700,125	640.0%	23,002,560	4500.5%
22	1,462,630	192.5%	4,070,137	714.0%	27,603,072	5420.6%
23	1,535,762	207.2%	4,477,151	795.4%	33,123,686	6524.7%
24	1,612,550	222.5%	4,924,866	885.0%	39,748,424	7849.7%
25	1,693,177	238.6%	5,417,353	983.5%	47,698,108	9439.6%

This simple example does not even take into consideration the effect of income generated, tax benefits, or principal reduction.

DEBT

In *The Complete Guide to Investing in Rental Properties* (New York: McGraw-Hill, 2004), I described the use of debt in the following excerpt.

Table 5.2 Effect of Leverage on Invested Capital Applying Annual Appreciation Only

Purchase Price:	$500,000
Percent Down:	15.0%
Down Payment:	$75,000

Number of Years	Annual Appreciation Rate					
	5.0%	Ret on Inv	10.0%	Ret on Inv	20.0%	Ret on Inv
1	525,000	33.3%	550,000	66.7%	600,000	133.3%
2	551,250	68.3%	605,000	140.0%	720,000	293.3%
3	578,813	105.1%	665,500	220.7%	864,000	485.3%
4	607,753	143.7%	732,050	309.4%	1,036,800	715.7%
5	638,141	184.2%	805,255	407.0%	1,244,160	992.2%
6	670,048	226.7%	885,781	514.4%	1,492,992	1324.0%
7	703,550	271.4%	974,359	632.5%	1,791,590	1722.1%
8	738,728	318.3%	1,071,794	762.4%	2,149,908	2199.9%
9	775,664	367.6%	1,178,974	905.3%	2,579,890	2773.2%
10	814,447	419.3%	1,296,871	1062.5%	3,095,868	3461.2%
11	855,170	473.6%	1,426,558	1235.4%	3,715,042	4286.7%
12	897,928	530.6%	1,569,214	1425.6%	4,458,050	5277.4%
13	942,825	590.4%	1,726,136	1634.8%	5,349,660	6466.2%
14	989,966	653.3%	1,898,749	1865.0%	6,419,592	7892.8%
15	1,039,464	719.3%	2,088,624	2118.2%	7,703,511	9604.7%
16	1,091,437	788.6%	2,297,486	2396.6%	9,244,213	11659.0%
17	1,146,009	861.3%	2,527,235	2703.0%	11,093,056	14124.1%
18	1,203,310	937.7%	2,779,959	3039.9%	13,311,667	17082.2%
19	1,263,475	1018.0%	3,057,955	3410.6%	15,974,000	20632.0%
20	1,326,649	1102.2%	3,363,750	3818.3%	19,168,800	24891.7%
21	1,392,981	1190.6%	3,700,125	4266.8%	23,002,560	30003.4%
22	1,462,630	1283.5%	4,070,137	4760.2%	27,603,072	36137.4%
23	1,535,762	1381.0%	4,477,151	5302.9%	33,123,686	43498.2%
24	1,612,550	1483.4%	4,924,866	5899.8%	39,748,424	52331.2%
25	1,693,177	1590.9%	5,417,353	6556.5%	47,698,108	62930.8%

Other people's money can be provided to you in one of two forms—either debt or equity. The most common type of financing is debt. Debt is most often provided in the form of some type of loan which can come from any number of sources including banks, mortgage companies, family members, friends, credit cards, and home equity loans to name a few. Financing with debt typically requires that you repay a loan with predetermined terms and conditions such as the repayment term (number of years to repay the loan), the interest rate, and any prepayment penalties which may be imposed for paying off a loan early.

One primary advantage of using debt is its lower cost of capital than other forms of financing such as equity. Another advantage of using debt is that it is typically more readily available than equity. One key disadvantage of using debt is that the debt must be serviced. In other words, you have to make periodic payments on the loan. Using debt as a source of financing will usually have a direct negative impact on the cash flow from your rental house since loans usually require monthly payments. It should be obvious to you that the more you borrow for a particular investment, the greater your monthly payment will be, and the greater your monthly payment, the less the property's after tax cash flow will be. As a smart investor, you must be sure that you have structured the purchase of your rental house in such a manner that will allow you to service the debt on it, whatever the source of that debt is, without a negative cash flow. This is after all expenses have been accounted for. You should have a minimum of a 1.1 to 1.2 ratio of free cash flow left over after all expenses have been paid to ensure that you can adequately meet the debt requirements. Debt is a wonderful tool, but like any tool, you must exercise caution and respect when using it. Otherwise you can quickly find yourself in trouble. You must be in control of your debt. Do not allow your debt to control you.

From this excerpt, we learn that the primary advantages of using debt are that it is readily available and that it can typically be obtained at a lower cost than alternative financing sources such as equity. In Chapter 3, we examined the effect of different interest rates on the value and returns of an income-producing property. The lower the cost of funds, the greater the cash flow, and the greater the cash flow, the greater an investor's returns.

We also learned that one key disadvantage is that debt usually requires that some type of periodic payment be made. This is especially important because an investor purchasing a non-income-producing property may have a difficult time making the required periodic payments. For example, when I purchase land on which to build houses, my preference is to defer all interest and tax payments for as long as I can. If possible, I structure the financing in such a manner that no payments are due until a lot is released. When a house is ready to be built on a particular lot, all accrued interest and taxes are paid on the lot at that time. The payment is made from the construction loan used to build the house. Structuring the financing in this manner enables me to lever up without having the burden of making periodic payments on the land.

One additional advantage of using debt is that the interest portion of the payment is tax deductible, because interest is treated as an expense for tax purposes. Since the interest portion of a debt payment is tax deductible, the effective interest rate is lower than it otherwise would be. This provides investors with an added incentive to use debt rather than equity, since they are able to further reduce their cost of funds. Let's take a moment to look at an example to see how this works.

Loan amount = $100,000
Interest rate = 6.50%
Annual interest paid = $100,000 × 6.50% = $6,500
Investor's tax rate = 35%
Reduction in taxes = $6,500 × 35% = $2,275
Effective interest rate = ($6,500 − $2,275) = $4,225 ÷ $100,000
     = 4.225%

This example assumes a loan amount of $100,000 and cost of funds of 6,50 percent. An investor in a 35 percent tax bracket would realize $2,275 in savings as a result of the reduction in tax liability. The annual cost of funds is reduced from $6,500 to $4,225, which in turn reduces the effective tax rate to 4.225 percent.

EQUITY

Another common method of funding an investment is by raising capital in the form of equity. Whereas debt represents money that is borrowed, equity represents money that is invested. Equity financing can be provided by any number of sources and commonly involves the formation of a legal partnership or corporation. Family, friends, business associates, and private investors can all be good sources of equity financing. One of the main reasons for using equity financing is to minimize the cash flowing out of income-producing properties. The repayment of equity financing can be structured in any number of ways. For example, you can agree with the investor to pay a specified percentage of the profits at the end of each quarter, semiannually, or even annually. You could also agree to defer all payments until such time as the property is sold. Sharing profits with an equity investor can be based on income, capital gains, or any combination of the two. Preserving as much cash as possible, especially in the earlier years of investing when cash reserves tend to be smaller, can mean the difference between success and failure in the real estate business.

Although not as common as lenders who provide financing in the form of loans, or debt, a number of institutional investors are willing to fund investment projects in the form of equity. In other words, instead of *lending* money to buyers, investors contribute *capital* in the form of equity. In essence, they become shareholders. Capital contributions from equity investors allow the smaller private investors to leverage up into larger commercial or multifamily properties that they otherwise would not be capable of purchasing.

Equity investors typically require a minimum return on their investment that is higher than if the funds had been borrowed. Furthermore, because they are shareholders, equity investors also expect to share in the profits of a property that result from its sale. Most of the larger institutional investors are looking to place large sums of capital and oftentimes will not even consider a project less than $5 million in size. Since they will fund up to 80 or 90 percent of the capital required, the private investor will need to be prepared to invest a minimum of 10 to 20 percent. Let's look at an example to see how this might work for a commercial strip center with a purchase price of $5 million.

Purchase price = $5,000,000
Total equity = 20% = $5,000,000 × 20% = $1,000,000
Institutional share = 80% = $1,000,000 × 80% = $800,000
Investor share = 20% = $1,000,000 × 20% = $200,000

Structuring the financing in this manner allows smaller investors the opportunity to acquire larger income-producing properties than would otherwise be possible. In this example, the investor is able to purchase a $5 million commercial property with only $200,000. Instead of the normal 15 to 20 percent down, the investor has to come up with only 4 percent of the total purchase price, as follows:

$$\text{Investor share of total purchase price} = \frac{\$200,000}{\$5,000,000} = 4\%$$

Institutional firms like partnering with local investors who are familiar with the market in a specific area. Local investors often-times have a good idea of which areas are preferable for various reasons. For example, they may have insight into which areas are enjoying positive, even strong, growth and which areas are deteriorating and should likely be avoided. Local investors can also help with, or even be responsible for, the management of the property.

Don't assume that institutional firms are standing by with an open checkbook waiting to invest in the first property that you bring to them. That isn't the case. These investors have accumulated large pools of capital because they are very careful, not because they throw money at every opportunity presented to them. As a smaller investor who is familiar with the local market, you will have to carefully select a property that you believe has potential and represents a sound investment. Then you need to be prepared to put together a well-thought-out business plan, which will include data specific to the area and the property, such as the unemployment rate, average vacancy rates, and rental rates for similar properties. Institutional investors are very selective when they purchase properties, so be prepared to sell them not only on the property and the area, but on yourself as well.

PARTNERSHIPS

Combining your own resources with those of a partner is another way to raise financing for investment properties. The type of partner I am referring to in this section is a friend, family member, or business acquaintance. This differs from the large institutional investor described in the previous equity financing section. Partnerships can be structured in a variety of ways. For instance, capital infusions by partners can take the form of debt or equity, partners can play an active or a passive role, and terms for the repayment provisions can be defined in any number of creative ways. While bringing in a partner certainly has its advantages, probably one of the most challenging aspects is finding one you can work with.

If your partner participates simply by loaning money in the form of debt, then a fixed amount will be repaid to that partner under predefined terms and conditions. Unlike more traditional sources of debt financing, payments can be structured in any manner the two of you agree on. For example, you may agree to make both principal and interest payments, interest-only payments, or perhaps defer all payments until the property is sold. Regardless of how the payments are structured, the amount repaid is predetermined as set forth in a fully executed promissory note and is not based on the profitability of the property. Furthermore, the two of you may choose to secure the loan by the property, or you may choose to secure it by some other form of collateral, or you may choose not to secure the loan at all. At a minimum, the promissory note should be witnessed and recordable. The two of you may choose *not* to record the note for any number of reasons, but the partner loaning the money should have the right to record the instrument if he or she so chooses. An alternative to securing debt financing from a partner is to obtain equity financing. If your partner agrees to invest in your project using equity, then he or she will share the risk with you. If your project goes south, your partner's investment in the project goes south with you. On the other hand, if you hit a home run, your partner will score right along with you. Both you and your partner will enjoy the benefit of sharing in the profits.

Partners may take either an active or passive role in helping you manage and operate the property. For example, you may decide to have your partners actively participate by taking advantage of whatever skill sets they may have. If they have good management skills, for instance, you may want them to help manage the property. On the other hand, you may choose to have your partners play a completely passive role wherein their only contribution is investment capital. In summary, allowing partners to participate can be beneficial to you by providing additional capital for a project that otherwise may be out of reach financially. Finally, partners may be able to contribute services or specific skills that you may be lacking.

We've discussed several of the advantages of working with partners. Now let's take a moment to review some of the challenges. Perhaps the biggest of them is finding the right partner to work with. Just as a married couple who are in tune with each other can live and work and dream together in harmony year after year, so can partners work together to achieve great financial success. As in a marriage, success requires give and take in the relationship. The partners must be able to get along with each other and work together in a spirit of harmony. There must always be a cooperative effort exerted by each partner. This doesn't mean there can't be any disagreements, for certainly there will be; however, you need to have the ability to resolve your differences peaceably.

It also helps to clearly define each partner's duties and responsibilities and to then allow them to work within the agreed-upon framework. As with our spouses, we are sometimes too quick to criticize and too slow to compliment. It is tempting to micromanage other people's performance and point out that they are "not doing it the right way." Working closely together with a partner takes just the right balance of temperament and respect for each other. Husbands and wives often search for years to find the right companion; even then, marriages often result in divorce. Finding the right partner to work with does not happen overnight. Even when you think you may have found the right business partner, the relationship can fail for any number of reasons.

You should consider in advance before ever forming a partnership how its potential failure may affect the relationship you have with that individual, especially if it is a family member. I know of one particular instance where a father-in-law invested much of his savings in his son-in-law's residential construction business. Two years later, the family business went belly-up when the son-in-law declared bankruptcy. I'm sure this failure placed a tremendous strain on the family's relationships. On a more successful note, however, I am equal partners with my brother-in-law, Don Mahoney, in our residential construction company, Symphony Homes. I respect his role as the master builder of our homes, and he in turn respects my role as the master builder of our company. I don't try to tell him how to build the houses, and he doesn't try to tell me how to build the company. That's not to say that we don't have input for each other. He offers his comments and opinions to me, which I gratefully accept, and I offer my comments and opinions to him. Although we have our differences from time to time, it has definitely been a win-win partnership for us. Without Don to ensure that each and every home is built as it should be, I would not have been able to enjoy a fraction of the success in our company that I do today. Likewise, without me to develop our business, Don wouldn't have nearly as many houses to build as he does today.

BLENDED FINANCING AND THE
WEIGHTED AVERAGE COST OF CAPITAL

When purchasing income-producing properties, especially larger ones, investors often combine several sources of financing, including both debt and equity. For example, an investor may purchase a 450-unit apartment building using a first mortgage for 70 percent of the total purchase price plus improvements, then raising another 15 percent of the total purchase price plus improvements through equity arrangements, then borrowing an additional 10 percent of the total for capital improvements from another lender, and finally, investing 5 percent of his or her own capital. Since the four different sources that provide the financing will most likely charge different rates, a blended rate must be calculated. This blended rate is known as the *weighted average cost of capital* (WACC). A company's WACC is the average rate of return required by all of its creditors and investors.

Calculating the WACC for a business or company enables its owners to determine the threshold for future projects or investments. If a real estate firm holding a portfolio of properties, for instance, calculated its WACC at 7.40 percent, assuming the firm's cost of capital was held constant, it would have to be able to earn a minimum of 7.40 percent to justify investing in another property. If the expected return was less than 7.40 percent, the firm would retain its investment resources until a more favorable opportunity presented itself.

An investment firm's cost of capital is calculated by first determining the weight of each component of debt or equity and then multiplying that weight by its respective cost. Take a moment to study the following formula.

Weighted average cost of capital = (proportion of debt × cost of debt) + (proportion of equity × cost of equity) = WACC

The formula can also be written as follows:

$$\text{Weighted average cost of capital} = \left(\frac{\text{bonds}}{\text{bonds} + \text{securities}} \right)$$

$$\times \text{bond rate} + \left(\frac{\text{securities}}{\text{bonds} + \text{securities}} \right) \times \text{securities rate} = \text{WACC}$$

$$\text{WACC} = \left(\frac{B}{B+S} \right) \times R_B + \left(\frac{S}{B+S} \right) \times R_S$$

where

WACC is the firm's weighted average cost of capital
B is the value of bonds, or debt, used for financing
S is the value of stocks, or equity, used for financing
R_B is the cost of debt, or interest rate
R_S is the cost of equity, or the expected return on equity

Now let's apply the WACC formula to an example. Assume the following:

Value of real estate portfolio = $25 million
Total outstanding debt = $20 million
Total outstanding equity = $5 million
Average cost of debt = 6.20%
Average cost of equity = 10.40%

$$\text{WACC} = \left(\frac{\$20,000,000}{\$20,000,000 + \$5,000,000} \right) \times 6.20\%$$

$$+ \left(\frac{\$5,000,000}{\$20,000,000 + \$5,000,000} \right) \times 10.40\% = \left(\frac{\$20,000,000}{\$25,000,000} \right)$$

$$\times 6.20\% + \left(\frac{\$5,000,000}{\$25,000,000} \right) \times 10.40\% = (.80 \times .0620)$$

$$+ (.20 \times .1040) = .0496 + .0208 = .0704 = 7.04\% = \text{WACC}$$

In this example, the weighted average cost of capital for the real estate portfolio is 7.04 percent. If the investment firm that owned the portfolio decided to purchase another property, its managers would carefully examine the firm's cost structure. Assuming a similar cost structure was required to purchase the property, then the manager's threshold would be a minimum of 7.04 percent. That means the total return from the property must yield an income stream of at least 7.04 percent to increase the total return to the firm. Anything less than that means that the cost of financing the property would be greater than the income earned from it and would therefore have a negative impact on earnings.

Although the WACC calculation is a useful tool for individuals or businesses investing on a larger scale, it is just as useful for those individuals or businesses investing on a smaller scale. As an example, an investor buying a $1 million commercial building must pull $200,000 out of her mutual fund, which has been averaging a 12.0 percent rate of return. She will borrow the remaining $800,000 at an interest rate of 6.0 percent. The WACC in this example would be as follows:

$$\text{WACC} = \left(\frac{\$800,000}{\$800,000 + \$200,000} \right) \times 6.00\%$$

$$+ \left(\frac{\$200,000}{\$800,000 + \$200,000} \right) \times 12.00\% = \left(\frac{\$800,000}{\$1,000,000} \right)$$

$$\times 6.00\% + \left(\frac{\$200,000}{\$1,000,000} \right) \times 12.00\% = (.80 \times .0600)$$

$$+ (.20 \times .1200) = .0480 + .0240 = .0720 = 7.20\% = \text{WACC}$$

At first glance, it appears that because the WACC is 7.20 percent, our investor is better off leaving her money in the mutual fund so it can continue to earn 12.00 percent rather the 7.20 percent shown in the calculation; however, because financial leverage was introduced, this may or may not be the case. If the property was purchased at a capitalization rate of 8.50 percent, that means its net operating income would be $85,000 annually before interest. Applying a simple interest-only calculation would require annual debt service as follows:

Net operating income = $85,000
Debt service = $800,000 × 6.00% = $48,000
Net income before taxes = $37,000

Now let's compare the earnings of $37,000 to the yield on our investor's savings if left in her mutual fund.

Mutual fund savings = $200,000
Expected rate of return = 12.00%
Earnings before taxes = $24,000
Difference between investments = $37,000 − $24,000 = $13,000
Yield on investor's equity = $37,000/$200,000 = 18.50%

In this simple example, by introducing the concept of financial leverage, the investor would be able to earn an 18.50 percent rate of return by purchasing the commercial building versus a 12.00 percent rate of return by leaving her money invested in a mutual fund. Calculating the weighted average cost of capital enables the investor to better understand her true cost of capital. Although she is borrowing funds at an interest rate of 6.00 percent, because she is investing funds that would otherwise earn 12.00 percent, her true WACC is 7.20 percent.

OPTIONS

Option agreements are used by investors to gain control of an asset without having to take legal title to it. Options give investors the legal right to purchase an asset at a predetermined price. The use of options is used by investors every day in the stock market to gain control of the rights to either buy or sell various types of securities. An investor could purchase, for instance, a put option for 1,000 shares of Intel with a strike price of $35. This gives the investor the right to sell shares of Intel at $35. The Black-Scholes model is the standard by which options are valued. As with all options, time t is one of the variables that determine its value. Investors have the right to exercise an option at their discretion within a specified period of time. While it is possible that an investor will buy or sell at precisely the right time to lock in a gain, it is also possible that the option will expire worthless and that the investor will lose the money invested to purchase it. In the case of the investor who purchased a put option for 1,000 shares of Intel, it is hoped that the price of the stock will fall so that the investor can sell it at the higher strike price of $35 after having purchased it at any price less than its strike price.

An option works essentially the same way with real estate as it does with a stock. Some sellers may require the purchaser to meet additional obligations, such as assuming responsibility for interest and taxes; however, these items are negotiable. When an option is used with real estate, investors have the legal right to purchase a specified piece of property at a predetermined price within a given time frame. As with stocks, t will eventually expire worthless if the option is not exercised. At some point before the expiration of the option agreement, the investor may exercise her right to purchase the property at whatever price was established. In addition, since a legal interest is held in the property, that interest is usually transferable. This gives the investor the right to sell the property without ever taking title to it. Options are a terrific tool investors can use to purchase property with very little cash of their own. This is especially true if another buyer is found before actually having to take title to it. Another benefit of using options is that they provide investors with the ability to limit their risk exposure in a particular property to only the premium paid for the option. If the investor decides not to exercise the right to purchase, the option expires worthless, and only the premium paid for the option is lost. Depending on the value of the subject property, an option may potentially cost tens of thousands of dollars. While this may represent a substantial amount of money, keep in mind that the price paid for an option is relative to the value of the property being sought. Although the Black-Scholes model is the standard used to price options for stocks, option premiums for real estate are typically based on whatever price is negotiated by the parties that have an interest in it. I personally have paid anywhere from about 1 percent of the total purchase price to as much as 5 percent for an option.

Some of the real estate investment activities employed by Symphony Homes include the use of options for the development and construction of single-family houses. Options are used to acquire rights to property to build on without ever taking legal title until we are ready to begin construction. The company does, however, have a recordable interest in the property. In Chapter 2, I referred to a recent real estate transaction that was worth $3.3 million. An option agreement was used to acquire the rights to that property, which gives Symphony Homes the ability to build on any one of the lots in an entire community at a predetermined price. When our company has a purchase agreement to build a new home for a client on one of those lots, we then exercise the option on that lot and take legal title to it. Although we do have a predetermined strike price, or purchase price, on all of the lots, interest and taxes begin accruing from the date the agreement is signed. The advantage to us in this case is that even though we do eventually have to pay those costs, we are able to defer them until we are actually ready to begin construction on a lot. This provision allows us to minimize our outgoing cash flow and thereby retain as much working capital as possible to take advantage of other potential opportunities.

Let's take a moment to compare the use of an option agreement on this transaction to the use of traditional bank financing. By using an option, we were able to gain control of the lots in an entire community with only 1 percent down. By comparison, purchasing

developed land through more traditional means such as bank financing typically requires at least a 20 percent down payment.

	Scenario 1: Option Agreement	Scenario 2: Traditional Bank Financing
Purchase price	$3,300,000	$3,300,000
Option fee	1%	20%
Total cash required	$3,300,000 × 1% = $33,000	$3,300,000 × 20% = $666,000
Difference = $660,000 − $33,000 = $627,000		

In this example, using an option agreement allowed me to gain
control of an entire community with only $33,000. If I had
approached a bank to finance the project, it would have required
$660,000 in total cash. Using an option agreement provided me with
a net favorable reduction in the amount of cash required of
$627,000. I think you would agree with me that this is a significant
sum of money. The use of an option here allowed me to take full
advantage of the law of leverage by gaining control of real estate
valued in excess of $3 million for a meager 1 percent of the purchase
price. Now that's what I call leverage!

The advantages of using an option in this case are twofold. The
first advantage is that if we have difficulty selling new homes to
prospective buyers in this particular community, we are not stuck
with the ongoing burden and cost of owning the lots. The only thing
we have at risk is our option money. The second advantage is that if
we were to actually purchase the lots, the sale would trigger an
increase in taxes due to a new and much higher assessed value,
because the value of finished lots is much higher than when the
developer first starts improving the land. This is because in the state
of Michigan, property values are not reassessed until a transfer of
ownership has occurred. They are instead capped at a maximum
increase by a change in prices similar to that of the Consumer Price
Index (CPI). As the new owners, Symphony Homes would then be
obligated to assume the new, higher tax liability.

In summary, the use of options can be an incredibly effective tool
for real estate investors who are interested in gaining control of
investment property without having to take title to it. Options enable
investors to gain control of property with very little money down,

which thereby allows them to maximize the use of leverage. I recommend, however, that options agreements be used prudently. Remember that time is one of the variables of an option agreement, and when t expires, so does the option. Carefully study the market as it applies to your particular investment opportunity before committing any capital to it to determine whether the probability of the outcome is favorable. This will help minimize the risk of any loss of capital.

Chapter 6

Real Estate Investment Performance Measurements and Ratios

Investors use a variety of methods to help them evaluate potential investment opportunities. These range from as unscientific an approach as a hot tip from a real estate broker who supposedly has inside connections, to general rules of thumb, to advanced mathematical models that analyze every facet of a property's income and expenses. My experience has been that the majority of less experienced investors really have no idea how to go about properly analyzing real estate, especially when it comes to multifamily and commercial properties. Most of them rely on using comparable sales of similar properties to help assess value. Although this is a good place to start, it should by no means be considered exhaustive. A more comprehensive approach requires the use of all or part of the 10 essential performance measurements outlined in Exhibit 6.1. A thorough mastery of these measurements is crucial to your success in this business. Without understanding them, how can you possibly know whether you're paying too much for a property? Likewise, how can you know if you're getting a good deal? The answer is you can't.

One primary method of measuring relationships that exist between the variables of an investment's income components is through the

Exhibit 6.1
Ten essential performance
measurements.

1. Net income return on investment
2. Cash return on investment
3. Total return on investment
4. Net operating income
5. Capitalization ratio
6. Debt service coverage ratio
7. Turnover ratio
8. Gross rent multiplier
9. Operating ratio
10. Break-even ratio

use of ratios. A ratio is a mathematical equation used to express the relationship between sets or groups of numbers. The use of ratios for analyzing income-producing properties is essential to properly and fully understand their respective values. Furthermore, ratios provide a gauge or general rule of thumb so that a specific property's value can quickly be determined relative to similar properties that may be for sale.

Two precepts must be remembered when applying ratio analysis. The first is the notion that *value is relative.* In *The Complete Guide to Investing in Rental Properties* (New York: McGraw-Hill, 2004), I described this precept as follows:

The smart investor knows that perhaps more important than any other part of the investment process is having a thorough understanding of the concept of real estate values. I like to compare the process of purchasing rental houses to that of shopping for a new car. If you're anything at all like most people, before you buy a new car you're likely to look at all of the newspaper ads related to the type of car you want. Then you'll probably call several of the local dealers to gather some general information and determine which models they have in stock. After that, you'll begin comparison shopping by going around to several dealerships to see which one is offering the best deal. Somewhere along the way, you will have narrowed your selection of cars down to one or two models. Finally, you'll begin the arduous task of negotiating price and terms with the salesperson. Since you've shopped around quite a bit already, you are already familiar with the car's price and what represents a good value. A good value in this case means that the price is equal to or less than fair market value relative to all other cars that are similar in design and features. If you can't reach an agreement with the salesperson, then it's on to the next dealer to try again until finally, you've found just the right car at just the right price.

Since purchasing a rental house for investment purposes costs anywhere from five to ten times more than a new car, don't you think it would be in your best interests to spend at least as much time shopping for a house as you do a car? Yes, of course it would. The more houses you look at in a particular market, the greater you understand their relative values. The fact that a 1200-square-foot house with three bedrooms, two baths, and a two-car garage is priced at $125,000 in a particular neighborhood means absolutely nothing by itself. It is only when you compare the price of that house to the price of all other similar houses in the same area that its price becomes meaningful.

Using the logic described here, we have established the precept that indeed, value is relative. This logic leads us to the second precept, which is that *performance measurements are relative.* The notion that value is relative leads us to conclude that the performance measurements that capture those values must also be relative. For example, what might be considered a good cap rate in one area might very well be considered poor in another area. These areas do not have to be in different parts of the country, either. They can quite easily be in the same metropolitan area. Since cap rates are a function of property values, and property values are in part determined by the location of the property, an investment property in a less than desirable neighborhood would command a higher cap rate (and lower price) to attract buyers who prefer a higher yield. Conversely, an investment property in a highly desirable neighborhood would command a lower cap rate (and higher price) to attract buyers who prefer a higher-quality asset.

The notion that value and performance measurements are relative is essential for investors to both understand and apply. Without this knowledge, it would be very easy to overpay for a property. Be sure to factor these precepts in when analyzing potential investment opportunities.

NET INCOME RETURN ON INVESTMENT

One thing almost all investors have in common is a desire to know the answer to the question, "How much will I make on my investment?" Put another way, investors want to know what the return on their invested dollars will be, or what their return on investment (ROI) will be. The ROI performance measurement can be applied to measure the effectiveness of all types of assets and is especially useful in real estate. The ROI measurement captures the relationship between net income and invested capital, cash flow and invested capital, and the asset's total return and invested capital.

The first of these measurements, *net income return on investment,* captures the relationship between net income and invested capital. This is helpful to financial managers who focus primarily on the traditional income statement. Net income is derived by subtracting all items that are classified as expenses for reporting purposes from gross revenues. Net income is calculated both before and after taxes. It gets a little tricky in that whenever a payment is applied to a mortgage, not all of the payment is treated as an expense. For example, the interest, taxes, and insurance portion of a payment are treated as expenses. The principal portion of the payment, however, is treated as a balance sheet item and has no effect on the income statement. When a payment is applied to principal, two things happen. First, cash is reduced, and second, the loan balance is reduced. The balance sheet remains precisely in balance, as one asset is used to reduce a liability by an equivalent amount.

The net income ROI performance measurement is calculated as follows:

$$\text{Net income ROI}$$

$$= \frac{\text{gross income} - \text{operating expenses} - \text{interest} - \text{depreciation}}{\text{owner's equity}}$$

We explore this performance measurement more fully by studying a detailed example in Part 2, "Case Study Reviews."

CASH RETURN ON INVESTMENT

The second performance measurement is referred to as the *cash return on investment,* also known as the cash-on-cash return. It is the ratio between the remaining cash after debt service and invested capital, also known as owner's equity. This ratio differs from the net income ROI in that it excludes all noncash items, such as depreciation expense, and includes the nonincome portion of loan payments that are made to principal loan balances. As a general rule, investors tend to focus more on this performance measurement than they do on the net income ROI measurement since it represents the cash return on their investment.

The cash ROI performance measurement is calculated as follows:

$$\text{Cash ROI} = \frac{\text{remaining cash after debt service}}{\text{cash investment}}$$

The cash ROI, then, is the ratio between the remaining cash *after* debt service and invested capital, or owner's equity. This performance ratio is important to investors because it measures the monthly and annual cash returns on the cash they have invested.

TOTAL RETURN ON INVESTMENT

The third performance measurement is referred to as the *total return on investment*. The total return on investment is similar to the cash ROI with one important distinction—it accounts for that portion of return that is not cash, namely, the reduction in principal. In other words, it takes into account the portion of the loan that is reduced each period by the payments that are applied to the remaining loan balance, or the principal portion of the loan payment. The total ROI is the ratio between the remaining cash after debt service plus principal payments and invested capital. The total ROI is calculated as follows:

Total ROI

$$= \frac{\text{remaining cash after debt service} + \text{principal reduction}}{\text{cash investment}}$$

The total ROI performance ratio does exactly as its name implies. It provides a measurement of the total return of an investor's capital by capturing both the cash and noncash portions of the return. The noncash portion is similar to making a house payment amortized over a period of years. The value is there in the form of a buildup of equity and a decrease in the liability, or mortgage, as the loan balance is reduced a little at a time over several years. The gain is realized in the form of cash at the time of sale. The total ROI can be calculated as both before-tax and after-tax performance measurements.

NET OPERATING INCOME

The fourth performance measurement is known as *net operating income* (NOI). Net operating income is the income that remains after all operating expenses have been paid. It is also the amount of income available to service the property's debt—in other words, to pay on any outstanding loan balances such as a mortgage or seller-financed note. Net operating income is also the numerator in the quotient used to calculate the capitalization rate. NOI is calculated as follows:

Gross income – total operating expenses = net operating income

The net operating income is a key figure to understand because it is needed to calculate a property's cap rate. It can also be used to estimate the approximate sales price of an income-producing property. For example, if you know that office buildings in a given market are selling for an estimated cap rate of eight (8 percent), and the NOI from a particular building is $240,000, then the estimated selling price for the building should be approximately $3 million. The calculation is made as follows:

$$\frac{\text{Net operating income}}{\text{Cap rate}} = \text{sales price}$$

$$\frac{\$240,000}{.08} = \$3,000,000$$

Now take a moment to review Table 6.1. The table provides a detailed example of how NOI is derived in a typical apartment building. These figures will vary widely, of course, among apartment buildings depending on factors such as whether the tenant or the management is paying for utilities, local tax rates, labor costs, and other factors.

Table 6.1 Net Operating Income

Operating Revenues	Annual
Gross Scheduled Income	700,489
Less Vacancy	24,340
Net Rental Income	676,149
Utility Income	71,877
Other Income—Laundry, Misc.	16,760
Gross Income	764,786
Operating Expenses	
General & Administrative	
Management Fees	26,767
Office Supplies	4,691
Legal and Accounting	1,404
Advertising	1,938
Total General & Administrative	34,801
Repairs and Maintenance	
Repairs, Maintenance, Make Readies	69,664
Contract Services	5,088
Patrol Services	4,831
Grounds and Landscaping	4,751
Total Repairs and Maintenance	84,334
Salaries and Payroll	
Office	33,780
Maintenance	21,920
Payroll Taxes	9,176
Total Salaries and Payroll	64,876
Utilities	
Electric	82,459
Gas	20,056
Water and Sewer	54,548
Trash	8,387
Telephone	1,378
Total Utilities	166,827
Other	
Real Estate Taxes	38,536
Insurance	19,447
Total Other	57,982
Total Operating Expenses	408,821
Net Operating Income	355,965

CAPITALIZATION RATIO

The fifth performance measurement is referred to as the *capitalization ratio,* or cap rate, which is the ratio between net operating income and sales price. Like the other performance measurements, the cap rate is a relevant measurement, which means that a favorable cap rate in one market may be considered unfavorable in another market. The cap rate is calculated as follows:

$$\frac{\text{Net operating income}}{\text{Sales price}} = \text{capitalization rate}$$

The cap rate is an indicator of value that measures the conversion a single payment or a series of payments, such as in a perpetuity, into a single value. The process of converting income into a single value then is what we refer to as *capitalization.* The cap rate captures this measurement in a single value. It is very similar to the *yield* on a financial instrument such as a certificate of deposit. In *The Complete Guide to Buying and Selling Apartments* (New Jersey: John Wiley & Sons, 2004), I discussed this crucial performance measurement at length. Following is an excerpt from Chapter 4.

As you can see, this ratio is really a very simple calculation used to measure the relationship between the income generated by the property and the price it is being sold for. To help put this in a better perspective for you, let's refer back to the beginning of this chapter when we discussed certificates of deposits. We knew the value of a CD was calculated by its respective yield. The cap rate measures that exact same relationship!

$$\text{Present value of CD} = \frac{\text{income}}{\text{rate}} = \frac{\$10,000}{.05} = \$200,000$$

Or to look at it another way . . .

$$\text{Rate} = \frac{\text{income}}{PV} = \frac{\$10,000}{\$200,000} = .05 = 5\%$$

Buying an apartment building as related to this equation is really no different than buying a CD from your local bank. As an investor, you are willing to pay or invest a certain amount of capital in order to achieve a desired return. You know that the rates paid by banks for CDs will vary within a given range, let's say 4%–6%, so you will most likely shop around a little bit to find the most favorable rate. The same is true of apartment complexes. The rate paid, or yield on your investment, will vary within a given range, generally 8%–12%, depending on a variety of market conditions including supply and demand issues, the current interest rate environment, and tax implications imposed by local, state, and federal authorities.

Let's look at an example. We know that NOI is derived by subtracting total operating expenses from gross income. If you were to pay all cash for an apartment building, then NOI represents the portion of income that is yours to keep (before taxes and capital improvements), or the yield on your investment. If you were considering purchasing an apartment building that yielded $50,000 annually and the seller had an asking price of $800,000, should you buy it? Let's plug in the numbers to our equation and find out.

Net operating income = $50,000

Sales price = $800,000

$$\text{Cap rate} = \frac{\text{NOI}}{\text{price}} = \frac{\$50,000}{\$800,000} = .0625 = 6.25\%$$

In this example, you can see that the asking price of $800,000 provides us with a yield of only 6.25%. Let's assume that comparable properties in this particular market are selling for cap rates of 10%. Armed with that knowledge, we can easily determine a more reasonable value for the property by solving for sales price as follows:

$$\text{Cap rate} = \frac{\text{NOI}}{\text{price}}$$

$$\text{Price} = \frac{\text{NOI}}{\text{cap rate}} = \frac{\$50,000}{.10} = \$500,000$$

So in this example, based on the limited information we have, we know the apartment is overpriced by $300,000. Understanding this simple, yet powerful equation is fundamental to properly assessing value. Armed with this knowledge, you can quickly determine if the asking price of an apartment building is reasonable.

The cap rate is one of the most important performance measurements available to investors. You can see by the example illustrated here that an investor who is unfamiliar with this key ratio could have potentially overpaid for the apartment building by an astonishing $300,000. I should add that you can't always rely on the advice or opinion of a real estate agent when it comes to analyzing income-producing properties such as apartment buildings. Many well-meaning agents don't understand value any better than the average person. Unless agents specialize in multifamily or commercial property, they will most likely *not* truly understand the value of an income-producing asset. I've also met my share of agents who do work in this industry and who still don't understand value. My advice to you is to familiarize yourself with cap rates by looking at and analyzing as many income-producing properties as you can. By doing so, you will be able to rely on your own judgment and not the opinions of others.

The cap rate is an important performance measurement to be used not only with apartment buildings, but with any kind of income-producing real estate. The cap rate is so important, in fact, that it is the premise on which one of three traditional appraisals methods are based. The *income capitalization method,* as it is referred to, is discussed in greater detail in Chapter 8, "The Valuation of Real Property."

DEBT SERVICE COVERAGE RATIO

The sixth performance measurement is known as the *debt service coverage ratio* (DSCR). The DSCR is a ratio that measures the relationship between available cash after operating expenses have been paid and the cash required to make the required debt payments. This ratio is especially important to lenders, as they want to ensure that the property being considered for investment purposes will generate enough cash to cover any and all debt obligations. In other words, they want and need to be assured that the real estate is throwing off enough cash to repay the loan. The debt service coverage ratio is calculated as follows:

$$\text{Debt service coverage ratio} = \frac{\text{net operating income}}{\text{principal} + \text{interest}} = \text{DSCR}$$

The ratio is a simple measure of the relationship of cash generated from an investment to the debt required to pay for that investment. The minimum DSCR varies from lender to lender, but in general it can be as low as 0.75 or as high as 1.40. Most lenders look for a minimum DSCR of 1.00 to 1.20.

Several factors can impact the DSCR. For example, if an investor increases the amortization period from 20 years to 30 years, the monthly payment will decrease. Since NOI isn't affected by a change in the amortization period, the DSCR will increase. Take a moment to review Tables 6.2 and 6.3. The two tables are identical except for the amortization period, which is 20 years in Table 6.2 and 30 years in Table 6.3.

Using a 20-year amortization period in Table 6.2 results in a DSCR of 116.03 percent. If the lender's minimum required DSCR was 120.00 percent, this property would fail, because it falls below the minimum. That doesn't necessarily mean the lender would reject the loan, however, as compensating factors may be taken into consideration. Now take a moment to study Table 6.3.

In this example, a 30-year loan amortization period is used, which results in a decrease in the amount of cash required to service the debt each month. The DSCR in this example is 138.65 percent, which compares favorably to the DSCR of 116.03 percent in Table 6.3. Since the lender's minimum required DSCR is 120.00 percent, the property structured with the longer amortization period of 30 years meets the lender's minimum requirement.

OPERATING EFFICIENCY RATIO

The next performance measurement is referred to as the *operating efficiency ratio* (OER). The OER is a computation that measures the operating expenses of an investment property relative to its size. The ratio is useful for both multifamily and commercial real estate properties. It is calculated as the ratio of total operating expenses to total square feet. The result provides a measure of how efficiently the property can be operated. The lower the number, the less it costs to manage and operate the property. The calculation is made as follows:

$$\text{Operating efficiency ratio} = \frac{\text{total operating expenses}}{\text{square feet}} = \text{OER}$$

In the examples illustrated in Tables 6.2 and 6.3, the total operating expenses in Year 1 are \$120,000 and the total square feet are 38,200. The resulting OER is 3.14, calculated as follows:

$$\text{OER} = \frac{\$120,000}{38,200} = 3.14$$

This calculation tells us is that it costs \$3.14 per square foot on average to operate the property. The operating efficiency ratio captures

Table 6.2 Debt Service Coverage Ratio

Financing and Income Analysis

Cost and Revenue Assumptions			Financing Assumptions		
Purchase Price	985,000		Total Purchase	100.00%	1,002,000
Improvements	0		Owner's Equity	15.00%	150,300
Closing Costs	17,000		Balance to Finc	85.00%	851,700
Total	1,002,000			Annual	Monthly
Estimated Monthly Rent Income	16,400		Interest Rate	6.000%	0.500%
Other Income	1,500		Amort Period	20	240
Total Income	17,900		Payment	73,222	6,102

Key Rent Ratios	
Total Square Feet	38,200.00
Total Price/Sq Ft	26.23
Fair Market Value/Sq Ft	27.50
Rental Income/Sq Ft	0.43
Total Income/Sq Ft	0.47
Capitalization Rate	8.48%
Gross Rent Multiplier	5.09
Operating Efficiency Ratio	3.14

		Year 1	Year 2	Year 3	Year 4	Year 5
Rental Increase Projections		0.00%	4.00%	3.50%	2.50%	2.00%
Average Monthly Rent		16,400	17,056	17,653	18,094	18,456
Operating Expense Projections		0.00%	-2.00%	-2.00%	-2.00%	-1.00%

		Actual			Projected		
Operating Revenues		Monthly	Year 1	Year 2	Year 3	Year 4	Year 5
Gross Scheduled Rental Income		16,400	196,800	204,672	211,836	217,131	221,474
Vacancy Rate	5.0%	820	9,840	10,234	10,592	10,857	11,074
Net Rental Income		15,580	186,960	194,438	201,244	206,275	210,400
Other Income		1,500	18,000	18,720	19,375	19,860	20,257
Gross Income	100.0%	17,080	204,960	213,158	220,619	226,134	230,657
Operating Expenses							
Repairs and Maintenance	14.1%	2,400	28,800	28,224	27,660	27,106	26,835
Property Management Fees	5.0%	850	10,200	9,996	9,796	9,600	9,504

■ 94 ■

	%						
Property Management Fees	5.0%	850	10,200	9,996	9,796	9,600	9,504
Taxes	9.4%	1,600	19,200	18,816	18,440	18,071	17,890
Insurance	7.0%	1,200	14,400	14,112	13,830	13,553	13,418
Salaries and Wages	10.5%	1,800	21,600	21,168	20,745	20,330	20,126
Utilities	5.9%	1,000	12,000	11,760	11,525	11,294	11,181
Professional Fees	0.9%	150	1,800	1,764	1,729	1,694	1,677
Advertising	2.9%	500	6,000	5,880	5,762	5,647	5,591
Landscaping	2.9%	500	6,000	5,880	5,762	5,647	5,591
Total Operating Expenses	58.5%	10,000	120,000	117,600	115,248	112,943	111,814
Net Operating Income	41.5%	7,080	84,960	95,558	105,371	113,191	118,843
Cash Flow From Operations							
Total Cash Available for Loan Servicing		7,080	84,960	95,558	105,371	113,191	118,843
Debt Service		6,102	73,222	73,222	73,222	73,222	73,222
Remaining CF From Ops		978	11,738	22,336	32,149	39,969	45,621
Plus Principal Reduction		1,843	22,739	24,141	25,630	27,211	28,889
Total Return		2,822	34,477	46,477	57,779	67,180	74,511
CF/Debt Servicing Ratio	116.03%	116.03%	116.03%	130.50%	143.91%	154.59%	162.31%
Net Operating Income ROI			56.53%	63.58%	70.11%	75.31%	79.07%
Cash ROI			7.81%	14.86%	21.39%	26.59%	30.35%
Total ROI			22.94%	30.92%	38.44%	44.70%	49.57%

Table 6.3 Debt Service Coverage Ratio

Financing and Income Analysis

Cost and Revenue Assumptions		Financing Assumptions				Key Rent Ratios	
Purchase Price	985,000	Total Purchase	100.00%	1,002,000		Total Square Feet	38,200.00
Improvements	0	Owner's Equity	15.00%	150,300		Total Price/Sq Ft	26.23
Closing Costs	17,000	Balance to Finc	85.00%	851,700		Fair Market Value/Sq Ft	27.50
Total	1,002,000					Rental Income/Sq Ft	0.43
			Annual	Monthly		Total Income/Sq Ft	0.47
Estimated Monthly Rent Income	16,400	Interest Rate	6.000%	0.500%		Capitalization Rate	8.48%
Other Income	1,500	Amort Period	30	360		Gross Rent Multiplier	5.09
Total Income	17,900	Payment	61,276	5,106		Operating Efficiency Ratio	3.14

Rental Increase Projections		0.00%	4.00%	3.50%	2.50%	2.00%
Average Monthly Rent		16,400	17,056	17,653	18,094	18,456
Operating Expense Projections		0.00%	-2.00%	-2.00%	-2.00%	-1.00%

Operating Revenues		Actual Monthly	Year 1	Year 2	Year 3	Year 4	Year 5
					Projected		
Gross Scheduled Rental Income		16,400	196,800	204,672	211,836	217,131	221,474
Vacancy Rate	5.0%	820	9,840	10,234	10,592	10,857	11,074
Net Rental Income		15,580	186,960	194,438	201,244	206,275	210,400
Other Income		1,500	18,000	18,720	19,375	19,860	20,257
Gross Income	100.0%	17,080	204,960	213,158	220,619	226,134	230,657

Operating Expenses							
Repairs and Maintenance	14.1%	2,400	28,800	28,224	27,660	27,106	26,835
Property Management Fees	5.0%	850	10,200	9,996	9,796	9,600	9,504

	%						
Taxes	9.4%	1,600	19,200	18,816	18,440	18,071	17,890
Insurance	7.0%	1,200	14,400	14,112	13,830	13,553	13,418
Salaries and Wages	10.5%	1,800	21,600	21,168	20,745	20,330	20,126
Utilities	5.9%	1,000	12,000	11,760	11,525	11,294	11,181
Professional Fees	0.9%	150	1,800	1,764	1,729	1,694	1,677
Advertising	2.9%	500	6,000	5,880	5,762	5,647	5,591
Landscaping	2.9%	500	6,000	5,880	5,762	5,647	5,591
Total Operating Expenses	58.5%	10,000	120,000	117,600	115,248	112,943	111,814
Net Operating Income	41.5%	7,080	84,960	95,558	105,371	113,191	118,843
Cash Flow From Operations	88.4%						
Total Cash Available for Loan Servicing		7,080	84,960	95,558	105,371	113,191	118,843
Debt Service		5,106	61,276	61,276	61,276	61,276	61,276
Remaining CF From Ops		1,974	23,684	34,282	44,094	51,915	57,567
Plus Principal Reduction		848	10,459	11,104	11,789	12,516	13,288
Total Return		2,822	34,143	45,386	55,883	64,431	70,855
CF/Debt Servicing Ratio	138.65%	138.65%	138.65%	155.95%	171.96%	184.72%	193.95%
Net Operating Income ROI			56.53%	63.58%	70.11%	75.31%	79.07%
Cash ROI			15.76%	22.81%	29.34%	34.54%	38.30%
Total ROI			22.72%	30.20%	37.18%	42.87%	47.14%

the relationship between operating expenses and size and can therefore be a useful measurement in evaluating similar properties. If the average OER in a specific market is 3.00, or $3.00 per square foot, then this property would be considered to be within range, but slightly above average.

GROSS RENT MULTIPLIER

The next performance measurement is referred to as the *gross rent multiplier* (GRM). The gross rent multiplier measures the relationship between the total purchase price of a property and its gross scheduled income. It is the ratio of price to income. The GRM calculation is made as follows:

$$\text{Gross rent multiplier} = \frac{\text{purchase price}}{\text{gross scheduled income}} = \text{GRM}$$

The GRM is similar to the cap rate in that it captures the relationship between revenues and price; however, there are two primary differences. The first is that while the GRM measures the relationship between gross revenues and price, the cap rate measures the relationship between net revenues, or NOI, and price. The second difference is that one ratio is inverted compared to the other. For example, purchase price is the numerator in the GRM quotient, but it's the denominator in the cap rate. While a higher cap rate is preferred to a lower cap rate, a lower GRM is preferred to a higher GRM. This is true because the ratio will decrease the lower the purchase price is relative to income. It will also decrease the higher the income is relative to the purchase price.

In the examples illustrated in Tables 6.2 and 6.3, the GRM of 5.09 measures the relationship between the total purchase price and the gross scheduled income in Year 1.

$$\text{GRM} = \frac{\$1,002,000}{\$196,800} = 5.09$$

In the model used to make the calculation, both improvements and closing costs have been factored into the analysis. Although there are no improvements in this example, they are typically included if major capital expenditures are expected. If the improvements are expected to increase the gross revenues, that, too, should be taken into consideration. The GRM can be calculated on either an as-is basis with no changes or improvements to the property, or on a pro forma basis, which includes both improvements and the expected increase in revenues that would result from the improvements.

OPERATING RATIO

The next performance measurement used to analyze income producing properties is the operating ratio (OR), which is the ratio between total operating expenses and gross income. Like the operating efficiency ratio, it provides a gauge of how efficiently a given property is being operated. Whereas the OER measures efficiency relative to a property's total square footage, the OR measures efficiency relative to a property's income. The calculation is made as follows:

$$\text{Operating ratio} = \frac{\text{total operating expenses}}{\text{gross income}} = \text{OR}$$

Depending on the type of income property, an OR can range from about 30 percent to as high as 70 percent or even more. Commercial properties tend to have a lower OR since most of the expenses are passed through to the tenant. Multifamily properties, on the other hand, tend to have a somewhat higher OR since the expenses that are passed through vary. For example, an apartment building being operated as an "all bills paid" property will certainly have higher expenses relative to its income compared to a similar property in which the utilities are paid by the tenants.

In the examples illustrated in Tables 6.2 and 6.3, the OR of

58.5 percent measures the relationship between total operating expenses and gross income and is calculated as follows:

$$OR = \frac{\$120,000}{\$204,960} = 58.5\%$$

The result in this example of 58.5 percent is somewhat on the high side, but does not fall outside the range of normal ratios. An investor looking to create value in an income-producing property would carefully examine each factor that contributes to the operating expenses. In other words, a high OR may signal that repairs and maintenance are abnormally high, or perhaps that management expenses could be trimmed. Conversely, an unusually low OR could signal that not all of the operating expenses are being reported. If repairs and maintenance, for example, are known to average 10 to 15 percent of gross income but are being reported as only 3 or 4 percent, then either the property is in exceptionally good condition or not everything is being reported.

BREAK-EVEN RATIO

The final investment performance measure we examine is known as the *break-even ratio* (BER), which measures the relationship between total cash inflows and total cash outflows. The BER is similar to the OR in that both ratios use total operating expenses as part or all of the numerator and gross income as the denominator. The difference between the two is that the BER includes as part of the numerator the debt service. The BER serves as a performance measurement of cash flows from a property, and the OR serves as a performance measurement of income and expenses.

As the break-even ratio's name implies, the break-even point is the point at which the total cash inflows are exactly equal to the total cash outflows. A property with a *negative cash flow* has a ratio greater than 1.0, which means that its cash outflows exceed its cash inflows; conversely, a property with a *positive cash flow* has a ratio less than 1.0, which means that its cash inflows exceed its cash out-flows. The break-even ratio is calculated as follows:

$$\text{Break-even ratio} = \frac{\text{total operating expenses} + \text{debt service}}{\text{gross income}}$$

$$= \text{BER}$$

In the examples illustrated in Tables 6.2 and 6.3, the BER would be calculated by adding the total operating expenses of $120,000 to the debt service of $61,276 and then dividing this sum by the property's gross income of $204,960. Take a moment to review the calculation.

$$\text{BER} = \frac{\$120,000 + \$61,276}{\$204,960} = 88.4\%$$

The property in this example has a positive cash flow since the BER is 88.4 percent, which is less than 1.0, or 100 percent. I strongly recommend to investors who have adopted a buy-and-hold strategy to invest in only those properties that have a positive cash flow and a BER of less than 1.0. To do otherwise means that addi-tional cash must be invested each month. A property with a negative cash flow is just like my three growing sons. They are constantly hungry and have to be fed all the time! Unless you have deep pock-ets, a hungry property will eat your lunch if you're not careful! If you're buying a property for the purpose of a quick rehab or flip, then a positive cash flow isn't as important, because you don't need as much cash to sustain the project. The negative cash flow, along with the building improvements, is factored into the analysis to determine whether the project represents a viable opportunity.

In summary, each of the 10 real estate investment performance measurements discussed in this chapter can be used by investors to assist in properly analyzing potential investment opportunities. Wise investors who elect to master these principles will no doubt gain greater insight into property values and their worth relative to alter-native opportunities.

Chapter 7

Advanced Real Estate Investment Analysis

In the previous chapter, we examined 10 different real estate investment performance measurements, which enabled us to better understand how an income-producing property was performing at a given point in time. These measurements are considered to be *static measurements,* meaning that they do not take into account a property's performance over more than one time period. Instead, performance is measured at either a specific point in time or over one period of time, for example, one month or one year. This chapter focuses on advanced methods of real estate investment analysis by measuring performance over multiple periods of time. These financial concepts deal with the time value of money and are especially helpful to individuals investing in real estate over a prolonged period of time.

FUTURE VALUE ANALYSIS

The first of these financial measurements is referred to as *future value* (FV). The future value concept seeks to determine the value of an investment over multiple periods of time by using the principle of compounding. This principle is used to attribute the interest earned on interest. For example, interest as it applies to money is simply the cost of money to the borrower and the income to the lender. Compound interest is the interest paid on the interest to the borrower and the interest earned on the interest by the lender. The future value concept helps investors to know what a particular property will be worth over a given period of time.

Let's look at a simple example to better understand the concept of future value and compounding. Banker Smith has offered to pay Investor Jones 5 percent annually for a certificate of deposit held for three years. How much will Investor Jones's initial investment of $1,000 be worth at the end of the three-year period? To find the solution, we start by introducing the following terms.

PV = present value = the value of an investment today
FV = future value = the value of an investment at some point in the future
i = the interest rate
n = the number of periods

In this example, our terms are applied as follows:

$PV = \$1,000$
$FV = ?$
$i = 5.00\%$
$n = 3$ years
FV in Year 1 = $\$1,000.00 \, (1 + .05) = \$1,000.00 \times 1.05 = \$1,050.00$
FV in Year 2 = $\$1,050.00 \, (1 + .05) = \$1,050.00 \times 1.05 = \$1,102.50$
FV in Year 3 = $\$1,102.50 \, (1 + .05) = \$1,102.50 \times 1.05 = \$1,157.63$

In this example, at the end of Year 3, Investor Jones would receive a total of $1,157.63 from Banker Smith. Now let's look at solving the same problem another way.

$FV = PV \, (1 + i)^3$
$FV = \$1,000 \, (1 + .05)^3$
$FV = \$1,000 \, (1.1576)$
$FV = \$1,157.63$

Applying future value principles to real estate helps investors determine the value of their invested capital at some distant point in the future. A working knowledge of the principle of compounding is essential to understanding the effects of returns which are generated over multiple periods of time. It is this compounding component that allows the growth of an investment to accelerate over time. Take a moment to review Exhibit 7.1.

Exhibit 7.1 illustrates the difference between growth rates in an initial investment of $1,000 earning 10 percent per year over a 25-year period. The line that curves up sharply is earning interest at a compounded rate, and the line that is linear is earning interest at a simple rate. The future value of a $1,000 investment earning 10 percent interest and compounded annually over 25 years is $9,850. By comparison, the future value of a $1,000 investment earning 10 percent simple interest annually over 25 years is only $3,400. In this example, the power of compounding has allowed one investment to grow at a rate almost three times faster than the other investment.

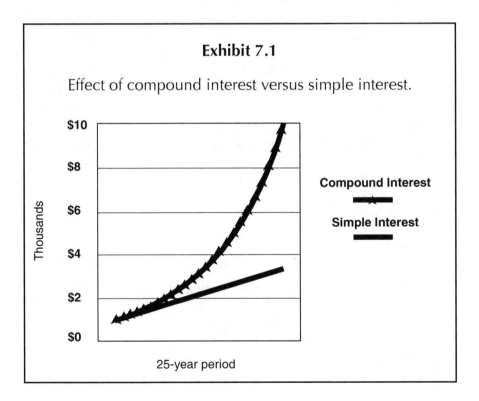

Exhibit 7.1

Effect of compound interest versus simple interest.

Now take a moment to study Table 7.1. This table provides the factor or value by which an investment can be multiplied to calculate its future value at a specific interest rate and time period. For example, to find out how much a $25,000 investment growing at a rate of 12 percent would be worth in 15 years, locate the corresponding value in the table and multiply it by the amount of the investment, as follows:

FV of $25,000 at 12% in 15 years, where
$PV = \$25,000$
$i = 12.00\%$
$n = 15$ years
Corresponding value from Table 7.1 = 5.47357
$FV = \$25,000 \times 5.47357 = \$136,839$

Although Table 7.1 is useful in helping to determine the future value of an investment, it is limited to the rates and time periods within the table. A financial calculator, on the other hand, can be used to calculate the future value of an investment of any size at any rate over any period of time. Most financial calculators are very easy to use. As long as any three of the four variables are known, the fourth one can easily be solved for. As an example, an investor with $5,000 wants to know how long she must hold an investment growing at an annual rate of 8 percent before her investment is worth $25,000. In this example, we must solve for n by entering into the calculator the known values as follows:

$PV = \$5,000$
$FV = \$25,000$
$i = 8.00\%$

Once these values have been entered, then simply solve for n.

$$n = 21 \text{ years}$$

In summary, the concept of future value enables businesses and individuals to determine the value of an investment at some point in

Table 7.1 Value of $1 at Various Compound Interest Rates and Time Periods

Year	2.00%	4.00%	6.00%	8.00%	10.00%	12.00%	14.00%	16.00%	18.00%	20.00%
1	1.02000	1.04000	1.06000	1.08000	1.10000	1.12000	1.14000	1.16000	1.18000	1.20000
2	1.04040	1.08160	1.12360	1.16640	1.21000	1.25440	1.29960	1.34560	1.39240	1.44000
3	1.06121	1.12486	1.19102	1.25971	1.33100	1.40493	1.48154	1.56090	1.64303	1.72800
4	1.08243	1.16986	1.26248	1.36049	1.46410	1.57352	1.68896	1.81064	1.93878	2.07360
5	1.10408	1.21665	1.33823	1.46933	1.61051	1.76234	1.92541	2.10034	2.28776	2.48832
6	1.12616	1.26532	1.41852	1.58687	1.77156	1.97382	2.19497	2.43640	2.69955	2.98598
7	1.14869	1.31593	1.50363	1.71382	1.94872	2.21068	2.50227	2.82622	3.18547	3.58318
8	1.17166	1.36857	1.59385	1.85093	2.14359	2.47596	2.85259	3.27841	3.75886	4.29982
9	1.19509	1.42331	1.68948	1.99900	2.35795	2.77308	3.25195	3.80296	4.43545	5.15978
10	1.21899	1.48024	1.79085	2.15892	2.59374	3.10585	3.70722	4.41144	5.23384	6.19174
11	1.24337	1.53945	1.89830	2.33164	2.85312	3.47855	4.22623	5.11726	6.17593	7.43008
12	1.26824	1.60103	2.01220	2.51817	3.13843	3.89598	4.81790	5.93603	7.28759	8.91610
13	1.29361	1.66507	2.13293	2.71962	3.45227	4.36349	5.49241	6.88579	8.59936	10.69932
14	1.31948	1.73168	2.26090	2.93719	3.79750	4.88711	6.26135	7.98752	10.14724	12.83918
15	1.34587	1.80094	2.39656	3.17217	4.17725	5.47357	7.13794	9.26552	11.97375	15.40702
16	1.37279	1.87298	2.54035	3.42594	4.59497	6.13039	8.13725	10.74800	14.12902	18.48843
17	1.40024	1.94790	2.69277	3.70002	5.05447	6.86604	9.27646	12.46768	16.67225	22.18611
18	1.42825	2.02582	2.85434	3.99602	5.55992	7.68997	10.57517	14.46251	19.67325	26.62333
19	1.45681	2.10685	3.02560	4.31570	6.11591	8.61276	12.05569	16.77652	23.21444	31.94800
20	1.48595	2.19112	3.20714	4.66096	6.72750	9.64629	13.74349	19.46076	27.39303	38.33760
21	1.51567	2.27877	3.39956	5.03383	7.40025	10.80385	15.66758	22.57448	32.32378	46.00512
22	1.54598	2.36992	3.60354	5.43654	8.14027	12.10031	17.86104	26.18640	38.14206	55.20614
23	1.57690	2.46472	3.81975	5.87146	8.95430	13.55235	20.36158	30.37622	45.00763	66.24737
24	1.60844	2.56330	4.04893	6.34118	9.84973	15.17863	23.21221	35.23642	53.10901	79.49685
25	1.64061	2.66584	4.29187	6.84848	10.83471	17.00006	26.46192	40.87424	62.66863	95.39622

the future by applying the principle of compounding to the amount of the initial investment. As long as any three of the four variables are known, the fourth unknown variable can be easily solved for.

PRESENT VALUE ANALYSIS

In the previous section, we examined the concept that deals with the time value of money as it applies to some point in the future. This concept, referred to as future value, allows us to determine the worth of an investment or financial instrument at a future time by introducing the notion of compounding. In this section, we examine the exact opposite concept, known as *present value* (PV). Present value is derived by adjusting the known future value of an asset at a predetermined interest rate, or *discount rate,* from a known future point in time backward to its value today. Present value analysis is a tool used by investment professionals every day in a myriad of business decisions, including investing in assets such as equipment to be used for expansion, financial instruments yielding a particular income stream, and income-producing real estate such as office buildings.

The notion of present value allows investors to calculate the known future value of an asset or financial instrument in today's dollars through a process referred to as *discounting.* For example, it answers a question such as, "How much do I need to invest today if I want to retire in 10 years with $1 million in an investment known to yield 12 percent?" In this example, our terms are applied as follows.

$PV = ?$
$FV = \$1{,}000{,}000$
$i = 12.00\%$
$n = 10$ years

To solve this problem, recall the future value equation as follows:

$$FV = PV\,(1 + i)^n$$

Now let's rewrite the equation to solve for the present value of an asset, as follows:

$$FV = PV (1 + i)^n$$
$$PV = FV\ 1\backslash(1 + i)^n$$
$$PV = \$1,000,000\ 1\backslash(1 + .12)^{10}$$
$$PV = \$1,000,000\ 1\backslash(3.1058)$$
$$PV = \$1,000,000 \times .321973$$
$$PV = \$321,973$$

You would need $321,973 to invest today in an asset yielding 12 percent to be able to retire in 10 years with $1 million. By experimenting with the time and interest rate elements of this equation, investors can explore various options that may be available to them. For example, if you don't have $321,973 today to invest, but you still want to retire with $1 million, you could either extend the value of time or increase the yield. Adjusting either one of these variables would decrease the amount of money needed to achieve your goal.

Now take a moment to review Table 7.2. This table provides the factor or value by which an investment can by multiplied to calculate its present value at a specific interest rate and time period. For example, to calculate the present value of an investment discounted at a rate of 12 percent that would be worth $25,000 in 15 years, locate the corresponding value in the table and multiply it by the amount of its future value, as follows:

PV of $25,000 at 12% in 15 years, where
$FV = \$25,000$
$i = 12.00\%$
$n = 15$ years
Corresponding value from Table 7.2 = .18270
$PV = \$25,000 \times .18270 = \$4,567$

The concept of present value calculations is a fundamental and essential tool used by firms in many aspects of operating their businesses. While future value calculations rely on the process of compounding to derive value, present value calculations rely on the process of discounting to derive value. Present value calculations allow investors to determine the worth of an asset whose future

Table 7.2 Present Value of $1 at Various Compound Interest Rates and Time Periods

Year	2.00%	4.00%	6.00%	8.00%	10.00%	12.00%	14.00%	16.00%	18.00%	20.00%
1	0.98039	0.96154	0.94340	0.92593	0.90909	0.89286	0.87719	0.86207	0.84746	0.83333
2	0.96117	0.92456	0.89000	0.85734	0.82645	0.79719	0.76947	0.74316	0.71818	0.69444
3	0.94232	0.88900	0.83962	0.79383	0.75131	0.71178	0.67497	0.64066	0.60863	0.57870
4	0.92385	0.85480	0.79209	0.73503	0.68301	0.63552	0.59208	0.55229	0.51579	0.48225
5	0.90573	0.82193	0.74726	0.68058	0.62092	0.56743	0.51937	0.47611	0.43711	0.40188
6	0.88797	0.79031	0.70496	0.63017	0.56447	0.50663	0.45559	0.41044	0.37043	0.33490
7	0.87056	0.75992	0.66506	0.58349	0.51316	0.45235	0.39964	0.35383	0.31393	0.27908
8	0.85349	0.73069	0.62741	0.54027	0.46651	0.40388	0.35056	0.30503	0.26604	0.23257
9	0.83676	0.70259	0.59190	0.50025	0.42410	0.36061	0.30751	0.26295	0.22546	0.19381
10	0.82035	0.67556	0.55839	0.46319	0.38554	0.32197	0.26974	0.22668	0.19106	0.16151
11	0.80426	0.64958	0.52679	0.42888	0.35049	0.28748	0.23662	0.19542	0.16192	0.13459
12	0.78849	0.62460	0.49697	0.39711	0.31863	0.25668	0.20756	0.16846	0.13722	0.11216
13	0.77303	0.60057	0.46884	0.36770	0.28966	0.22917	0.18207	0.14523	0.11629	0.09346
14	0.75788	0.57748	0.44230	0.34046	0.26333	0.20462	0.15971	0.12520	0.09855	0.07789
15	0.74301	0.55526	0.41727	0.31524	0.23939	0.18270	0.14010	0.10793	0.08352	0.06491
16	0.72845	0.53391	0.39365	0.29189	0.21763	0.16312	0.12289	0.09304	0.07078	0.05409
17	0.71416	0.51337	0.37136	0.27027	0.19784	0.14564	0.10780	0.08021	0.05998	0.04507
18	0.70016	0.49363	0.35034	0.25025	0.17986	0.13004	0.09456	0.06914	0.05083	0.03756
19	0.68643	0.47464	0.33051	0.23171	0.16351	0.11611	0.08295	0.05961	0.04308	0.03130
20	0.67297	0.45639	0.31180	0.21455	0.14864	0.10367	0.07276	0.05139	0.03651	0.02608
21	0.65978	0.43883	0.29416	0.19866	0.13513	0.09256	0.06383	0.04430	0.03094	0.02174
22	0.64684	0.42196	0.27751	0.18394	0.12285	0.08264	0.05599	0.03819	0.02622	0.01811
23	0.63416	0.40573	0.26180	0.17032	0.11168	0.07379	0.04911	0.03292	0.02222	0.01509
24	0.62172	0.39012	0.24698	0.15770	0.10153	0.06588	0.04308	0.02838	0.01883	0.01258
25	0.60953	0.37512	0.23300	0.14602	0.09230	0.05882	0.03779	0.02447	0.01596	0.01048

value is known in today's dollars by discounting it back at a specified or required rate. Understanding the principle of present value enables business owners to make prudent decisions relating to the use of available capital for investment purposes.

NET PRESENT VALUE ANALYSIS

In the previous section, we learned about using present value formulas to determine the value of an asset in today's dollars of a known future value at a specific discount rate and period of time. In this section, we examine another financial tool used to measure investments. It's known as *net present value* (NPV). The financial analysis of assets using net present value calculations is identical to that of present value calculations with one exception. In a present value calculation, an investor simply wants to determine how much should be invested today to earn a particular rate of return over a given period of time, so solving for PV is all that is required. In a net present value calculation, however, the cost of the investment is already known. Because of this, investors seeking to purchase an income-producing asset use the PV formula to discount the value of the asset back at a predetermined minimum expected rate of return. If the present value of the asset exceeds its cost, the difference is a positive NPV. In this case, the investor would approve the purchase of the asset since it met or exceeded her minimum expected rate of return. If, however, the present value of the asset is less than its cost, the difference results in a negative NPV in which case, the investor would reject the purchase since it did not meet her minimum expected rate of return.

Let's look at an example to better understand how the net present value calculation can be useful to a business. Assume a business that has a minimum required rate of return of 8 percent is considering the purchase of an income-producing asset with a purchase price of $500,000. The future value of the asset in eight years is expected to be $1.1 million. Using the minimum required rate of return of 8 percent, should the company purchase the asset? To answer that question, we must first solve for its present value.

PV of $1.1 million at 8% in 10 years, where
FV = $1,100,000
i = 8.00%
n = 10 years
Corresponding value from Table 7.2 = .46319
PV = $1,100,000 × .46319 = $509,512

To determine the net present value of this investment, the initial cost of the asset must now be subtracted from the present value.

NPV = *PV* − cost
NPV = $509,512 − $500,000 = $9,512
NPV = $9,512

Since the NPV is positive, it meets the minimum rate of return required by the business and therefore merits further consideration. A NPV greater than zero means that not only does the asset meet the minimum rate of return, but by definition, it actually exceeds it. By substituting the actual cost of the asset for PV, we can solve for *i* using a financial calculator, as follows:

PV = $500,000
FV = $1,100,000
n = 10 years
i = ?

Using a financial calculator, enter the values as illustrated for each of the three known variables. Be sure to enter the PV of $500,000 as a negative value since it represents a cash flow out. All other variables should be entered as positive values. The solution for *i* is as follows:

PV = $500,000
FV = $1,100,000
n = 10 years
i = 8.20%

To summarize, the yield on this investment is 8.20 percent, which exceeds the minimum rate of return required by the business. When analyzing these types of investment opportunities, recall that firms must take into consideration their cost of capital. In this example, if the company's cost of capital was 6.00 percent, investing in the asset would yield an incremental 2.20 percent. The net present value calculation is a tool commonly used by investors from many different industries, including real estate.

INTERNAL RATE OF RETURN

In the previous section, the financial analysis principle of net present value enabled us to first calculate the present value of an investment and then subtract the actual cost of the asset from its present value. The NPV calculations were made with a minimum rate of return already established by the firm. In this section, instead of solving for the NPV, we solve for the *internal rate of return* (IRR). The IRR calculation measures the yield or rate of return on an investment rather than its present value. The present value is assumed to be the initial cost of the asset. The IRR calculation measures the yield from a series of cash flows across a specified period of time and includes the cost of the asset, the cash flows from the asset, and the salvage value of the asset at the end of its useful life. In the case of plant and equipment, an asset's useful life may be exhausted at the end of a period due to functional or technical obsolescence. The useful life of real estate, which may actually increase in value over time, is said to be exhausted when the property is divested.

Let's look at an example. Assume Investor Lincoln wants to add an additional space to a small retail strip center. Construction costs to add the space are estimated to be $100,000. As illustrated in Table 7.3, Lincoln has two choices. In Scenario 1, he can lease the space to Tenant A on a lease-option agreement for three years at a rate of $10,000 per year and then sell the space at the end of the three-year period for $110,000. In Scenario 2, he can lease the space to Tenant B on a lease option agreement for six years at a rate of $10,000 per year for the first three years and $12,500 for the next three years, then sell the space at the end of the six-year period for $120,000.

The internal rate of return in Scenario 1 is 12.94 percent. The income generated from three years' worth of cash flows is the equivalent of earning an annualized rate of return of 12.94 percent on Investor Lincoln's initial investment of $100,000. If, however, Investor Lincoln chooses to hold the property for six years, his yield increases to 13.40 percent. Because the IRRs in this example are marginally close, there may be other factors such as tax issues that could affect Lincoln's decision to choose one scenario over the other; however, with all other things being equal, the higher yield in Scenario 2 suggests that Investor Lincoln should choose this alternative over Scenario 1.

Let's look at another example using The Value Play Income Analyzer, a proprietary model used for analyzing income properties such as apartment buildings. In Table 7.4, the cash flows of a 50-unit apartment building are examined to determine its respective internal rate of return.

In Table 7.4, note the net cash flows from investment section in the lower portion of the table. This section is used to display the net cash flows from the property. The first value in the Year 1 exit section of −$514,250 is a cash-flow-out value that represents the owner's initial equity. This is followed by a cash-flow-in value of $683,618, derived by adding the following values.

Table 7.3 Internal Rate of Return

Cash Flows	Scenario 1	Scenario 2
Initial Investment	(100,000)	(100,000)
Cash Flow in Year 1	10,000	10,000
Cash Flow in Year 2	10,000	10,000
Cash Flow in Year 3	120,000	10,000
Cash Flow in Year 4		12,500
Cash Flow in Year 5		12,500
Cash Flow in Year 6		132,500
Internal Rate of Return	12.94%	13.40%

Owner's equity	$514,250
After-tax cash flows	$97,983
Principal reduction	$46,385
Gain on sale	$25,000
Total	$683,618

The cash flow in value of $683,618 assumes the owner sells the property at the end of Year 1 at a cap rate of 9.43 percent, which is comparable to the 9.50 cap rate at the time of purchase (shown in the key ratios section). If the property was sold at the end of the first year, based on its projected cash flows it would earn an internal rate of return of 32.93 percent. Take a moment to review the net cash flows from investment in Year 3. The initial cash flow out, which is the owner's equity, of $514,250 is the same as in the Year 1 scenario. The income earned from Years 1, 2, and 3 is then factored in, as well as the reduction in principal and gain on sale of $450,000. Based on the projected cash flows in the Year 3 scenario, the property would generate an IRR of 46.05 percent. Now take a moment to examine the net cash flows from investment in Year 5. The cash flows are derived in the same manner as in the previous two scenarios, but include income and principal reduction for Years 4 and 5 as well. Based on the projected cash flows in the Year 5 scenario, the property would earn an internal rate of return of 40.21 percent.

While the internal rate of return calculation is widely used by investors to measure the yield on a series of cash flows, there is one caveat. The IRR calculation works best when the initial cash flow is negative and all subsequent cash flows are positive. Additional negative values in the cash flow stream can potentially create multiple solutions. In an excerpt taken from *Investment Analysis for Real Estate Decisions* (Chicago: Dearborn Trade, 1997, p. 222), authors Greer and Kolbe note that the IRR calculation can be problematic under certain conditions. The authors assert the following.

Table 7.4 Property Analysis Worksheet
The Value Play Income Analyzer

Cost and Revenue Assumptions

Land	500,000
Building	2,500,000
Improvements	0
Closing Costs	25,000
Total	3,025,000
Number of Units	60
Average Monthly Rent	700
Gross Monthly Revenues	42,000

Financing Assumptions

Total Purchase	3,025,000	100.00%
Owner's Equity	514,250	17.00%
Balance to Finc	2,510,750	83.00%
	Annual	Monthly
Interest Rate	5.750%	0.479%
Amort Period	25	300
Payment	189,543	15,795

Key Ratios

Total Square Feet	52,500.00
Avg Sq Ft/Unit	875.00
Avg Rent/Sq Ft	0.80
Avg Cost/Sq Ft	57.62
Avg Unit Cost	50,416.67
Capitalization Rate	9.50%
Gross Rent Multiplier	6.00
Expense/Unit	3,307.90
Expense/Foot	3.78

	Year 1	Year 2	Year 3	Year 4	Year 5
Rental Increase Projections	0.00%	3.00%	3.50%	3.00%	3.00%
Average Monthly Rent	700	721	746	769	792
Operating Expense Projections	0.00%	-2.00%	-1.00%	1.50%	2.00%

		Actual Monthly	Year 1	Year 2	Projected Year 3	Year 4	Year 5
Operating Revenues							
Gross Scheduled Income		42,000	504,000	519,120	537,289	553,408	570,010
Vacancy Rate	5.0%	2,100	25,200	25,956	26,864	27,670	28,501
Net Rental Income		39,900	478,800	493,164	510,425	525,737	541,510
Other Income		600	7,200	7,416	7,676	7,906	8,143
Gross Income	100.0%	40,500	486,000	500,580	518,100	533,643	549,653
Operating Expenses							
Repairs and Maintenance	13.0%	5,265	63,180	61,916	61,297	62,217	63,461
Property Management Fees	3.5%	1,418	17,010	16,670	16,503	16,751	17,086
Taxes	7.9%	3,200	38,400	37,632	37,256	37,815	38,571
Insurance	2.0%	812	9,744	9,549	9,454	9,595	9,787
Salaries and Wages	4.4%	1,800	21,600	21,168	20,956	21,271	21,696
Utilities	5.2%	2,120	25,440	24,931	24,682	25,052	25,553
Trash Removal	0.3%	125	1,500	1,470	1,455	1,477	1,507
Professional Fees	0.7%	300	3,600	3,528	3,493	3,545	3,616
Advertising	1.2%	500	6,000	5,880	5,821	5,909	6,027
Other	2.5%	1,000	12,000	11,760	11,642	11,817	12,053
Total Op. Exp.	40.8%	16,540	198,474	194,505	192,559	195,448	199,357

Net Operating Income		23,961	287,526	306,075	325,541	338,195	350,296
	59.2%						
Interest on Loan	29.7%	12,031	143,158	140,420	137,520	134,448	131,195
Dep. Exp. - Building		7,576	90,909	90,909	90,909	90,909	90,909
Dep. Exp. - Equip.		0	0	0	0	0	0
Net Income Before Taxes		4,354	53,459	74,747	97,112	112,838	128,191
Income Tax Rate	0.0%	0	0	0	0	0	0
Net Income After Taxes		4,354	53,459	74,747	97,112	112,838	128,191

Cash Flow From Operations							
Net Income After Taxes		4,354	53,459	74,747	97,112	112,838	128,191
Dep. Exp.		7,576	90,909	90,909	90,909	90,909	90,909
Total CF From Ops.		11,930	144,368	165,656	188,021	203,747	219,101
Interest on Loan		12,031	143,158	140,420	137,520	134,448	131,195
Total Cash Available for Loan Servicing		23,961	287,526	306,075	325,541	338,195	350,296
Debt Service		15,795	189,543	189,543	189,543	189,543	189,543
Remaining After Tax CF From Ops		8,165	97,983	116,532	135,997	148,652	160,752
Plus Principal Reduction		3,865	46,385	49,124	52,024	55,095	58,348
Total Return		12,031	144,368	165,656	188,021	203,747	219,101

CF/Debt Servicing Ratio	151.69%	151.69%	161.48%	171.75%	178.43%	184.81%

Net Income ROI		10.40%	14.54%	18.88%	21.94%	24.93%
Cash ROI		19.05%	22.66%	26.45%	28.91%	31.26%
Total ROI		28.07%	32.21%	36.56%	39.62%	42.61%

Net CFs From Investment - 1 Yr Exit	(514,250)	683,618				
Net CFs From Investment - 3 Yr Exit	(514,250)	97,983	116,532	1,222,780		
Net CFs From Investment - 5 Yr Exit	(514,250)	97,983	116,532	135,997	148,652	1,610,979

	Exit Price	Gain on Sale	Cap Rate
Estimated Exit Price/Gain On Sale - 1 Yr	3,050,000	25,000	9.43%
Estimated Exit Price/Gain On Sale - 3 Yr	3,450,000	425,000	9.44%
Estimated Exit Price/Gain On Sale - 5 Yr	3,700,000	675,000	9.47%

	IRR
Annualized IRR - 1 Yr	32.93%
Annualized IRR - 3 Yr	46.05%
Annualized IRR - 5 Yr	40.21%

Problems associated with the internal rate of return can result in conflicting decision signals from this and other discounted cash flow approaches. Generally, such a conflict arises because the internal rate of return signal is distorted. If heeded, it might result in serious investment error. Potential dissonance stems from peculiarities of the internal rate of return equation, which can yield more than one solution, and from problems associated with the reinvestment assumption inherent in choices among alternative investments that exhibit different patterns of anticipated after tax cash flows.

Mathematicians and analysts alike have attempted to resolve the problems that occur with IRR calculations resulting from the reversal in signals in a series of cash flows. Three of the more common methods used to address these issues are (1) the modified internal rate of return, or MIRR, (2) the adjusted rate of return, and (3) the financial management rate of return. According to Greer and Kolbe, the MIRR method "solves the multiple root problem by discounting all negative cash flows back to the time at which the investment is acquired and compounding all positive cash flows forward to the end of the final year of the holding period." The modified approach eliminates the reversal-of-signals problem and provides a unique solution for a series of cash flows. The adjusted rate of return method assumes the investor has in essence borrowed funds from one period and repaid them in another period, again attempting to deal with positive and negative changes in values. Finally, the financial management rate of return method, developed by M. Chapman Findley and Stephen D. Messner, integrates two intermediate rates. The first, a cost-of-capital rate, is applied to negative that which are discounted back to the beginning of the investment time period where $t = 0$. The second rate is a reinvestment rate and is applied to positive values that are compounded forward to the end of the investment time period.

In summary, this chapter has focused on several advanced methods of real estate investment analysis by measuring performance over multiple periods of time. These financial analysis tools enable individuals and businesses to evaluate investments extending over various periods of time and having various streams of cash flow. Most financial analysis methods use discounting and compounding calculations to express the sum of a stream of cash flows in either present value or future value terms, thereby enabling investors to make decisions based on predetermined minimum rates of return.

Chapter 8

The Valuation of Real Property

APPRAISAL DEFINED

An appraisal is an estimate of an object's worth or value. Appraisals are used to determine the value of both personal property and real property. For example, you may want to have an independent appraisal done on a diamond ring with a $20,000 price tag before investing that kind of money in it. The appraisal could then be used for insurance purposes in the event the ring was lost or stolen. Appraisals are also used to determine the worth and value of real property, such as land or buildings. In *Income Property Valuation* (Massachusetts: Heath Lexington Books, 1971, p. 9), author William N. Kinnard states the following as it relates to the appraisal process:

> An appraisal is a professionally derived conclusion about the present worth or value of specified rights or interests in a particular parcel of real estate under stipulated market conditions or decision standards. Moreover, it is (or should be) based on the professional judgment and skill of a trained practitioner. Its conclusions should be presented in a thoroughly logical and convincing way to a client or an interested third party who requires the value estimate to help make a decision or solve a problem involving the real estate in question.

An appraisal opinion is usually delivered in written form. A professional appraisal report should contain as a minimum the essential ingredients of an appraisal identified as (1) the identity and legal description of the real estate; (2) the type of value being estimated; (3) the interests being appraised; (4) the market conditions or decision standards in terms of which the value estimate is made (frequently identified by specifying an "as of" date or effective date for the appraisal); and (5) the value estimate itself. Moreover, the report should indicate the data and reasoning employed by the appraiser in reaching his value conclusion, any special or limiting conditions that impinged on his analysis and conclusion, and the appraiser's certification and signature.

THE NATURE OF PRICE AND VALUE

As Kinnard clearly states, the process for appraising real property is well defined and specific. Although objective in its format, property values vary widely for many reasons. A 1,000-square-foot house with three bedrooms and two baths, for example, may be worth only $60,000 in Dallas, Texas, while in Hollywood, California, that same house may sell for $150,000. Real estate values are impacted by many different micro- and macroeconomic forces, including supply and demand issues, the current interest rate environment, local and national economic conditions, the desirability of the location, and differences in tax rates. The same appraisal standards applied to a particular piece of real property in one region may yield entirely different results for a similar piece of real property in another region. Likewise, an appraisal of those same properties today would almost certainly be different than an appraisal conducted 10 years ago.

Although the terms *price* and *value* are similar in meaning, they are not the same. An appraisal is an estimate of value and provides no indication of what price will actually be paid for a piece of real property. For example, an individual shopping for a new refrigerator will first determine all the desired features she must have, and then begin to shop for one matching her requirements. Once a model is selected, she will then most likely shop around at several locations to determine which store is offering the best price. By purchasing the refrigerator at the lowest price available, not only is the buyer able to save money, but she is also said to have received the best value. Although two identical refrigerators at two different locations may have the same resell value, the one that originally sold for less money has a greater equivalent value.

The appraisal provides the basis for price, but buyers and sellers are free to negotiate. Kinard asserts, "In the perfect market of economic theory, informed and rational buyers would pay no more, and informed and rational sellers would accept no less, than the present worth of the anticipated future benefits from ownership of an asset." As a result of various differences in economic conditions, however, the actual price paid may be, and often is, different than the stated value in an appraisal report. Price is therefore a reflection of the past. It is what has already occurred. Value, on the other hand, reflects the price that should be paid "in the perfect market of economic theory." Value is therefore a forecast of price. It is what *may* occur at some point in the future, not what *has* occurred at some point in the past.

THREE PRIMARY APPRAISAL METHODS

Three primary methods are used by appraisers to determine the value of real estate: the replacement cost method, the sales comparison method, and the income capitalization method. (See Exhibit 8.1). Each method of valuation has its place and serves a unique function in assessing the worth of real property. Commercial properties such as retail centers, office buildings, and apartment complexes, for example, rely primarily on the income method, while single-family houses typically rely on the sales comparison method.

REPLACEMENT COST METHOD

The *replacement cost method,* or cost approach, is most commonly used for estimating the replacement value of physical assets for

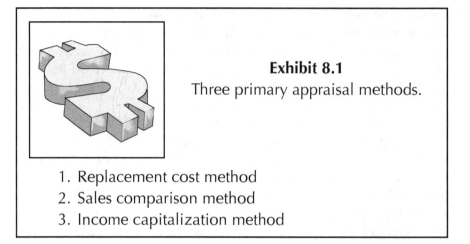

Exhibit 8.1
Three primary appraisal methods.

1. Replacement cost method
2. Sales comparison method
3. Income capitalization method

insurance purposes. For example, should a house be destroyed in a hurricane, an insurance company would want to know the actual cost to replace it. The income method and the sales comparison method are of little or no consequence in estimating replacement costs. The insurance policy you have on your personal residence most likely includes a replacement cost policy with built-in premium adjustments that automatically increase each year due to rises in labor and material costs. Butler Burgher, Inc., an appraisal firm in Houston, Texas, stated the following in an appraisal report that was completed for one of my apartment projects.

The cost approach is based on the premise that the value of a property can be indicated by the current cost to construct a reproduction or replacement for the improvements minus the amount of depreciation evident in the structures from all causes plus the value of the land and entrepreneurial profit. This approach to value is particularly useful for appraising new or nearly new improvements.

The replacement cost approach is most commonly used when estimating the actual costs associated with replacing the physical assets of a house or building. For example, for an office building completely destroyed by fire, the value established from the cost approach would be useful in helping to determine exactly how much an insurance company would pay for the resulting damages.

An additional factor taken into consideration when the replacement cost approach is used is *depreciation,* which encompasses deterioration, functional obsolescence, and external obsolescence. *Deterioration* is said to occur when property loses value because of average wear and tear over a period of time. For example, a 10-year-old roof that has a 25-year life is said to have deteriorated, or depreciated, by 10/25, or 40 percent. *Functional obsolescence* is described as a loss in property value resulting from outdated home designs or mechanical equipment. The value of a house with only gas space heaters rather than central heating, for example, would be adversely affected. Finally, *external obsolescence* is described as a loss in property value resulting from changes in the surrounding neighborhood or community. For instance, the value of a house would be adversely affected if it were located in a neighborhood that had experienced a significant increase in crime. An increase in traffic and noise levels may also contribute to a decline in value.

The underlying rationale of the replacement cost approach is that an informed buyer would not be willing to pay more for a particular house than the cost of building an identical house on a comparably sized lot in a similar neighborhood. The basic formula for calculating the replacement cost approach is as follows:

$$\text{Replacement cost} = \text{cost of construction} - \text{depreciation} + \text{land value}$$

Let's look at an example. Assume the subject property is similar in design, size, and quality to a new house that costs $100,000 to build, not including the lot. The subject property is 30 years old and has depreciated in value by 25 percent due to normal wear and tear, as well as a general decline in the neighborhood in which it is located. The value of the lot is estimated at $20,000. Using the replacement cost approach, the value of the subject property is calculated as follows:

Replacement cost = $100,000 − ($100,000 × 25%) + $20,000

Replacement cost = $100,000 − $25,000 + $20,000 = $95,000

In this example, since the subject property has declined in value, using the replacement cost approach indicates a value of $95,000. This compares to a total value of $120,000 for a new house, which includes a comparable lot, for a difference of $25,000, the amount of loss suffered by the subject property from depreciation.

SALES COMPARISON METHOD

The second primary appraisal method is the *sales comparison method,* or market approach, which is the method deemed most appropriate for the proper determination of value for single-family houses. This includes both owner-occupied and non-owner-occupied single-family dwellings. The sales comparison method is by far the most commonly used approach of the three methods, because the number of single-family dwellings is much greater than any other type of property. This method is based on the logic that the price paid for recent sales of like properties represents the price buyers are willing to pay and is therefore representative of true market value. The price paid may vary for many reasons, including changes in interest rates, changes in unemployment rates, changes in general economic conditions, as well as changes in the cost of materials and land. All of these factors combine to cause changes in the supply and demand of available properties.

The sales comparison method is based on the premise of substitution and maintains that a buyer would not pay more for real property than the cost of purchasing an equally desirable substitute in its respective market. This method also assumes that all comparable sales used in the appraisal process are legitimate arm's-length transactions to help ensure accuracy of the data used in the report. The sales comparison method furthermore provides that comparable sales used have occurred under normal market conditions. For example, this assumption would exclude properties bought and sold under foreclosure conditions—that is, those purchased from a bank's real estate owned, or REO, portfolio.

The sales comparison method typically examines three or more like properties and adjusts their value based on similarities and differences among them. For example, if the subject property had a two-car garage and the comparable property had a three-car garage, an adjustment would be made for the difference to bring the values more in line with each other. In this case, the comparable property's value would be adjusted downward to compensate for the additional garage unit. In other words, the value of the additional garage unit is subtracted to make it the equivalent of a two-car garage. Butler Burgher provides further clarification of the sales comparison method:

> The sales comparison approach is founded upon the principle of substitution which holds that the cost to acquire an equally desirable substitute property without undue delay ordinarily sets the upper limit of value. At any given time, prices paid for comparable properties are construed by many to reflect the value of the property appraised. The validity of a value indication derived by this approach is heavily dependent upon the availability of data on recent sales of properties similar in location, size, and utility to the appraised property.
>
> The sales comparison approach is premised upon the principle of substitution—a valuation principle that states that a prudent purchaser would pay no more for real property than the cost of acquiring an equally desirable substitute on the open market. The principle of substitution presumes that the purchasers will consider the alternatives available to them, that they will act rationally or prudently on the basis of their information about those alternatives, and that time is not a significant factor. Substitution may assume the form of the purchase of an existing property with the same utility, or of acquiring an investment which will produce an income stream of the same size with the same risk as that involved in the property in question. . . .

The actions of typical buyers and sellers are reflected in the comparison approach.

According to Butler Burgher, the sales comparison appraisal method examines like properties and adjusts their respective values based on similarities and differences between them. This method is most often used in valuing single-family houses. Recall that the objective of using this method is to determine the subject property's value. Unlike the cost approach, which seeks to establish the cost of reconstruction for the subject property, the sales comparison approach seeks to establish its market value. Recall also that the market value of a property is *not* the same as its price. The appraiser's objective is to determine a value that reflects the *most likely* price a buyer is willing to pay for a particular property given similar properties to choose from.

While the use of sales comparables, or *comps,* as they are also referred to, is an important factor to consider in the analysis of estimating the value of larger income-producing properties, greater weight is usually given to the income capitalization method discussed in the next segment. The sales comparison method is designed to examine and compare the physical attributes of real property, not the income generated by it.

INCOME CAPITALIZATION METHOD

The third primary appraisal method is the *income capitalization method,* used to value real property that generates some type of income, which is employed for investment purposes. In *Income Property Valuation,* author Kinard describes the process of capitalization as follows:

> Real estate is a capital good. This means that the benefits from owning it—whether in the form of money income or amenities, or both—are received over a prolonged period of time. Operationally, this means more than one year; in fact, it is typically for 10, 20, 40 or more years.

In all economic and investment analysis, of which real estate appraisal is an integral part, the value of a capital good is established and measured by calculating the *present worth,* as of a particular valuation date, of the anticipated future benefits (income) to the owner over a specified time period. The process of converting an income stream into a single value is known as *capitalization.* The result of the capitalization process is a present worth estimate. This is the amount of capital that a prudent, typically informed purchaser-investor would pay as of the valuation date for the right to receive the forecast net income over the period specified.

Kinard's succinct description of capitalizing an asset clarifies the process and is so profound that it bears repeating: "The process of converting an income stream into a single value is known as *capitalization.*" The income capitalization method, then, is appropriately used to value buildings like retail centers, office buildings, mini storage units, industrial buildings, mobile home parks, and multifamily apartment buildings, to name a few. The capitalized value from income-producing real estate is derived directly from the net cash flow or income generated by the asset. Investors compare the rates of return produced from various types of assets against their perceived risks and invest their capital accordingly. Assuming that risk is held constant, an investor's return on capital is the same regardless of whether it is derived from real estate, stocks, or bonds. To more fully understand the income capitalization method, let's turn once again to Butler Burgher.

> The income capitalization approach is based on the principle of anticipation which recognizes the present value of the future income benefits to be derived from ownership of real property. The income approach is most applicable to properties that are considered for investment purposes, and is considered very reliable when adequate income/ expense data are available. Since income producing real estate is most often purchased by investors, this approach is valid and is generally considered the most applicable.
>
> The income capitalization approach is a process of estimating the value of real property based upon the principle

that value is directly related to the present value of all future net income attributable to the property. The value of the real property is therefore derived by capitalizing net income either by direct capitalization or a discounted cash flow analysis. Regardless of the capitalization technique employed, one must attempt to estimate a reasonable net operating income based upon the best available market data. The derivation of this estimate requires the appraiser to 1) project potential gross income (PGI) based upon an analysis of the subject rent roll and a comparison of the subject to competing properties, 2) project income loss from vacancy and collections based on the subject's occupancy history and upon supply and demand relationships in the subject's market . . . , 3) derive effective gross income (EGI) by subtracting the vacancy and collection income loss from PGI, 4) project the operating expenses associated with the production of the income stream by analysis of the subject's operating history and comparison of the subject to similar competing properties, and 5) derive net operating income (NOI) by subtracting the operating expenses from EGI.

To summarize Butler Burgher's remarks, the present value of a capital asset is directly related to its future net operating income. To more fully understand the income capitalization method, let's break it down to its most basic level by analyzing a simple financial instrument such as a certificate of deposit, or CD. When people buy CDs, they invest a specified dollar amount that earns a predetermined rate of interest for a predetermined period of time. Let's look at a simple example. Assuming a market interest rate of 4.0 percent, how much would an investor be willing to pay for an annuity yielding $4,000 per annum? The answer is easily solved by taking a ratio of the two values, as follows:

$$\text{Present value} = \frac{\text{income}}{\text{rate}} = \frac{\$4,000}{.04} = \$100,000$$

In other words, if an investor purchased a certificate of deposit for $100,000 that yielded 4.0 percent annually, she could expect to earn $4,000 over the course of a one-year period. It doesn't matter whether the income continues indefinitely. The present value, or *capitalized value,* remains the same and will produce an income stream of $4,000 as long as she continues to hold the $100,000 certificate of deposit. In this example, we have converted the income stream of $4,000 into a single value, which is $100,000. The process for estimating multifamily and commercial properties is essentially the same. The expected future income stream is converted into a single capital value. Let's take a moment to compare the formula for calculating the present value of a CD to the formula for calculating the present value, or capitalized value, of an income-producing property such as an apartment building.

$$\text{Present value of CD} = \frac{\text{income}}{\text{rate}} = \frac{\$4,000}{.04} = \$100,000$$

Present value of apartment building

$$= \frac{\text{net operating income}}{\text{capitalization rate}} = \frac{\$4,000}{.08} = \$50,000$$

$$\text{Cap rate} = \frac{\text{net operating income}}{\text{price}} = \frac{\$4,000}{\$50,000} = 8.0\%$$

Can you see how similar these formulas are? In principle, they are identical. In this example, an individual who invests $100,000 in a certificate of deposit with a yield of 4.0 percent will earn an income of $4,000. Since the yield on the apartment building is higher at 8.0 percent, only $50,000 is needed to earn an income of $4,000. In both examples, the income stream produced by the two assets is converted into a single capital value. The process is very much the same for determining the value of a company's stock. The ratio is referred to as a P/E ratio. It is the ratio of the price of a given company's share of stock to the earnings generated by that company, as follows:

$$\text{P/E ratio} = \frac{\text{price}}{\text{earnings}} = \frac{\$10.00}{\$1.00} = 10$$

$$\text{Inverse of P/E ratio} = \text{E/P ratio} = \frac{\text{earnings}}{\text{price}} = \frac{\$1.00}{\$10.00} = .10$$

$$\text{Present value of stock} = \frac{\text{income}}{\text{rate}} = \frac{\$1.00}{.10} = \$10.00$$

In this example, an investor purchasing one share of stock for a price of $10.00 could expect to earn a 10 percent return, or $1.00. Whether you are attempting to estimate the value of a certificate of deposit, an income-producing property, or a share of stock, the process is the same. The income stream from each asset is converted into a single capital value. The yield on each asset is different, however, as a result of various risk premiums assigned by their respective markets. The certificate of deposit is essentially a risk-free investment with a guaranteed rate of return and therefore offers the lowest yield. The apartment building carries more risk due to the dynamics of the both micro- and macroeconomics, which affects housing and therefore offers a somewhat higher yield. Finally, the share of company stock carries even greater risk due to the volatility inherent in the stock market, measured as *beta,* and therefore offers the highest yield among the three asset classes.

In summary, each of the three primary appraisal methods serves a unique function by estimating value using different approaches. Depending on the type of property being appraised, all three approaches may be taken into consideration, each with its respective weight applied as deemed appropriate. Butler Burgher asserts, "The appraisal process is concluded by a reconciliation of the approaches. This aspect of the process gives consideration to the type and reliability of market data used, the applicability of each approach to the type of property appraised and the type of value sought."

Chapter 9

Financial Statements and Schedules

$\mathbb{F}$inancial statements are crucial to those who use them by providing information necessary to make decisions regarding an organization. Users of financial statements are classified as either internal or external. *Internal users* of financial statements include accounting and finance groups, managers, senior executives, and board members. This group uses statements to measure the progress of the company, to evaluate its strength, and to identify areas where improvement is needed. *External users* of financial statements typically fall into one of three categories: investors, the government, and the general public. Investors include both creditors and debtors, who rely on information from financial statements to make funding decisions regarding equity and debt. Government agencies include local, state, and federal tax authorities, as well as various regulatory agencies. Finally, for corporations that are publicly traded, information is provided to the general public.

Financial statements represent the end product of the accounting process. For example, all of the information contained on an income statement is the end result of hundreds or even thousands of individual inputs. The information presented on the report is the end result of those individual inputs. Every time inventory is purchased and later resold, an entry must be made in the accounting system. Inventory becomes a cost of goods sold and flows through the system as an expense; when the item is sold, that sale is treated as revenue. The difference between revenue and cost of goods sold is income. When operating an income-producing property, services, not inventory, generate the revenue, and items such as administrative costs, employees, interest, and taxes are treated as expenses. The difference between the revenue and the expenses is income.

When setting up an accounting system, there are several things to consider. For example, a business must determine whether it will operate on an accrual system of accounting or on a cash system. Under the accrual method of accounting, revenue is recognized when goods and services are rendered, not when cash is received. For example, if the owner of a commercial office building operating under the accrual method purchased a one-year insurance policy in June, she would record each month the expense associated with the portion of the premium that had been used. When the policy is initially purchased, rather than recording it as an expense, it is recorded as an asset, typically under the category of prepaid insurance. With each passing month, one-twelfth of the premium is removed from the prepaid insurance and treated as an expense. The accrual method of accounting attempts to more closely match both revenues and expenses with the period in which they occur rather than when cash is exchanged. This method is said to have a smoothing effect on a company's income statement. Almost all larger businesses use the accrual method of accounting, and many smaller business do as well.

The cash method of accounting, on the other hand, recognizes both revenues and expenses at the time payment is made. If, for example, the owner of several rental houses purchased individual insurance policies at various times throughout a given period and expensed the entire amount at the time the policies were paid for, he would be using the cash method of accounting. The cash method of accounting matches both revenues and expenses with the period in which cash is exchanged rather than with the period in which they occur. Although some smaller businesses use the cash method of accounting, very few, if any, larger businesses use this method.

All standards of accounting are governed by what are called *generally accepted accounting principles* (GAAP). Financial accounting and reporting assumptions, standards, and practices that an individual business uses in preparing its statements are all regulated by

GAAP. The standards for GAAP are prescribed by authoritative bodies such as the Financial Accounting Standards Board (FASB). The FASB is an independent, nongovernmental body which consists of seven members. The standards applied by FASB are based on practical and theoretical considerations that have evolved over a number of years in reaction to changes in the economic environment. Rulings issued by the board are recognized as being authoritative.

The three common financial statements most useful for income-producing properties are the income statement, balance statement, and cash flow statement. (See Exhibit 9.1.) These statements are used to report the financial condition of a company on a periodic basis, such as monthly, quarterly, or annually. A prospective purchaser of an income-producing property would be classified as an external user of these financial statements. In order to properly and accurately assess the financial condition of this type of property, the broker or seller should furnish the prospective buyer with the most recent two or three years of historical operating statements. The ability to review several periods provides investors with a more complete picture of the property's capacity to perform over an extended period of time. Investors should be able to detect any trends that are present, such as the regular increase of rents. Conversely, an investor who observed flat or declining rents with corresponding increases in the vacancies would possibly conclude the market in that particular area has softened. This could also indicate management problems, which can be much more easily overcome than a deteriorating market.

Historical operating statements are not always readily available for one reason or another, and when they are, they are not always accurate, especially on smaller properties where no formal accounting system is used. Sellers or their brokers should be able to provide a minimum of the most recent 12-month period of operating data. The trailing 12-month period is the most important because it will enable prospective buyers to accurately evaluate an income-producing property's most recent performance. By examining in detail each of the past 12 months, investors can gauge the relative stability of the revenues, expenses, and net operating income of an enterprise.

INCOME STATEMENT

The first financial statement most commonly used by investors is the *income statement.* The income statement is used to measure a firm's revenues and expenses over a specified period of time. It reports the net income or net loss from a property's operating activities and forms the basis for investment-related decisions. The income statement presents a summary of an income-producing property's earnings activities for a stated period of time, such as for an entire fiscal year or for a particular quarter. It reports the revenues generated and any expenses that occurred. Operating revenues less operating expenses is equal to the property's net operating income. An in-depth analysis of the income statement can provide investors with insight into the level of existing profitability of a property and an indication of its future profitability. Investors commonly use the historical performance of a property to help predict or forecast its ability to earn future income.

Since the income statement is used to capture the earnings of a business, it must take into account factors that impact those earnings. While a retail chain such as Wal-Mart generates income primarily from the sale of goods, a real estate investor's income is

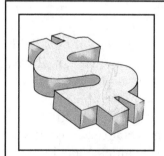

Exhibit 9.1
Three primary financial statements.

1. Income statement
2. Balance statement
3. Statement of cash flows

derived from rents. Investors may also derive revenue through the sale of property, but if this is not their primary business, the revenue thus generated may be treated as a capital gain rather than as income. For example, in the residential construction business, we are in the business of selling houses. Our income statement is set up much like a manufacturing firm's in that all of the labor and materials required to build a house are not expensed until the house is actually sold. The sale of the house produces revenue, and in this case, income, labor, and materials flow through what is referred to as the *cost of goods sold*. Although income statements vary from business to business and company to company, they generally share several of the same basic components. All income statements must reflect both the revenues that flow through the business and the expenses. These two primary categories are typically referred to as *operating revenues* and *operating expenses*. The difference between these two is known as *net operating income*. Since interest expense can vary widely due to a property's capital structure, it is not included under operating expenses, but is treated as a separate category called *interest expense*. Finally, the difference between net operating income and interest expense produces *pretax net income*.

Take a moment to study Table 9.1 to better understand how the various components of an income statement work together. The income statement presented in this example is designed to serve an investor in the rental business and would be used primarily for a multifamily property. It can easily be modified by eliminating categories that are not needed or by adding additional categories to suit the needs of the individual business or entity. For example, the owner of a commercial building would not need all of the items shown in this example. Many of the expenses, such as common area maintenance and taxes, are passed directly through to the tenants. The income statement can easily be modified to reflect the specific needs of the company it serves. Investors who take the time to study and review the income statements of many properties will soon be able to understand their informational content and make sound buy-and-sell decisions based on the information presented in them.

Table 9.1 Sample Income Statement

	Actual				Annual
Operating Revenues	**Qtr 1**	**Qtr 2**	**Qtr 3**	**Qtr 4**	
Gross Scheduled Income	175,200	176,952	178,722	180,509	711,382
Less Vacancy	8,760	8,848	8,936	9,025	35,569
Net Rental Income	166,440	168,104	169,785	171,483	675,813
Utility Income	11,030	13,796	17,375	12,548	54,749
Other Income - Laundry, Misc.	3,862	3,900	3,939	3,979	15,680
Gross Income	181,332	185,800	191,099	188,010	746,242
Operating Expenses					
General & Administrative					
Management Fees	5,440	5,574	5,733	5,640	22,387
Office Supplies	1,831	1,849	1,868	1,886	7,434
Legal and Accounting	470	475	480	484	1,909
Advertising	166	168	170	171	676
Total General & Administrative	7,907	8,066	8,250	8,182	32,406
Repairs and Maintenance					
Repairs, Maintenance, Make Readies	14,910	15,059	15,209	15,361	60,539
Contract Services	1,084	1,095	1,106	1,117	4,401
Patrol Services	1,205	1,217	1,229	1,241	4,891
Grounds and Landscaping	329	332	335	338	1,334
Total Repairs and Maintenance	17,526	17,702	17,879	18,057	71,164

Salaries and Payroll					
Office	7,500	7,500	7,500	7,500	30,000
Maintenance	6,500	6,500	6,500	6,500	26,000
Payroll Taxes	1,057	1,057	1,057	1,057	4,228
Total Salaries and Payroll	15,057	15,057	15,057	15,057	60,228
Utilities					
Electric	11,913	14,899	18,765	13,552	59,129
Gas	4,330	3,747	2,485	3,380	13,942
Water and Sewer	10,456	11,145	13,114	11,887	46,602
Trash	1,425	1,425	1,425	1,425	5,700
Telephone	355	371	388	341	1,455
Total Utilities	28,479	31,587	36,177	30,585	126,828
Other					
Real Estate Taxes	11,200	11,200	11,200	11,200	44,800
Insurance	5,025	5,112	5,112	5,112	20,361
Total Other	16,225	16,312	16,312	16,312	65,161
Total Operating Expenses	85,194	88,724	93,674	88,194	355,786
Net Operating Income	96,138	97,076	97,425	99,816	390,456
Interest Expense	56,064	56,064	56,064	56,064	224,256
Net Income (Pretax)	40,074	41,012	41,361	43,752	166,200

The first primary category on the income statement is *operating revenues.* Operating revenues for rental property consist of all sources of revenue such as gross scheduled income, vacancy loss, utility income, and other income. Gross scheduled income represents 100 percent of the potential income of a rental property if every single unit or space were occupied. In other words, if the vacancy rate were zero and every tenant paid 100 percent of their respective rent, the rental income for the property would be maximized. Vacancy loss represents the amount of income lost due to the unrented units. Promotional discounts and concessions, as well as delinquencies, also fall under the vacancy loss category. Other income includes income collected for late fees, application fees, laundry room income, vending machine income, and any income that may be collected for utilities. It can also include income for interest earned on money held in interest-bearing accounts such as money market accounts.

The second primary category on the income statement is *operating expenses.* This includes all of the expenses having to do with actually operating an income-producing property, such as general and administrative, payroll, repairs and maintenance, utilities, and taxes and insurance. It does *not* include depreciation expense, interest expense, or any debt service. Depreciation is, of course, expensed for tax purposes, but that is treated separately on a statement prepared explicitly for federal tax purposes. The purpose in this section is to better understand the income statement so that it can be used to evaluate a property for its value using the income capitalization method, and also to enable us to better forecast the property's potential for future earnings. Since depreciation is not a true expense in the sense that it affects the cash account (except for smaller capital improvements), it is not usually included on a standard income statement for financial reporting purposes. Since we are not concerned with the tax consequences at this juncture, we will disregard depreciation.

General and administrative expenses include disbursements for items such as office supplies, legal and accounting fees, advertising and marketing expenses, and property management fees. Payroll expenses would consist of all expenses related to those personnel directly employed by the entity operating the rental property. Related expenses include payroll for office personnel, maintenance and grounds employees, payroll taxes, workers' compensation, state and federal employee taxes, and benefits such as insurance and 401(k) programs. Payroll expenses should *not* include any costs for work performed by subcontractors, even though you may furnish all of the materials and pay the subcontractors only for their labor. These types of expenses fall under repairs and maintenance. Make-readies for apartments, contract services, security and patrol services, general repairs and related materials, and landscaping services should all be included in repairs and maintenance. Utility expenses consist of all disbursements related to a rental property's utility usage, such as electric, gas, water and sewer, trash removal, cable services, and telephone expenditures. In many instances, these costs are passed on directly to the tenants and would therefore not be included here.

Taxes and insurance expense also fall into the operating expenses category. They typically include disbursements for real estate taxes and insurance premiums for physical assets such as the building and any loss of income resulting from damage to the premises. Insurance premiums for boiler equipment, pumps, swimming pool equipment, and other machinery also fall into this category. Depending on the specific type of property being operated, many of these subcategories may or may not be required. In addition, there may also be some missing for your particular purposes. This section is provided to give investors a general idea of items that can be found on an income statement and is not intended to be all-inclusive.

The third primary category on the income statement is *net operating income* (NOI). Although NOI is generally just a single line item, this is the most important element of an income statement. Net operating income is calculated as follows:

Gross income – total operating expenses = net operating income

Net operating income is the income remaining after all operating expenses have been accounted for. It is also the amount of income available to service any of the property's related debt. In addition, net operating income is the numerator in the quotient used to calculate the capitalization rate, or cap rate, which was discussed in detail in Chapter 8 under the "Income Capitalization Method" of valuing income-producing properties.

The fourth primary category on the income statement is *interest expense.* This category includes the interest portion of any debt payments being made on the property. Interest expense is placed below net operating income rather than above it in operating expenses since the method in which a particular piece of investment property is funded and capitalized varies widely. For example, Investor A might purchase a commercial strip center using 85 percent debt and only 15 percent equity, while Investor B may choose to purchase an identical building using 50 percent debt and 50 percent equity. If interest expense were treated under the operating expense category, the resulting net operating income for both properties would be different. This is because Investor A's interest expense is higher because he is using 85 percent debt. Meanwhile, Investor B's interest expense would be lower because she is using a financing structure comprised of only 50 percent debt. If Investor C wanted to purchase one of the two buildings for her own investment portfolio, she would not be able to evaluate them consistently, because the financing structures are different. It would appear to Investor C that Investor B's retail strip center was more profitable than Investor A's property, because Investor B has a lower interest expense.

If this seems a little confusing, review the income statement shown in Table 9.1 and experiment with interest expense by moving it above the NOI category. Recall also that net operating income is the numerator in the quotient used to calculate the cap rate. Since NOI would be different for Investor A's property and Investor B's property, either the resulting cap rate would be different or the property value itself would have to be different to achieve the same cap rate.

The fifth primary category on the income statement is *net income.* Net income is simply the difference between net operating income and interest expense. In the example in Table 9.1, the figure shown is pretax net income and not after-tax net income. External users of financial statements are not necessarily concerned with how much tax the owner or seller of a property is paying because their tax rate is likely to be different. After-tax net income would very likely be different from owner to owner for smaller to midsized properties.

BALANCE STATEMENT

The second financial statement most commonly used by investors is the *balance statement,* or balance sheet as it is sometimes referred to, which is used to report a property's assets, liabilities, and equity. It reports a property's financial position at a specific point in time. In effect, the balance statement provides both internal and external users with a snapshot of an income-producing property's financial position on a specific date. Reports are most often printed at monthly, quarterly, and annual intervals. The balance statement can be useful in providing information about a property's liquidity and its financial flexibility, which can be critical at times to meet unexpected short-term obligations. An external user such as a lender, for example, may examine the debt-to-equity ratio and determine that the business is already highly leveraged and that no remaining borrowing capacity exists.

The balance sheet can also be used in measuring the profitability of an income-producing property. For example, by relating a company's net income to the owner's equity or to the total assets, returns can be calculated and used to assess the company's level of profitability relative to similar businesses.

The return on assets (ROA) is used to measure the relationship between net income and total assets. In other words, the ratio measures the return on the total assets deployed by a business. It is calculated as follows:

$$\text{Return on assets} = \frac{\text{net income}}{\text{total assets}} = \text{ROA}$$

$$\text{ROA} = \frac{\$166,200}{\$3,727,060} = 4.46\%$$

The Return On Equity, or ROE, is used to measure the relationship between Net Income and Total Capital. This ratio helps measure the return on an investor's total equity in a property. It is calculated as follows:

$$\text{Return on equity} = \frac{\text{net income}}{\text{total capital}} = \text{ROE}$$

$$\text{ROE} = \frac{\$166,200}{\$654,764} = 25.38\%$$

Now take a look at Table 9.2 to better understand how the various components of a balance statement work together. The balance statement illustrated in this example is designed to serve an investor in the rental business and could be used for owners of single-family, multifamily, or commercial properties. The statement can easily be modified by eliminating those categories that are not needed or by adding additional categories to suit the needs of the individual business or entity.

Three primary categories are part of every balance statement: assets, liabilities, and equity. Take a moment to review the following balance sheet equations.

$$\text{Assets} = \text{liabilities} + \text{equity}$$

$$\text{Assets} - \text{liabilities} = \text{equity}$$

$$\text{Assets} - \text{equity} = \text{liabilities}$$

Observe that the two sides of the equation are equal, hence the name *balance* statement. The two sides of the balance sheet must always equal each other, since one side shows the resources of the business and the other side shows who furnished the resources (i.e., the creditors). The difference between the two is the equity.

The first primary category on a balance statement is known as a company's *assets*. The assets of a business are the properties or economic resources owned by the business and are typically classified as either current or noncurrent assets. Current assets are those that are expected to be converted into cash or used or consumed within a relatively short period of time, generally within a one-year operating cycle. Noncurrent, or fixed assets, are those assets whose benefits extend over periods longer than the one-year operating cycle. For income-producing properties, current assets include amounts owed but not yet collected, such as accounts receivable, cash, security deposits (with utility companies or suppliers, for example), prepaid items such as insurance premiums, and supplies. Fixed assets include items such as buildings, equipment, and land.

The second primary category on a balance statement is known as a company's *liabilities*. The liabilities of a business are its debts, or any claim another business or individual may have against the operating entity. Liabilities can also be classified as current or noncurrent. Current liabilities are those that will require the use of current assets or that will be discharged within a relatively short period of time, usually within one year. Noncurrent, or long-term liabilities, are those liabilities longer than one year in duration. Current liabilities include amounts owed to creditors for goods and services purchased on credit, such as accounts payable, salaries and wages owed to employees or contractors, security deposits (deposits made by the tenants prior to moving in), taxes payable, and notes payable. Long-term liabilities include mortgages payable and any kind of secondary financing secured against the property, such as loans for capital improvements or equipment financing.

The third primary category on a balance statement is known as a company's *equity*. The equity of a business represents that portion of value remaining after all obligations have been satisfied. In other words, if an investor's position in an entity were to be completely liquidated by selling off all of the assets and subsequently satisfying all of the creditors, any remaining proceeds would represent the equity. Since the law gives creditors the right to force the sale of the assets of the business to meet their claims, the equity in a business is considered to be subordinate to the debt. In the event a company declares bankruptcy, obligations to the creditors are satisfied first, and obligations to owners or shareholders are satisfied last.

Table 9.2 Sample Balance Statement

Assets	
Current	
Operating Cash	50,212
Petty Cash	818
Accounts Receivable	1,851
Supplies	965
Prepaid Insurance	10,827
Utility Deposits	14,684
Total Current Assets	79,357
Fixed	
Buildings	3,201,900
Equipment	76,353
Land	369,450
Total Fixed Assets	3,647,703
Total Assets	3,727,060

Liabilities	
Current	
Accounts Payable	4,376
Wages Payable	5,254

Employee Taxes Payable	814
Property Taxes Payable	36,617
Line of Credit	250,000
Security Deposits	25,615
Total Current Liabilities	322,677
Long Term	
Mortgages Payable	2,335,840
Notes Payable - Secondary Financing	256,894
Notes Payable - Capital Improvements	156,885
Total Long Term Liabilities	2,749,619
Total Liabilities	3,072,296

Equity

Capital	
Owner's Contributions	670,871
Owner's Withdrawals	(191,529)
Retained Earnings	175,422
Total Capital	654,764

Total Liabilities and Capital

3,727,060

The two primary categories of equity are (1) owner's contributions and (2) retained earnings. The owner's equity represents that portion of capital that an investor has personally invested. For example, if an investor put down $400,000 on a $2.5 million commercial building and later spent an additional $150,000 in capital improvements, the owner's equity would be $550,000. Retained earnings represent that portion of income left in or retained by the business. If a business generates positive earnings, those earnings are referred to as net income and consequently increase the retained earnings account. Conversely, if a business generates negative earnings, those earnings are referred to as a net loss and consequently decrease the retained earnings account. If the company has positive earnings, and those earnings are not left in the company but are instead paid out to the owner, then the equity decreases by a corresponding amount as a result of the owner's draw.

STATEMENT OF CASH FLOWS

The third financial statement most commonly used by investors is the *statement of cash flows,* which is used to measure the cash inflows and outflows produced by the various operating, investing, and financing activities of a business. These activities affect companies and their respective financial statements in different ways. For example, income may flow into an investor's apartment building from its rental operations and subsequently flow out of it through the purchase of new equipment. In this example, both the income statement and the balance statement are affected, since cash flows in from rents and is then disbursed to purchase assets such as equipment.

Whereas the balance statement measures a firm's assets, liabilities, and equity at a specific point in time, the statement of cash flows measures a firm's operating, investing, and financing activities over a period of time. It can be used to measure cash flows over a month, a quarter, or an entire year. The statement of cash flows is intended to be used in conjunction with both the income statement and the balance statement. By using all three financial statements together, both internal and external users can better evaluate the strengths and weaknesses of a company. Take a moment to review the statement of cash flows in Table 9.3.

Cash flow activities are commonly categorized as either operating, investing, or financing activities. Cash inflows from operating activities as they pertain to income-producing properties include income collected from rents, deposits, utility income, laundry and vending income, and interest income. Essentially, any source of cash that flows through the income statement under the heading of operating revenues qualifies as a cash inflow from operating activities. Cash outflows from operating activities includes expenditures made, such as those for management, repairs and maintenance, landscaping, property taxes, insurance, and payments to suppliers. Essentially, any source of cash that flows out of the business under the heading of operating expenses qualifies as a cash outflow from operating activities.

Cash inflows from investing activities as they pertain to income-producing properties include the sale of assets, collections on loans or credit that have been extended (e.g., accounts receivable), and the sale of debt or equity instruments. A real estate investment company that holds several properties in its portfolio may, for example, sell one of its buildings. Doing so would be classified as a cash inflow from investing activities, since one of the assets, a building, was sold. Cash outflows from investing activities include the purchase of assets, the extension of credit or loans, and the purchase of debt or equity instruments. A real estate investment company, for instance, may decide to diversify by investing its excess cash in the securities of another company in an unrelated industry. Doing so would be classified as a cash outflow from investing activities, since an asset such as securities was purchased.

Cash inflows from financing activities as they pertain to income-producing properties include the issuance of long-term debt or equity securities, as well as funds obtained through any type of borrowing activity. For example, a real estate investment company may obtain a mortgage to purchase an office building to add to its portfolio of properties, or it may secure a line of credit to make capital improvements. Cash outflows from financing activities include the

Table 9.3   Sample Statement of Cash Flows

Cash Flows From Operating Activities	
Cash Inflows	
Rental Income	711,382
Deposits	12,455
Utility Income	54,749
Laundry Income	11,541
Vending Income	4,139
Interest Income	2,258
Total Cash Inflows	796,524
Cash Outflows	
Deposit Refunds	4,975
General and Administrative	32,406
Repairs and Maintenance	71,164
Salaries and Payroll	60,228
Utilities	126,828
Taxes	44,800
Insurance	224,256
Interest Expense	20,361
Total Cash Outflows	585,018
Net Cash Flows From Operating Activities	211,506

Cash Flows From Investing Activities	
Cash Inflows	
Accounts Receivable	7,112
Sale of Property A	455,000
Sale of Equity	100,000
Total Cash Inflows	562,112

Cash Outflows
Accounts Receivable   9,621
Purchase of Land   210,000
Purchase of Property B   761,890
 Total Cash Outflows   981,511

Net Cash Flows From Investing Activities   (419,399)

Cash Flows From Financing Activities

Cash Inflows
Mortgage on Property B   647,607
Line of Credit for Property B   125,000
 Total Cash Inflows   772,607

Cash Outflows
Mortgage on Property A   386,750
Line of Credit for Property A   100,000
 Total Cash Outflows   486,750

Net Cash Flows From Financing Activities   285,857

Net Change In Total Cash   77,964

Beginning Cash   50,212
Ending Cash   128,176

payment of dividends on equity issued, repurchasing debt or equity that had been issued, and the repayment of borrowed funds. A real estate investment company may, for example, decide to repurchase a series of bonds that were issued to raise cash. Doing so would be classified as a cash outflow from financing activities.

Finally, the net changes in cash flow from operating, investing, and financing activities are aggregated to provide the total change in cash flows for a company. To reconcile the statement of cash flows, the cash at the beginning of the period is added to the net change in total cash, which should match the cash at the end of the period. For example, in Table 9.3, assume the period measured was from the beginning of the calendar year, or January 1, to the end of the calendar year, or December 31. The beginning cash on January 1 is $50,212. That figure is then added to the net change in total cash of $77,964 to provide the ending cash of $128,176. This amount should match exactly the amount of cash shown on the balance statement on December 31.

In summary, the income statement, balance statement, and statement of cash flows provide both internal and external users with vital information about the financial well-being of a company or business. They are equally as useful to investors evaluating potential income-producing properties. The balance statement is a static instrument that reflects a company's financial position at a specific point in time. The income statement and statement of cash flows, on the other hand, are dynamic instruments that reflect a company's financial position, and changes in its position, over a period of time Using these financial statements in conjunction with each other will provide the most benefit to investors evaluating potential investment opportunities.

Part 2

Case Study Review: Practical Application of Valuation Analysis

Chapter 10

Case Study 1: Single-Family Rental House

$\mathbb{I}$n this case study, we examine a single-family house to determine whether it is worthy of our investment capital for rental purposes. To properly analyze this type of property, two tests must be applied. The first test applied to our subject property is the comparable sales analysis test. Any type of asset, whether it be gold, silver, stocks, bonds, or real estate, should be purchased at a price less than or equal to its fair market value (FMV). To pay more than FMV implies that a premium has been assessed. Any type of premium paid must be fully justified. The second test applied to our subject property is a cash flow analysis test. An investment property must have cash flow sufficient to break even, at a minimum. If a negative cash flow exists, the investor must be prepared to inject capital into the asset on an ongoing basis. If capital must be continuously invested, negative returns will likely result. If a property has negative returns, like any other type of asset, there is little point in investing in it.

In this first case study, we analyze the property by applying the comparable sales test and the cash flow analysis test. In the next case study, we look at an alternative use for this same property to evaluate it for a better and higher use. The property in this first case study is an actual investment opportunity that I purchased several months ago. The house is located directly across the street from a beautiful all-sports lake in Lake Orion. The property is not considered to be lake-front, but rather lake view. While houses on the lakefront typically sell for $200 per square foot and up, lake-view houses sell for between $120 and $140 per square foot. The subject property falls into the second category, with a couple of exceptions, which is the reason I'm interested in it to begin with. The house sits directly across the street from the lake on a little more than three-fourths of an acre and happens to be the only parcel of land uniquely situated with buildable lot space and zoned *residential multiple* (RM). That means it is not a single-family parcel, but rather a multifamily parcel that will accommodate more than one house or condominium unit. As you'll learn in the next case study, the alternative use as residential multiple is where the property's true value lies.

An additional bonus included in this deal is that along with the land and the house are two boat slips. The seller of the property happened to own 28 feet of lake frontage right across the street from the house, and this parcel is currently home to two boat slips and a motorized hoist, or boat lift. This small piece of land also happens to be deeded separately from the main property, which allowed me to take possession of the boat slips free and clear immediately upon closing. The deal was structured with the main house and property purchased under one contract for the agreed-on price, with the boat slip on anther contract for only $10.

Take a few minutes to examine Table 10.1, carefully studying the property's income as it flows through the model. In this table, the property is analyzed using the seller's original asking price of $370,000. The worksheet you see is a proprietary model I developed to quickly and easily analyze potential rental house investment opportunities. I call it *The Value Play Rental House Analyzer.* Once the necessary data has been gathered, it can be input into the model, and in just a few minutes, the user can know with a fairly high degree of accuracy whether a deal makes sense based on predetermined investment criteria. The user need only key in the variables, and the model performs all of the calculations automatically. Although at first glance the model may appear complex, it is actually quite easy to use.

We start by analyzing this property as though it were going to be used as a rental house only. The ultimate goal in this particular example is to rent the house out while the necessary approvals from the local planning commission are being obtained. The rent from the house in this situation is a bonus, since most of the time, new construction does not include income-producing property such as this. The income from the rents is intended to help offset the carrying costs of the construction project, which will be further discussed in the next case study. For now, however, let's start by analyzing it as a single-family rental house to determine whether it meets the criteria as set forth in our two tests, the comparable sales test and cash flow test.

TEST 1: COMPARABLE SALES ANALYSIS

The first section of the model allows the user to enter information for comparable home sales. This information is needed to help make accurate projections of the estimated resale value of an investment property and can be easily obtained by almost any local real estate sale agent. In fact, if you ask them, real estate agents can send the comps online to your e-mail address, which you can then access via the Internet. Next in this section is a provision that allows users to make adjustments to the sales price of the comps. This section provides users with the ability to compare properties on an apples-to-apples basis, just as an appraiser would do. For example, if the subject property has a central air-conditioning system and the comparable sale property does not, the price of the comparable sale will need to be revised upward in the adjustments to price section. This is exactly how real estate agents and appraisers derive the market value of a house. They start with an average price per square foot of several similar houses that have recently sold and make adjustments to compensate for differences in value.

The comp averages section simply takes an average of the three comps' sales prices to come up with an average sales price. This number is then divided by the average price per square foot. The result is a weighted average price per square foot. There is also a provision that allows users to turn the comps section off or on. As users become more and more familiar with a specific market or neighborhood, they are likely to already know what the average sales price per square foot is, so the sales data really doesn't need to be keyed in. Instead, the comps section can be turned off and the user's own estimate entered in.

Table 10.1 Property Analysis Worksheet. The Value Play Rental House Analyzer

Property Value Analysis

Comp #1		Comp #2		Comp #3	
Address:	123 S. Sample Drive	Address:	456 N. Sample Drive	Address:	789 S. Sample Drive
Sales Price	365,500.00	Sales Price	289,900.00	Sales Price	294,000.00
Adjustments to Price	1,600.00	Adjustments to Price	(2,400.00)	Adjustments to Price	3,200.00
Adjusted Price	367,100.00	Adjusted Price	287,500.00	Adjusted Price	297,200.00
Square Feet	2,645.00	Square Footage	2,096.00	Square Feet	2,200.00
Price Per Square Foot	138.79	Price Per Square Foot	137.17	Price Per Square Foot	135.09

Comp Averages	
Sales Price	316,466.67
Adjustments to Price	800.00
Adjusted Price	317,266.67
Square Feet	2,313.67
Price Per Square Foot	137.13

Adjustment to Comps	2.50	0.00
	390,956	383,956
	370,000	370,000
	20,956	13,956

	2.50
	(2.50)
	376,956
	370,000
	6,956

Subject Property 421 Moroni Blvd.		Property Values	
Purchase Price	370,000	Fair Market Value	370,000
Square Feet	2,800.00	Actual Price	2,800.00
Price/Sq Ft	132.14	Difference	132.14
Turn Comps Off/On		ON	
Est Price/Sq Ft If Turned OFF		135.00	

Financing and Income Analysis

Cost and Revenue Assumptions	
Purchase Price	370,000
Improvements	0
Closing Costs	3,500
Total	373,500
Estimated Monthly Rent Income	1,750
Other Income	250
Total Income	2,000

Financing Assumptions		
Total Purchase	100.00%	373,500
Owner's Equity	10.00%	37,350
Balance to Finc	90.00%	336,150
	Annual	Monthly
Interest Rate	6.000%	0.500%
Amort Period	30	360
Payment	24,185	2,015

Key Rent Ratios	
Total Square Feet	2,800.00
Total Price/Sq Ft	133.39
Fair Market Value/Sq Ft	137.13
Rental Income/Sq Ft	0.63
Total Income/Sq Ft	0.71
Capitalization Rate	4.10%
Gross Rent Multiplier	17.79
Operating Efficiency Ratio	2.72

Rental Increase Projections	0.00%	4.00%	3.50%	3.50%	
Average Monthly Rent	1,750	1,820	1,884	1,950	2,018
Operating Expense Projections	0.00%	2.00%	2.00%	1.50%	1.50%

Operating Revenues	Actual Monthly	Year 1	Year 2	Year 3	Year 4	Year 5
				Projected		
Gross Scheduled Rental Income	1,750	21,000	21,840	22,604	23,396	24,214
Vacancy Rate	5.0% 88	1,050	1,092	1,130	1,170	1,211
Net Rental Income	1,663	19,950	20,748	21,474	22,226	23,004
Other Income	250	3,000	3,120	3,229	3,342	3,459
Gross Income	100.0% 1,913	22,950	23,868	24,703	25,568	26,463
Operating Expenses						
Repairs and Maintenance	5.2% 100	1,200	1,224	1,248	1,267	1,286
Property Management Fees	5.5% 105	1,260	1,285	1,311	1,331	1,351
Taxes	18.3% 350	4,200	4,284	4,370	4,435	4,502
Insurance	2.9% 55	660	673	687	697	707
Salaries and Wages	0.0% 0	0	0	0	0	0
Utilities	0.0% 0	0	0	0	0	0
Professional Fees	1.3% 25	300	306	312	317	322
Advertising	0.0% 0	0	0	0	0	0
Other	0.0% 0	0	0	0	0	0
Other	0.0% 0	0	0	0	0	0
Other	0.0% 0	0	0	0	0	0
Total Operating Expenses	33.2% 635	7,620	7,772	7,928	8,047	8,167
Net Operating Income	66.8% 1,278	15,330	16,096	16,776	17,521	18,295
Cash Flow From Operations						
Total Cash Available for Loan Servicing	1,278	15,330	16,096	16,776	17,521	18,295
Debt Service	2,015	24,185	24,185	24,185	24,185	24,185
Remaining CF From Ops	(738)	(8,855)	(8,089)	(7,409)	(6,663)	(5,889)
Plus Principal Reduction	335	4,128	4,383	4,653	4,940	5,245
Total Return	(403)	(4,727)	(3,707)	(2,756)	(1,724)	(645)
CF/Debt Servicing Ratio	63.39%	63.39%	66.55%	69.36%	72.45%	75.65%
Net Operating Income ROI		41.04%	43.09%	44.91%	46.91%	48.98%
Cash ROI		-23.71%	-21.66%	-19.84%	-17.84%	-15.77%
Total ROI		-12.66%	-9.92%	-7.38%	-4.61%	-1.73%

In this example, three comparable sales of properties similar in characteristics and close in size to the subject property were used. The objective was to use houses in desirable locations also having lake views. In the subject property section, simply enter in the purchase price of the house being analyzed. In this example, the original asking price by the seller was $370,000. The asking price is a good place to begin the analysis, but users can also easily experiment with the model by merely changing the asking price, which is exactly what we are going to do in Table 10.2. After entering the purchase price, the square footage of the subject property is entered, which in this example is 2,800. The average sales price per square foot from the comps section is then fed into the subject property section. The purchase price per square foot is automatically calculated and then multiplied by the square footage of the subject property under the property values and adjustment to comps sections.

The adjustment to comps cell is used to create an estimated fair market value (FMV) using a range of property values for three different scenarios—best case, most likely, and worst case. In this case study, $2.50 per square foot is used; however, the number can be changed to anything you want it to be. For the best-case estimated fair market value, the model adds $2.50 to the price per square foot cell in the comp averages section, and then multiplies the sum of the two by the square feet of the subject property. The positive value of $2.50 is visible under the adjustment to comps heading. Here's how the calculation works:

Best-Case Estimate of Fair Market Value

(Average price per square foot + adjustment to comps)

× subject property square feet = best-case estimate

of FMV ($137.127 + $2.50) × 2,800 = $390,956

The most likely estimate of the FMV calculation in the model neither adds nor subtracts the value of $2.50 to the price per square foot cell in the comp averages section. As you can see in Table 10.1, it is set to zero. This calculation is merely the product of the average price per square foot and the number of square feet. Take a moment to examine the calculation.

Most Likely Estimate of Fair Market Value

Average price per square foot × subject property square feet

= most likely estimate of FMV $137.127 × 2,800 = $383,956

For the worst-case estimate of FMV, the model subtracts $2.50 from the price per square foot cell in the comp averages section, and then multiplies the difference of the two by the number of square feet of the subject property. Take a minute to review the calculations.

Worst-Case Estimate of Fair Market Value

(Average price per square foot − adjustment to comps)

× subject property square feet = worst-case estimate

of FMV ($137.127 − $2.50) × 2,800 = $376,956

The purpose of creating three different scenarios in the model is to provide a range of estimated fair market values. This allows the user to evaluate the very minimum FMV that might be expected on the low end of the price range, and the very highest FMV that might be expected on the high end of the price range. In this example, using $2.50 provides a total range of $5.00 per square foot—from +$2.50 to −$2.50.

Now let's take a moment to interpret the output. What is the model telling us? The three different values provide us with a minimum estimate for FMV and a range of values up to a maximum estimate for FMV. In order for the subject property to pass the first of the two tests, which is the comparable sales test, it must meet a minimum threshold of any value greater than zero by taking the difference of the FMV and the actual purchase price. In this example, the subject property passes the test under all three price scenarios reflected in the model, with positive values of $20,956 for the best-case estimate, $13,956 for the most likely estimate, and $6,956 for the worst-case estimate. If everything else looks good in the rest of the model, it is acceptable to have a negative value under the worst-case estimate. The most likely and best-case estimates, however, must have positive values. The difference in values shown in each of these three scenarios represents a discount of the actual purchase price to the market. So far, so good. Our subject property has passed the first test.

TEST 2: CASH FLOW ANALYSIS

The second test involves analyzing all income and expenses that affect the cash flow of the property. Under the cost and revenue assumptions heading, the purchase price, cost of improvements, and closing costs are entered and their values summed to provide the total cost of the investment. Below the cost assumptions are the revenue assumptions. To determine the appropriate rent to charge, I contacted a local property management company familiar with the rents in the area, which recommended charging approximately $1,750 per month in rent. Under other income, I included $250 per month, which represents the rent I could charge for the two boat slips that come with the property. Although a local marina on the same lake charges $2,000 per season for boat slips, I chose $1,500 per season for each of the two boat slips to be a little more competitive. This averages out to a rate of $250 per month. The total income estimated for the subject property, including the boat slips, is $2,000 per month.

In the owner's equity section under financing assumptions, a value of 10.00 percent was entered, since this value was initially intended to be my investment in the property. Below that, a value of 6.000 percent was entered for the interest rate, and 30 years was entered for the amortization period in the annual column. The model automatically calculates both the annual and the monthly payment. The owner's equity, interest rate, and amortization period are all variables that can easily be changed. Experimenting with these variables allows users of the model to see how changing them affects the output.

The key rent ratios section is especially important and captures data vital to the overall analysis of the subject property. All of these calculations are made automatically and change only when the variables affecting them are changed. The rental income per square foot, for example, provides a gauge with which to measure the relative rental income to the market as a whole. Although this measurement is calculated on a monthly basis, it could also be calculated annually. In our example, the value is $.63 per square foot which is low compared to smaller rental houses. This is because the rent per square foot is usually higher for smaller houses and drops as houses get bigger. The same relationship also holds true for buying a house. Generally speaking, the price per square foot goes down the larger the home, because with each house built, certain fixed costs must be overcome (land, heating, ventilation and air-conditioning equipment, etc.). Once these fixed costs have been overcome, the cost of adding additional square feet becomes much lower.

Also under the key rent ratios heading is the capitalization rate, which was discussed extensively in Chapter 8. Recall that the cap rate is the ratio between the net operating income and the purchase price. As you can see, this ratio is really a very simple calculation used to measure the relationship between the income generated by the property and the price it is being sold for. Recall also that this ratio measures the same relationship as for a certificate of deposit. The *price* we are willing to pay for the CD is a function of its *yield,* or rather, the *income* it generates. This is precisely consistent with the relationship between the *price* of an income-producing property, the *yield* an investor expects to receive on his or her investment, and the property's ability to generate *income.*

$$\frac{\text{Net operating income}}{\text{Purchase price}} = \text{capitalization rate}$$

$$\text{cap rate} = \frac{\$15,330}{\$373,500} = 4.104\%$$

Under the key rent ratios section in this example, notice the cap rate of 4.10 percent. This number represents the yield of the property as a whole since it is based on its total purchase price and not the equity. It is the return on investment, or ROI, that measures that relationship. A cap rate of only 4.10 percent for the experienced investor should immediately raise a red flag. This rate is anemic at best. As you gain more experience analyzing single-family rental houses, you will begin to more fully appreciate the importance of understanding capitalization rates. As you will see, this low cap rate corresponds directly with the property's ability to generate enough income to satisfy all of its related expenses and to service its debt obligation. Without even looking at the rest of the output, I know that this property will not have positive cash flow because of the low cap rate.

The gross rent multiplier (GRM) measures the relationship between the scheduled gross income and the total purchase price. The high GRM in this example should raise another red flag to the experienced investor. The lower the GRM, the better. This is true because the lower the purchase price relative to the property's income, the lower the ratio. Also, the higher the income relative to the purchase price, the lower the ratio will be.

$$\frac{\text{Purchase price}}{\text{Gross scheduled rental income}} = \text{gross rent multiplier}$$

$$\text{GRM} = \frac{\$373,500}{\$21,000} = 17.786\%$$

Finally, in the key rent ratios section is also a computation that measures the operating expenses of the property relative to its size. It is calculated as the ratio of total operating expenses to square feet. The result provides a measure of how efficiently the property can be operated. The lower the number, the less it costs to manage and operate the property. The calculation is made as follows.

$$\frac{\text{Total operating expenses}}{\text{Square feet}} = \text{operating efficiency ratio}$$

$$\text{OER} = \frac{\$7,620}{2,800} = \$2.72$$

The next section of the model allows the user to key in rental increases and changes in operating expenses to forecast over a five-year time horizon the profitability of the rental house. In this example, I entered in 0 percent for the first year for both rental increases and operating expenses because that best represents my expectations for the property. In Years 2 to 5, I have allowed for modest increases in both income and expenses. Using a five-year time horizon gives you a better idea of how an investment will perform over a longer period of time, as opposed to analyzing it only as it is operating today.

The next section of the model is operating revenues. The model determines the gross scheduled rental income based on the estimated monthly rental income entered under the cost and revenue assumptions section. In this example, a vacancy rate of 5.0 percent was used, which represents about two and a half weeks out of the year. The value for other income is the rental income from the two boat slips, which is again derived from the cost and revenue assumptions section.

Under the operating expenses section, expenses are estimated based on what you know to be true about the property, and also on information that is assumed or estimated. In this example, the repairs and maintenance expense is relatively low, representing only 5.2 percent of the property's gross income. Repairs and maintenance often run as high as 10 to 15 percent, sometimes even higher. Since the subject property is fairly new and in very good condition, I assumed a lower rate of only $100 per month. Property management fees typically range from about 3.5 percent to as much as 10.0 percent, depending on the size and type of rental unit. The value entered for taxes is estimated to be $350 per month. Since I will not be using any employees for this property, salaries and wages are assumed to be zero. The tenants are responsible for their own utilities, so this value, too, has been set to zero. I used $25 per month for professional fees in the event I need my attorney to review any of the documents. Advertising expenses are assumed to be zero because the property management company is responsible for that. There are also three other variables that can be set to anything that is needed, but in this case, all are assumed to be zero. Finally, all operating expenses are summed to provide the total operating expenses.

Net operating income is calculated by simply taking the difference between gross income and total operating expenses, which is $1,278 per month in this example. This number then flows down to the cash flow from operations section and becomes the total cash available for loan servicing. In the monthly column, the value of $2,015 for debt service is derived from the model's calculations under the financing assumptions section. Remember the anemic cap rate of 4.10 percent that we discussed earlier? We concluded that there is a direct correlation between this ratio and the ability of the investment property to generate enough income to satisfy all of its obligations, including the debt. In this example, we have a negative value of $738 per month. This means that, based on all of the information we know about the subject property and given the assumptions which have been used, an investor who purchases this property under these terms and conditions will have to shell out an extra $738 per month just to break even. Sounds like a great deal, doesn't it? Of course not. The principal reduction value of $335 in the monthly column does help somewhat, but this amount goes to pay down the property's debt and therefore still represents cash that is being paid out. It is only used here to help measure the overall return and profitability of the project.

Although the subject property passed the first test under the comparable sales section of the model, it failed the second test miserably. This is why it is absolutely critical for those individuals who are considering purchasing rental houses to understand how to properly analyze potential investment opportunities. An investor must be able to understand the value of a property relative to its surrounding community, and must then ensure that it can generate enough income to meet all of its obligations, including debt instruments.

Before we move on, let's take a moment to examine the last few ratios in the model. The first ratio is the debt service coverage ratio (DSCR), discussed at length in Chapter 3. Recall that the ratio is used to measure the ability of available cash to service the debt. A value of 1.0 percent means that there is exactly enough cash to cover all debt obligations. Anything less than 1.0 percent means that there is not enough cash to cover those debt obligations and anything greater than 1.0 percent means that not only is there enough to cover the debt, but also that there will be some left over. It is the portion left over that we are most interested in. That portion represents the cash return on an investment, also known as the *cash ROI*. The ratio in this case study is calculated as follows:

$$\frac{\text{Total cash available for loan servicing}}{\text{Debt service}}$$

$$= \text{CF debt servicing ratio}$$

$$\text{DSCR} = \frac{\$1,278}{\$2,015} = 63.39\%$$

The cash ROI is the central focus of an investor's objective. Recall that this ratio measures the cash portion of the return against the total dollar amount of cash invested into a property. In this example, the ratio is negative, meaning there is a negative return on investment, because the cash flow is not sufficient to meet all the obligations. The cash flow is itself negative. The ratio is calculated as follows:

$$\frac{\text{Remaining CF from ops}}{\text{Owner's equity}} = \text{cash return on investment}$$

$$\text{cash ROI} = \frac{-\$8,855}{\$37,350} = -63.39\%$$

The primary purpose of analyzing the subject property in Table 10.1 was to determine its value relative to comparable sales and to determine its ability to generate enough income to satisfy all of its obligations using the seller's asking price. According to the analysis in this case study, we have thus far concluded that while the investment property meets the comparable sales test, it does not meet the cash flow test. At this point, we could either reject the property as a viable investment opportunity and move on to the next deal, or we could experiment with the variables to determine what it would take for the property to conform to our criteria. My preference is to experiment with the model since, by doing so, I can go back to the seller and explain with logic and reasoning why the property is overpriced, at least for my purposes. Most sellers are willing to listen, and after having done so, will often grant at least some concessions.

With that in mind, the next step in the analysis is to begin experimenting with the variables. Let's start by posing the following question: At what price can the property be purchased using the existing total monthly income of $2,000 so that a break-even cash flow can be achieved? Using the model, we can quickly solve for the correct purchase price by simply adjusting the price downward until the remaining cash flow from operations is exactly zero. Now take a minute to examine Table 10.2.

In order to achieve a break-even point of zero in the cash flow analysis, the purchase price must be adjusted to a surprisingly low $233,250! Remember that the seller's asking price was $370,000. That's a difference of $136,750. Do you think most sellers would be willing to accept that much less for their property? In most cases, the answer is no. On larger and more expensive commercial or multifamily properties, however, sellers know that valuations are based on income and that the price of their property must reflect the going market rate. If they're not prepared to sell at market rates, there's a good chance their property will sit on the market for a long time.

Since it is unlikely the seller would be willing to reduce the asking price by $136,750, let's look at changing yet another variable. In this example, we pose the following question, "How much rent has to be charged to exactly cover all expenses associated with the property?" Solving for the answer is done by simply increasing the rental income just enough to break even while leaving the purchase price at the original asking price of $370,000. Now take a minute to examine Table 10.3.

After reviewing Table 10.3, you can see that an additional $777 per month of rental income would be required to achieve our objective of breaking even. Unfortunately, the market will not support that level of rent for this property, so increasing the rents by $777 per month is not practical. You can see the value of having a tool such as the model used in these examples. The kind of objective and analytical information provided by the model can be used very effectively to an investor's advantage simply by sharing the output from the model with the seller.

In this particular example, I had several follow-up discussions with the seller explaining to him that my initial assessment of his property had determined that the price he was asking was too high and would not support the debt required to finance it. I further explained to him that I have relationships with several lenders and that obtaining the proper financing to buy his house would be no problem. I also told him that since the property would be used for investment purposes, the lender would want to make sure that there was adequate rental income to cover all of the expenses, and in particular, the note to the bank. After listening to my explanation about why it would be difficult to buy his house at full asking price, the seller agreed that maybe there was some room to negotiate. I threw out a number of $330,000, which didn't seem to scare him off. We both agreed to think about it for a few days and then get back together. In the next chapter, as we explore an alternative use for the property, we'll also look at the purchase details of this transaction.

In summary, in this case study we examined a single-family house to determine whether it would be suitable for rental purposes based on our analysis. To properly analyze this property, two tests were applied. The first test was the comparable sales test, which the subject property passed according to the output from the model. We determined that the house could be purchased at a price less than or equal to its fair market value (FMV) and that no premium would be required based on the seller's asking price. The second test applied to our subject property was the cash flow analysis test. In this case study, the property had a significant negative cash flow and therefore failed the test according to the output from the model. We then experimented with different variables in the model to ascertain what would be required to bring this property in line with our investment criteria. We learned that by either

Table 10.2 Property Analysis Worksheet. The Value Play Rental House Analyzer

Property Value Analysis

Comp #1	
Address:	123 S. Sample Drive
Sales Price	365,500.00
Adjustments to Price	1,600.00
Adjusted Price	367,100.00
Square Feet	2,645.00
Price Per Square Foot	138.79

Comp #2	
Address:	456 N. Sample Drive
Sales Price	289,900.00
Adjustments to Price	(2,400.00)
Adjusted Price	287,500.00
Square Footage	2,096.00
Price Per Square Foot	137.17

Comp #3	
Address:	789 S. Sample Drive
Sales Price	294,000.00
Adjustments to Price	3,200.00
Adjusted Price	297,200.00
Square Feet	2,200.00
Price Per Square Foot	135.09

Comp Averages

Sales Price	316,466.67
Adjustments to Price	800.00
Adjusted Price	317,266.67
Square Feet	2,313.67
Price Per Square Foot	137.13

Subject Property 421 Moroni Blvd.

Purchase Price	233,250
Square Feet	2,800.00
Price/Sq Ft	83.30
Turn Comps Off/On	ON
Est Price/Sq Ft If Turned OFF	135.00

Property Values

Fair Market Value	233,250
Actual Price	2,800.00
Difference	83.30

Adjustment to Comps

2.50	0.00	2.50 (2.50)
390,956	383,956	376,956
233,250	233,250	233,250
157,706	150,706	143,706

Financing and Income Analysis

Financing Assumptions

Total Purchase	100.00%	236,750
Owner's Equity	10.00%	23,675
Balance to Finc	90.00%	213,075

	Annual	Monthly
Interest Rate	6.000%	0.500%
Amort Period	30	360
Payment	15,330	1,277

Cost and Revenue Assumptions

Purchase Price	233,250
Improvements	0
Closing Costs	3,500
Total	236,750

	Annual	Monthly
Estimated Monthly Rent Income	1,750	
Other Income	250	
Total Income	2,000	

Key Rent Ratios

Total Square Feet	2,800.00
Total Price/Sq Ft	84.55
Fair Market Value/Sq Ft	137.13
Rental Income/Sq Ft	0.63
Total Income/Sq Ft	0.71
Capitalization Rate	6.48%
Gross Rent Multiplier	11.27
Operating Efficiency Ratio	2.72

Rental Increase Projections

Average Monthly Rent	0.00%	4.00%	3.50%	3.50%	
	1,750	1,820	1,884	1,950	2,018
Operating Expense Projections	0.00%	2.00%	2.00%	1.50%	1.50%

Operating Revenues	%	Actual Monthly	Year 1	Year 2	Projected Year 3	Year 4	Year 5
Gross Scheduled Rental Income		1,750	21,000	21,840	22,604	23,396	24,214
Vacancy Rate	5.0%	88	1,050	1,092	1,130	1,170	1,211
Net Rental Income		1,663	19,950	20,748	21,474	22,226	23,004
Other Income		250	3,000	3,120	3,229	3,342	3,459
Gross Income	100.0%	1,913	22,950	23,868	24,703	25,568	26,463
Operating Expenses							
Repairs and Maintenance	5.2%	100	1,200	1,224	1,248	1,267	1,286
Property Management Fees	5.5%	105	1,260	1,285	1,311	1,331	1,351
Taxes	18.3%	350	4,200	4,284	4,370	4,435	4,502
Insurance	2.9%	55	660	673	687	697	707
Salaries and Wages	0.0%	0	0	0	0	0	0
Utilities	0.0%	0	0	0	0	0	0
Professional Fees	1.3%	25	300	306	312	317	322
Advertising	0.0%	0	0	0	0	0	0
Other	0.0%	0	0	0	0	0	0
Other	0.0%	0	0	0	0	0	0
Other	0.0%	0	0	0	0	0	0
Total Operating Expenses	33.2%	635	7,620	7,772	7,928	8,047	8,167
Net Operating Income	66.8%	1,278	15,330	16,096	16,776	17,521	18,295
Cash Flow From Operations							
Total Cash Available for Loan Servicing		1,278	15,330	16,096	16,776	17,521	18,295
Debt Service		1,277	15,330	15,330	15,330	15,330	15,330
Remaining CF From Ops		0	0	766	1,446	2,191	2,966
Plus Principal Reduction		212	2,617	2,778	2,949	3,131	3,324
Total Return		212	2,617	3,544	4,395	5,323	6,290
CF/Debt Servicing Ratio	100.00%	100.00%	104.99%	109.43%	114.29%	119.34%	
Net Operating Income ROI		64.75%	67.99%	70.86%	74.01%	77.28%	
Cash ROI		0.00%	3.23%	6.11%	9.26%	12.53%	
Total ROI		11.05%	14.97%	18.56%	22.48%	26.57%	

Table 10.3 Property Analysis Worksheet. The Value Play Rental House Analyzer

Property Value Analysis

Comp #1		Comp #2		Comp #3	
Address:	123 S. Sample Drive	Address:	456 N. Sample Drive	Address:	789 S. Sample Drive
Sales Price	365,500.00	Sales Price	289,900.00	Sales Price	294,000.00
Adjustments to Price	1,600.00	Adjustments to Price	(2,400.00)	Adjustments to Price	3,200.00
Adjusted Price	367,100.00	Adjusted Price	287,500.00	Adjusted Price	297,200.00
Square Feet	2,645.00	Square Footage	2,096.00	Square Feet	2,200.00
Price Per Square Foot	138.79	Price Per Square Foot	137.17	Price Per Square Foot	135.09

Comp Averages		Subject Property 421 Moroni Blvd.		Property Values		Adjustment to Comps		
						2.50	0.00	2.50
								(2.50)
Sales Price	316,466.67	Purchase Price	370,000	Fair Market Value		390,956	383,956	376,956
Adjustments to Price	800.00	Square Feet	2,800.00	Actual Price		370,000	370,000	370,000
Adjusted Price	317,266.67	Price/Sq Ft	132.14	Difference	ON	20,956	13,956	6,956
Square Feet	2,313.67	Turn Comps Off/On						
Price Per Square Foot	137.13	Est Price/Sq Ft If Turned OFF	135.00					

Financing and Income Analysis

Cost and Revenue Assumptions

Purchase Price	370,000
Improvements	0
Closing Costs	3,500
Total	373,500
Estimated Monthly Rent Income	2,527
Other Income	250
Total Income	2,777

Financing Assumptions

Total Purchase	373,500	100.00%
Owner's Equity	37,350	10.00%
Balance to Finc	336,150	90.00%

	Annual	Monthly
Interest Rate	6.000%	0.500%
Amort Period	30	360
Payment	24,185	2,015

Key Rent Ratios

Total Square Feet	2,800.00
Total Price/Sq Ft	133.39
Fair Market Value/Sq Ft	137.13
Rental Income/Sq Ft	0.90
Total Income/Sq Ft	0.99
Capitalization Rate	6.48%
Gross Rent Multiplier	12.32
Operating Efficiency Ratio	2.72

Rental Increase Projections	0.00%	4.00%		3.50%	3.50%
Average Monthly Rent	2,527	2,628	2,720	2,815	2,914
Operating Expense Projections	0.00%	2.00%	2.00%	1.50%	1.50%

	%	Actual Monthly	Year 1	Year 2	Year 3	Year 4	Year 5
Operating Revenues						Projected	
Gross Scheduled Rental Income		2,527	30,324	31,537	32,641	33,783	34,966
Vacancy Rate	5.0%	126	1,516	1,577	1,632	1,689	1,748
Net Rental Income		2,401	28,808	29,960	31,009	32,094	33,217
Other Income		250	3,000	3,120	3,229	3,342	3,459
Gross Income	100.0%	2,651	31,808	33,080	34,238	35,436	36,677
Operating Expenses							
Repairs and Maintenance	3.8%	100	1,200	1,224	1,248	1,267	1,286
Property Management Fees	4.0%	105	1,260	1,285	1,311	1,331	1,351
Taxes	13.2%	350	4,200	4,284	4,370	4,435	4,502
Insurance	2.1%	55	660	673	687	697	707
Salaries and Wages	0.0%	0	0	0	0	0	0
Utilities	0.0%	0	0	0	0	0	0
Professional Fees	0.9%	25	300	306	312	317	322
Advertising	0.0%	0	0	0	0	0	0
Other	0.0%	0	0	0	0	0	0
Other	0.0%	0	0	0	0	0	0
Other	0.0%	0	0	0	0	0	0
Total Operating Expenses	24.0%	635	7,620	7,772	7,928	8,047	8,167
Net Operating Income	76.0%	2,016	24,188	25,308	26,310	27,389	28,509
Cash Flow From Operations							
Total Cash Available for Loan Servicing		2,016	24,188	25,308	26,310	27,389	28,509
Debt Service		2,015	24,185	24,185	24,185	24,185	24,185
Remaining CF From Ops		0	3	1,123	2,125	3,205	4,324
Plus Principal Reduction		335	4,128	4,383	4,653	4,940	5,245
Total Return		335	4,131	5,506	6,778	8,145	9,569
CF/Debt Servicing Ratio		100.01%	100.01%	104.64%	108.79%	113.25%	117.88%
Net Operating Income ROI		64.76%	64.76%	67.76%	70.44%	73.33%	76.33%
Cash ROI		0.01%	0.01%	3.01%	5.69%	8.58%	11.58%
Total ROI		11.06%	11.06%	14.74%	18.15%	21.81%	25.62%

decreasing the purchase price of the house or by increasing its rental income, the property could conform to our investment standards. In this example, however, the reduction in purchase price and the increase in rents were quite significant and would therefore not be practical, since neither the seller nor the market would be accepting of them.

Chapter 11

Case Study 2: Single-Family to Multifamily Conversion

EXPLORING ALTERNATIVE POSSIBILITIES

In the previous case study, we examined a single-family rental house situated across the street from an all-sports lake to determine whether it would be suitable for investment purposes. While the subject property passed the fair market value test, it failed the cash flow analysis test. After experimenting with several of the variables to ascertain what it would take to bring the property in line with our investment criteria, it was determined that the required changes were too substantial and that it would be impractical to do so. This being the case, let's now turn our attention to an alternative use for the property. The house sits directly across the street from the lake on a little less than one acre of land and, as mentioned in the previous chapter, happens to be the only parcel of land uniquely situated with buildable lot space and zoned residential multiple (RM). The underlying value of this property is *not* in its current use as a single-family parcel, but rather, its true value lies in the RM zoning, which the property already has, and the size of the lot it is situated on.

The primary purpose of this chapter is to encourage readers to think outside the box. In other words, I want you to always be thinking of different ways to create value in the investment opportunities you consider. Start by looking at the property for what it is and analyzing it accordingly. Then consider any alternative uses for the property to determine whether there is not perhaps a better and higher use for it. There may also be other ways of creating or adding value to a property, such as by making various improvements to it, by converting unused storage space to rentable space, by expanding or enlarging an existing facility, or perhaps by adding rentable garage or storage space to an office or apartment building. The point is, investors should get in the habit of shifting their minds into high gear by looking for opportunity wherever it may exist—and especially wherever it doesn't exist.

In the previous chapter, we learned that the seller indicated he might be willing to consider a sales price of $330,000. As agreed, we allowed several days to pass before getting back together. I knew that the seller was anxious to sell and wanted to return to Colorado where his family lived. He also told me that his grandmother gave him the house about six years ago, which led me to believe that he didn't owe very much on it. With that in mind, I decided to probe lower by offering $275,000, a figure that I thought he would likely reject. My true objective was to settle at $300,000, thinking that he would probably walk away with $200,000 or so. As it turned out, the seller did in fact reject the lower offer of $275,000, but was willing to accept the somewhat higher figure of $300,000. Recall that since his original asking price was $375,000, the agreed-upon lower price represented a direct cost savings to me of $75,000. This savings did not come easily, but instead required constant nurturing of the relationship between us, as well as the use of various negotiating tactics discussed in *The Complete Guide to Investing in Rental Properties* (New York: McGraw-Hill, 2004).

In the previous chapter, we established that it would take a selling price of $236,750 to exactly break even on the property's cash flow. With that being the case, why do you suppose I would be willing to pay more than the cash flows from the property would support? My purpose for purchasing this property from the outset was twofold. First, I wanted the two boat slips that came with the deal for personal use, especially since they were already deeded separately from the main parcel. Second, I wanted the slightly less than one acre of land on which the house was sitting to build several condominium units for Symphony Homes. The existing house on the property happens to be of modular construction, which means that it can be disassembled and moved to another lot just before construction on the condominiums begins. Although the rental income from the house is not sufficient to cover all of the property's obligations, it will certainly help offset them over the next several months while getting the project approved through the local planning commission. Even though I expect a negative cash flow for several months, these carrying costs have been factored into the overall cost of the project. This project, by the way, has been officially named "65 Park Island Condominiums." The 65, incidentally, refers to the project's physical address and not to the number of condominium units.

In this chapter, we analyze the Park Island project and look at ways of achieving the property's highest and best use. The fact that the property is currently zoned for multiple units, combined with the fact that it has only one single-family dwelling on it tells us that it is being underused, especially since it sits on nearly an acre of land. Although one acre of land is small compared to many other condominium projects, the existing density ordinances will allow us to build a total of nine two-bedroom units. In addition, since the appeal of the site is that it is located directly across the street from a very popular lake, the land will also accommodate three additional boat storage units. They are designed to be 25 feet in length, which will allow owners to store their boats and thereby provide them with convenient access. Owners would otherwise have to store their boats off-site, which would actually end up costing them more than purchasing one of the three available units. Since there are only three boat storage units, they are expected to sell quickly.

In order to maximize the profitability of this project, we must first identify its constraints. For example, we know that the size of the land on which to build the units is just under one acre. We also know that existing density requirements will permit a maximum of nine condominium units on a parcel of land this size. The next constraint to identify is really a function of marketing. According to the research we conducted, the ideal price point for units such as these is between $175,000 and $200,000. From a purely psychological perspective, it is best to keep the prices below $200,000, for example, $199,000 or less.

We have identified the first two of a total of three primary constraints. First, we have established that a maximum of nine units can be built, and second, that the price points should fall between $175,000 and $199,000. The remaining constraint is a function of both profit and marketing and is one that must be solved for. The question is, what size condominium units should be built to provide the optimum level of profit while at the same time meeting the demands of the market and being considered to be a good value? In the previous chapter, we established that lake-view property typically sells for between $120 and $140 per square foot. The question then becomes, what size units should be built that will provide the optimum level of profit, be priced between $175,000 and $199,000, and at the same time average between $120 and $140 per square foot?

Solving for the optimum-sized units requires that the overall profitability of the project be maximized while working within the known constraints. To do this, all of the fixed and variable costs of the project must first be identified and then input into a model. The next step is to create a *profit matrix* in which various levels of profitability are calculated based on the fixed and variable costs related to the construction of various-sized units within the known parameters. Since this is not a book about residential construction, I won't bother providing the detail for the related costs or the profit matrix. You may rest assured, however, that they do exist and that a great deal of time and energy went into their creation. What I will provide, though, is a summary of the costs, size of units, and expected profits associated with the project. Take a moment to examine Table 11.1.

By reviewing the summary information contained in Table 11.1, it should be immediately evident that the subject property in this case study was being significantly underused as a single-family residence. In the previous case study, the project was rejected because it failed the cash flow analysis test. Even after experimenting with the variables in our model, it was deemed impractical to pursue with our investment capital because it was so far out of line. The seller would have rejected the abnormally low sales price of $233,250 and the market would have rejected the abnormally high total rental rate of

Table 11.1   65 Park Island Condominiums: Projected Costs and
Revenues

Item Description	Total Sq Ft Cost/Foot	Number of Units Per Unit	Total
Condominium Units	1,497	1	9
Projected Costs			
Land	22.27	33,333	300,000
Development	5.51	8,250	74,250
Construction	72.63	108,700	978,300
Interest and Taxes	1.78	2,667	24,000
Marketing	0.67	1,000	9,000
Closing and Commissions	4.05	6,067	54,606
Total Projected Costs	106.92	160,017	1,440,156
Projected Revenues			
Ballad	1,301	2	349,800
Mozart I	1,406	2	379,800
Mozart II	1,600	1	209,900
Waltz	1,614	4	799,600
Boat Storage	250	3	50,100
Site Premiums	0	0	31,000
Total Projected Revenues			1,820,200
Projected Earnings			380,044

$2,777. Less experienced investors would have likely walked away from this project under these conditions. An astute investor such as yourself, however, understands how important it is to think outside the box for any possible way to create value where none existed before.

In this particular example, the culmination of three unique factors gave birth to an opportunity that may otherwise never have come to life had we not been in the habit of exploring alternative possibilities. First, the fact that this parcel of land was already zoned RM naturally facilitated the construction of condominium units. Second, the fact that the parcel of land was large enough to accommodate several units provided ample profitability for a project of this size. Finally, our willingness to examine this opportunity from another perspective resulted in the birth of a project that will eventually prove to be quite profitable for our company, Symphony Homes.

THE RELATIONSHIP BETWEEN RISK AND REWARD

Most investors are aware of the relationship between the two concepts of risk and reward. The two terms are said to be highly correlated in that the greater the potential risk in an investment, the greater the potential reward. There is, of course, no guarantee that there will be any reward, since a potential risk implies that there is also a potential chance of loss. This relationship is known as the *beta* when referring to stocks. An individual stock that has a correlation exactly equal to that of the market is said to have a beta of 1.0. A stock with a beta of 1.0 can on average be expected to earn a return equal to that of the market given an equal level of risk. A stock with a beta greater than 1.0 can on average be expected to earn a return higher than the market, but also carries a higher level of risk than that of the market, which is evident by its increased volatility. Conversely, a stock with a beta less than 1.0 can on average be expected to earn a return lower than the market, but also carries a lower level of risk than that of the market, which is evident by its increased volatility.

The relationship between risk and reward exists among all asset classes, including our favorite, that being real estate. Perhaps one of the biggest drawbacks and greatest risks to any real estate development project is having to deal with any number of unknowns, which can cause delays and potential setbacks, thereby driving up the cost of the project and reducing its profitability. Typical problems that may arise from a development project include dealing with legal challenges, engineering issues, zoning changes, and the required approvals by local authorities.

In the case of the Park Island project, the biggest challenge I faced was fighting city hall. The project already had the proper zoning, so no zoning changes were required. No variances were being requested, either, which can also cause potential delays. The planning commission's legal obligation in this matter was to review the project to ensure that it conformed to the local ordinances as they were currently written. Our team of architects, engineers, and attorneys worked together from the very beginning to take every precaution to ensure that the project was designed to conform with all laws, codes, and ordinances to minimize any delays that might otherwise arise. After reviewing the project and determining that it was in fact in compliance, the planning commission's obligation was to then approve it and allow our company to begin construction after having obtained the necessary permits. Unfortunately, things didn't go as smoothly as we had hoped.

I had every expectation from the very beginning that this project would go smoothly since no zoning changes or variances were required, so I had anticipated having the final approvals from the planning commission no later than the month of February. This would allow our crews to get started with construction of the project by March, which was the prime building and selling season, and we would have the project sold and completed no later than July or August, just in time for the start of the new school session. Unfortunately, we were met with resistance at every level by the planning commission. The resistance stemmed from two key members of the commission who had a reputation for being antigrowth. Quite by chance, we became aware of several derogatory comments made by these key members in a public forum at which a newspaper reporter happened to be present. The following article was brought to my attention the day after it was published on February 4 in the *Lake Orion Review:*

News Headline: Condo Newspaper Ad Irks Council

Village officials were surprised to see an ad for Park Island condominiums in the Oakland Press on Jan. 21. Village of Lake Orion Council members expressed dismay on Jan. 26 at the timing of the ad. According to LO Village Manager JoAnn Van Tassel, the developer, Symphony Homes, is a long way from getting any final OK from the village. "They've only been here once and March is the earliest they'll be back at the planning commission," she added. "I think it's deplorable. This reflects on the credibility of the applicant."

Council president Bill Siver, who is also a member of the PC, said it's (the ad) a waste of Symphony Homes' money.

"They're no further along than when they came to us at the planning commission. If they took any money from anybody, I would think it was fraud," he added.

The ad mentions the development consists of nine resort-like condominiums with a lake view. The ad shows a drawing of one and two story units. Symphony Homes' web site mentions the development is coming soon—2004. Location maps are listed. One photo shows two young children playing on a very sandy beach.

The site says the community will provide a resident with easy access to a variety of lake activities including boating, fishing, skiing, swimming, snowmobiling and ice fishing.

Within five minutes of reading this rather shocking newspaper article, I was on the phone with my attorney. After faxing a copy of the article to him, he, too, expressed shock and disbelief that comments of that nature were being freely made by public officials in a public forum. My attorney recommended that as a principal of Symphony Homes, I respond with a letter to the editor to present our side of this issue. He drafted his own letter to the attorney who represents the village requesting that the responsible parties immediately issue a statement of retraction and that if they did not, we would seriously consider any and all legal remedies available to us.

I called the editor of the newspaper the next day to discuss with her the article that had been printed. She indicated a willingness to print my response in the next issue of the paper, which would be the following Wednesday (the newspaper is issued weekly). Here is the letter I sent to her:

Friday February 6

The Lake Orion Review
Response to article printed on February 4: **Condo Newspaper Ad Irks Council** Letter to the Editor:

As Principal of Symphony Homes, my initial reaction was one of shock and outrage to the article printed in your February 4th newspaper edition regarding the approval of the proposed condominium project at 65 Park Island Drive in the Village of Lake Orion.

Our company elected to begin advertising the proposed condominium project in January in an effort to generate interest and potential pre-sales of the homes. This is a common practice among builders and developers and is certainly within our legal right to do so.

In the spirit of cooperation, I met personally with Ms. Van Tassel in the summer of 2003 and was given the assurance that the Village would be supportive of our desire to develop this parcel of land. It was determined that the project would be designed with no request for zoning changes since it already had the proper zoning in place, and also that no requests for variances would be made. Our intent was to minimize delays in order to take advantage of the optimum construction period in the spring of 2004. The project has been designed from the very outset to be in full compliance with the existing laws and ordinances as they are currently written.

Your article stated that Lake Orion Village Manager JoAnn Van Tassel said "the developer, Symphony Homes, is a long way from getting any final OK from the village." Ms. Van Tassel is then quoted as saying, "They've only been here once and March is the earliest they'll be back at the planning commission," she added. "I think it's deplorable. This reflects on the credibility of the applicant."

Ms. Van Tassel is somehow mistakenly operating under the false premise that we have no right to advertise our project. To publicly state that our actions are "deplorable" and that this somehow reflects on our credibility is deeply offensive. Ms. Van Tassel has forgotten who the client is in this application process. It is *not* the Village who has paid the application fee, but Symphony Homes. The members of the council have a legal obligation to review our project in a timely manner. Their job is to ensure that our project complies with ordinances as they are currently written, and then to approve it once it has been determined that it is in compliance. I have personally been treated with extreme disrespect by Ms. Van Tassel on more than one occasion. I find this behavior quite troubling.

Your article also quotes Council president Bill Siver, who is also a member of the PC as saying, "it's (the ad) a waste of Symphony Homes' money." Mr. Siver further states, "They're no further along than when they came to us at the planning commission. If they took any money from anybody, I would think it was fraud," he added.

Mr. Siver's claim that our activities are somehow fraudulent not only deeply offends me and the other members of the Symphony Homes team, but also makes me ashamed to think that I am a member of the same community as this man. My partner, Don Mahoney, and I are both Lake Orion residents. This is where we have chosen to raise our families, this is where our children are attending school, and this is where we are spending our tax dollars.

I am saddened by the actions and statements made by members of the Lake Orion Village council, and in particular, those made by Ms. Van Tassel and Mr. Siver. These slanderous and libelous statements have been made with absolutely no basis of fact and with no regard for the character and integrity of our company. I expect nothing short of a retraction by the council and a public apology printed on the front page of your newspaper.

I welcome the opportunity to further discuss this matter with you or a representative of the newspaper. I would also ask that as a journalist and in fairness to Symphony Homes, you consider printing this letter in *The Lake Orion Review.*

Respectfully yours,
Steve Berges
Principal
Symphony Homes

As it turned out, the *Lake Orion Review* printed my letter to the editor in its entirety on the following Wednesday. In the interim, both Van Tassel and Siver issued retraction statements after counseling with the village attorney. Although their letters were written individually, they were similar in both tone and format. The two letters were printed in the *Lake Orion Review* on the same day and on the same page as my letter to the editor. Following is the letter written by Mr. Siver and printed in the newspaper.

The Village Attorney has forwarded to me a February 6 letter from . . . , attorney for Symphony Homes and its principal, Steve Berges, regarding the following statement attributed to me by *The Lake Orion Review* in its February 4 edition—"If they took any money from anybody, I would think it was fraud."

Although I do not recall if the quoted language is exactly what I said during Council Comments at the January 26 meeting, I was concerned with the fairness of the 65 Park Island Condominium project being advertised as if it was an approved project when it did not have site plan approval from the Village.

However, having reviewed the Village Attorney's February 9 memo to the Council, I now understand that the developer of this proposed condominium project may be able to take deposits under preliminary reservation agreements before Village site plan approval and recording of Master Deed with the Register of Deeds.

Therefore, if that is true, to the extent I made them, I retract the comments attributed to me in the February 4 Lake Orion Review. They were nothing more than an expression of my personal opinion of and frustration with the situation without the benefit of the legal opinion just received and without any intent to accuse Symphony Homes or Mr. Berges of any unlawful conduct.

Dated: February 9   Signed: William Siver

Although I was glad to see a swift retraction of their inappropriate remarks, I was disappointed in the tone of both letters. Neither Siver nor Van Tassel expressed any degree of remorse that I could detect in their letters. The bottom line is that someone finally stood up to the abuse of power exhibited by them and they had no choice but to respond. They were in effect backed into a corner. Sadly enough, our public officials sometimes forget who pays their salaries. They forget who the customer is and for whom they are working. Some public officials become so intoxicated with power that they lose sight of their civic duties and, in so doing, become blind to the needs of the very people they are called to serve.

Although the relationship between risk and reward is highly correlated, it is a relationship that can be carefully managed to provide investors with the highest probability of a favorable outcome. The biggest challenge I find among people with whom I visit is their inability to assume risk. For many different reasons, they fear the unknown and are afraid of failure. What I try to help them understand is that it's okay to fail at something. Just because we are not successful every time we try to do something doesn't mean that we are failures. It is only when we stop trying that we become failures. Can you imagine teaching children to ride a bike and then asking them to quit or give up the first time they fall off? Of course not. The following is an excerpt relating to risk taken from *The Complete Guide to Buying and Selling Apartments* (New Jersey: John Wiley & Sons, 2004).

> I believe that for a variety of reasons, some people are naturally more comfortable with risk than others. The upbringing we receive within our families is one of the most significant factors that contributes to our self-esteem and self-confidence. When I reflect back upon my own childhood, it is with great fondness that I remember my mother's encouraging words. She reminded me many, many times over the years that God had given me talents and that they were to be used and not wasted. She often told me that I could do anything that I set my mind to. During my adolescent years, unfortunately, I didn't set my mind to much of anything worthwhile. It wasn't until later that I heard her inspiring words over and over in my mind, prodding me along, and it wasn't until then that I finally began to believe her. For those of you with children, you may remember the

story of *The Little Engine That Could.* The Little Engine struggles mightily to pull a heavy load of toys to be delivered up a steep hill. As the Little Engine struggles up the hill, he says, "I think I can, I think I can, I think I can . . ." Whenever my five-year-old and three-year-old sons tell me, "Daddy, I can't do it," I gently remind them of the Little Engine. As I remember the lessons from my mother who sang the songs of praise and encouragement at every opportunity, I strive to carry on this legacy in her memory within my own family.

Regardless of whether or not you received guidance from a parent, family member, or friend, establishing an acceptable level of comfort with risk is a process that can be developed one step at a time through your life experiences. While this process may come more naturally for some, each and every one of you has the ability to assume risk in varying degrees. Sometimes you may have to push yourself to take that initial step, but you must be willing to step outside of your comfort zone, to push the boundaries a little bit. This is the only way you can learn and progress. With each and every step, you will gain confidence in your abilities. It is this confidence which will ultimately enable you to achieve your goals and reach your full potential.

In summary, we learned that it is quite possible to take a project that may appear to be dead in the water and find a way to resuscitate it. In the previous case study, the subject property passed the sales comparison test, but failed the cash flow test, thus rendering it apparently dead in the water. In this chapter, however, an alternative use for the property was discovered by our willingness to think outside the box. To think outside the box, remember to take every opportunity to think of different ways to create value in the investment opportunities you consider. Start by looking at the property for what it is and analyzing it accordingly. Then consider any alternative uses for the property to determine whether one will work. Get in the habit of shifting your mind into high gear by looking for opportunity wherever it may exist—and especially wherever it doesn't exist.

Chapter 12

Case Study 3: Multifamily Apartment Complex

In the previous case study, we examined the conversion of a single-family rental house situated across the street from an all-sports lake into a multifamily condominium property and discussed the notion of thinking outside the box. We also discussed some of the pitfalls that challenge investors when working with local officials. In this chapter, we analyze a multifamily project that already has 24 units, but also has some additional land that could potentially accommodate another 80 units. We evaluate this investment opportunity on its ability to generate an acceptable rate of return on a purely stand-alone basis. In other words, although the property can support the construction of additional units, its valuation must be based on its ability to generate income as it currently exists. While value can be attributed to the extra land, an investor purchasing this property solely for its current operating income should not be willing to invest additional capital without having a use for it. Doing so would result in overpaying for the property. At the time I evaluated this opportunity, I had no interest in building the additional condominium units in this particular market.

This 24-unit property was first brought to my attention by a real estate broker I had been working with for some time. After relocating to Michigan, I discovered that the properties I was looking at here were not nearly as competitively priced as those in Texas, where I had just come from. My experience in Texas had taught me to maintain a disciplined and patient approach to investing in real estate. I had learned that if I was patient enough, the right opportunity would eventually present itself. I was hopeful that this particular project would meet my investment criteria, as I had been searching for close to a year.

Before ever going to look at a property, I make it a habit to review the related financial statements first. If the deal makes sense after running it through my model on the first pass, it may be worth taking a look at. In this case, the output from my model indicated that the returns were weak at best. I thought, however, that it was still worth taking a look at to see whether there might be a way that I could add or create value and also to get direct feedback from the seller to determine if there were any flexibility in his asking price. It had been a while since anything had even come close to showing up on my radar screen worth looking at, so with this in mind, I arranged to meet with the broker and the seller.

A few days later, my partner and I met with the broker, the seller, and a prospective property manager at the apartment building. My first impression of the property was that although it was off the beaten path, it appeared to be fairly well maintained. According to the seller, he had no problem keeping it rented. This statement, however, was inconsistent with the fact that two units had been empty for over a month. Although one of them was in obvious need of repair, the other one was clean and ready to go. According to the seller, he had a prospective tenant who was interested in one unit, but had not made up her mind. I tucked that fact into the back of my mind, thinking that since the property was not as visible as others, it may have an adverse effect on its vacancy rate. Both the broker and the seller did their best to sell me on the property's upside potential with the construction of additional units and did not seem to be very flexible on the asking price. I asked them why, if developing the additional units was such a good opportunity, the seller wasn't doing that. The seller responded that he "just wanted to sell the property" so he could retire. I've heard the "retire" reason for selling more times than I care to count. I think when sellers use that term, what they really mean is they are tired of fooling with the management of their property.

Table 12.1 contains the data in our model, The Value Play Income Analyzer, which was used to analyze this property. Take a moment now to review it.

In the upper left-hand corner of Table 12.1 is a box labeled "Cost and Revenues Assumptions." This box is used to input the basic assumptions by which much of the model's output will be determined. In this example, the total purchase price of the apartments was $1,550,000. I estimated the value of land at $400,000 and the value of the building at $1,150,000. The values attributed to the land and building inputs affect a depreciation calculation made in the model, but are essentially irrelevant if the tax rate further down in the model is set to zero. My initial input value for the improvements was zero, since the property was in relatively good condition and I did not anticipate making any capital improvements. Closing costs in this example were estimated to be $20,000. These values are then summed to assume a total cost of $1,570,000. Following the cost assumptions are the revenue assumptions. The property consisted of 24 units, which, according to the seller, were rented at an average rate of $720 per month. The model calculates product of these two values to determine the gross monthly revenues, which in this example are $17,280.

Now take a look at the box labeled "Financing Assumptions." We know that the total purchase price is $1,570,000 based on the inputs from our cost assumptions. The owner's equity is a variable input by the user to determine the amount of money required to purchase the property. Since improvements and closing costs are included in the total purchase price, this must be taken into consideration when entering the amount of equity. Sometimes some of the closing costs can be rolled into the financing, and sometimes the seller will pay some of them. Since every closing transaction is different, the model provides the user with the flexibility to estimate his or her total cash outlay in this section. Whether or not some of the closing costs are rolled into the loan or paid for by the seller is irrelevant. The total amount of cash required by the investor,

Table 12.1 Property Analysis Worksheet. The Value Play Income Analyzer

Cost and Revenue Assumptions

Land	400,000
Building	1,150,000
Improvements	0
Closing Costs	20,000
Total	1,570,000
Number of Units	24
Average Monthly Rent	720
Gross Monthly Revenues	17,280

Financing Assumptions

Total Purchase	100.00%	1,570,000
Owner's Equity	17.50%	274,750
Balance to Finc	82.50%	1,295,250
	Annual	Monthly
Interest Rate	8.000%	0.667%
Amort Period	25	300
Payment	119,963	9,997

Key Ratios

Total Square Feet	25,700.00
Avg Sq Ft/Unit	1,070.83
Avg Rent/Sq Ft	0.67
Avg Cost/Sq Ft	61.09
Avg Unit Cost	65,416.67
Capitalization Rate	7.62%
Gross Rent Multiplier	7.57
Expense/Unit	3,397.32
Expense/Foot	3.17

Rental Income Projections
Average Monthly Rent
Operating Expense Projections

	0.00%	3.50%	4.00%	3.00%	3.00%
	720	745	775	798	822
	0.00%	-2.50%	0.00%	1.50%	2.00%

Operating Revenues

		Actual Monthly	Year 1	Year 2	Projected Year 3	Year 4	Year 5
Gross Scheduled Income		17,280	207,360	214,618	223,202	229,898	236,795
Vacancy Rate	5.0%	864	10,368	10,731	11,160	11,495	11,840
Net Rental Income		16,416	196,992	203,887	212,042	218,403	224,956
Other Income		350	4,200	4,347	4,521	4,657	4,796
Gross Income	100.0%	16,766	201,192	208,234	216,563	223,060	229,752

Operating Expenses

		Actual Monthly	Year 1	Year 2	Year 3	Year 4	Year 5
Repairs and Maintenance	14.7%	2,462	29,544	28,805	28,805	29,237	29,822
Property Management Fees	4.0%	671	8,048	7,846	7,846	7,964	8,123
Taxes	12.2%	2,050	24,600	23,985	23,985	24,345	24,832
Insurance	2.8%	465	5,580	5,441	5,441	5,522	5,633
Salaries and Wages	1.5%	250	3,000	2,925	2,925	2,969	3,028
Utilities	2.2%	365	4,380	4,271	4,271	4,335	4,421
Trash Removal	0.5%	82	984	959	959	974	993
Professional Fees	0.6%	100	1,200	1,170	1,170	1,188	1,211

	%	Monthly	Year 1	Year 2	Year 3	Year 4	Year 5
Advertising	0.9%	150	1,800	1,755	1,755	1,781	1,817
Other	1.2%	200	2,400	2,340	2,340	2,375	2,423
Total Op. Exp.	40.5%	6,795	81,536	79,497	79,497	80,690	82,304
Net Operating Income	59.5%	9,971	119,656	128,736	137,066	142,370	147,448
Interest on Loan	51.5%	8,635	103,007	101,600	100,076	98,425	96,637
Dep. Exp. - Building		3,485	41,818	41,818	41,818	41,818	41,818
Dep. Exp. - Equip.		0	0	0	0	0	0
Net Income Before Taxes		(2,148)	(25,169)	(14,682)	(4,828)	2,127	8,993
Income Tax Rate	0.0%	0	0	0	0	0	0
Net Income After Taxes		(2,148)	(25,169)	(14,682)	(4,828)	2,127	8,993

Cash Flow From Operations

		Monthly	Year 1	Year 2	Year 3	Year 4	Year 5
Net Income After Taxes		(2,148)	(25,169)	(14,682)	(4,828)	2,127	8,993
Dep. Exp.		3,485	41,818	41,818	41,818	41,818	41,818
Total CF From Ops.		1,336	16,649	27,137	36,990	43,945	50,811
Interest on Loan		8,635	103,007	101,600	100,076	98,425	96,637
Total Cash Available for Loan Servicing		9,971	119,656	128,736	137,066	142,370	147,448
Debt Service		9,997	119,963	119,963	119,963	119,963	119,963
Remaining After Tax CF From Ops		(26)	(307)	8,773	17,102	22,407	27,485
Plus Principal Reduction		1,413	16,956	18,364	19,888	21,538	23,326
Total Return		1,387	16,649	27,137	36,990	43,945	50,811

		Monthly	Year 1	Year 2	Year 3	Year 4	Year 5
CF/Debt Servicing Ratio		99.74%	99.74%	107.31%	114.26%	118.68%	122.91%
Net Income ROI			-9.16%	-5.34%	-1.76%	0.77%	3.27%
Cash ROI			-0.11%	3.19%	6.22%	8.16%	10.00%
Total ROI			6.06%	9.88%	13.46%	15.99%	18.49%
Net CFs From Investment - 1 Yr Exit		(274,750)	321,399				
Net CFs From Investment - 3 Yr Exit		(274,750)	(307)	8,773	402,060		
Net CFs From Investment - 5 Yr Exit		(274,750)	(307)	8,773	17,102	22,407	582,307

	Exit Price	Gain on Sale	Cap Rate		IRR
Estimated Exit Price/Gain On Sale - 1 Yr	1,600,000	30,000	7.48%	Annualized IRR - 1 Yr	16.98%
Estimated Exit Price/Gain On Sale - 3 Yr	1,625,000	55,000	8.43%	Annualized IRR - 3 Yr	14.43%
Estimated Exit Price/Gain On Sale - 5 Yr	1,750,000	180,000	8.43%	Annualized IRR - 5 Yr	18.69%

including closing costs or improvements, is input into this cell. The interest rate and amortization period are then input by the user to calculate both the annual and monthly payments. At the time I looked at this property, a competitive market rate of interest was considered to be 8.0 percent, and my lender offered 25 years as the amortization period. Based on the financing assumptions entered into the model, the monthly debt service is calculated to be $9,997, or $119,963 annually.

The next box in the model is labeled "Key Ratios." The only input for this section is the first value, which is identified as the total square feet; all other data in this section are outputs that are calculated automatically by the model. In this example, the total square feet was 25,700, which gives us an average number of square feet per unit of 1,070. These were fairly good-sized units for two-bedroom apartments, which I considered to be a plus for the property. The average rent per square foot was calculated to be $.67. The average cost per square foot was calculated at $61.09, giving us a total cost per unit of $65,417, which was a little pricey for apartments rented at this lower rate. I've paid as little as $15,000 to $20,000 per unit for apartments, so I wasn't very excited about paying more than $65,000 per unit for these. The gross rent multiplier, discussed in Chapter 6, was calculated to be 7.57. Next is the expenses per unit, which divides the total operating expenses by the number of units, resulting in $3,448. This number is then divided by the average square feet per unit to provide the average expense per unit, which in this example resulted in $3.22. Both of these expense calculations were considered to be in line with the market.

The next section of the model is used to forecast changes that may affect both revenues and expenses. For example, if the rents for the property were below market, an adjustment to increase them could be made. Likewise, if expenses appeared to be out of line, they, too, could be increased or decreased as deemed appropriate. In this example, the rents were in line with current market conditions, so there was little room to increase them in Year 1. The property's expenses also appeared to be in line with the market, so the value was set to zero.

The next section of the model is operating revenues. The model reads the gross monthly revenues value from the cost and revenues section and inputs it automatically into gross scheduled income, which in this example is $17,280. A vacancy factor consistent with the local market is then subtracted from gross scheduled income to produce net rental income. The next value, other income, includes any type of income such as application fees, late fees, utility income, vending income, and interest income. This particular apartment building earned approximately $350 per month in other income, derived primarily from laundry and vending services. The sum of net rental income and other income results in gross income. In this example, gross income is $16,766 per month, or $201,192 per year.

After accounting for all of the operating revenues, we then move to operating expenses. Operating expenses include all of the day-to-day costs incurred to operate the property with the exception of interest, which is accounted for later. For example, operating expenses include such items as repairs and maintenance, management fees, taxes, insurance, utilities, landscaping, and any other day-to-day operating expenses. This section would not, however, include long-term capital improvements such as replacing an entire roof or expanding the parking lot. In this example, total operating expenses amount to $6,795 per month and $81,536 per year. As indicated in the model, this figure represents approximately 40 percent of the property's gross income.

Depending on the type of income-producing property, total operating expenses can range anywhere from about 25 percent of gross income to as much as 65 percent of gross income. If expenses run higher than that, the property will most likely have a difficult time with cash flow. Commercial buildings that use a triple net lease arrangement, in which expenses are passed on to the tenants, tend to have lower operating expenses, while multifamily properties typically fall into the 40 to 60 percent range. One primary factor that significantly affects operating expenses is whether the property is submetered. For example, some older apartment buildings had a master meter installed at the time of construction. In this type of situation, the apartments are often rented out as "all bills paid," and the landlord or owner assumes the responsibility for paying all of the utilities. Conversely, in most newer apartment buildings, the units are individually metered, and tenants are responsible for their own utilities. This significantly reduces the total operating expenses for the owner.

The next section of the model is net operating income. Recall that the value for NOI is crucial, as it is the numerator in the cap rate calculation. The annual NOI is this example is $119,656, which gives us a cap rate of 7.62 percent, as follows:

$$\text{Cap rate} = \frac{\text{net operating income}}{\text{price}} = \frac{\$119,656}{\$1,570,000} = 7.62\%$$

The model then calculates the annual first-year interest based on the loan amount, interest rate, and amortization period, which in this example is $103,007. Depreciation is then factored in for tax purposes; however, I prefer to evaluate income-producing properties on a before-tax basis, because this is the way a lender will evaluate it. The tax rate was therefore set to zero, which means the value determined for depreciation is irrelevant in this example.

The next section of the model, cash flow from operations, is especially important since it tells us how much cash is available to service any debt related to the property. The model begins by adding back in the net income after taxes, depreciation, and interest to give us the total cash available to service the debt, which in this example is the $119,656—the same value as NOI since the tax rate is set to zero. The annual debt service is $119,963, which means that the property will generate a negative cash flow of $307 per year on a before-tax basis. Below that is principal reduction, which is the amount applied to pay down the loan in Year 1. When the principal reduction of $16,956 is factored in, the total return on this property is $16,649.

Below the cash flow from operations section, the model provides us with information necessary to make a decision on the viability of this opportunity. In this example, the cash flow to debt service ratio, also known as the debt service coverage ratio (DSCR), is less than 1. Most lenders require a minimum DSCR of 1.00 to 1.20. I personally prefer to see the DSCR above 1.20 as a minimum standard to ensure that the property has adequate cash flow to cover any debt-related obligations. Notice also that both the net income and cash ROIs are negative and that only the total ROI is slightly positive. None of the returns shown here are acceptable. Below the returns is a section that shows the net cash flows from investment, followed by my favorite section, estimated exit price and gain on sale. This section of the model allows the user to evaluate the potential resale value of a property based on cap rates specific to its area. In this example, the value of $1.6 million in Year 1 has a corresponding cap rate of 7.48 percent.

Since the property would not generate sufficient income to cover the debt and provide an acceptable rate of return, I opted not to purchase it. The seller was not willing to negotiate on price, and experience has taught me that it's better to walk away from a deal than to purchase something I'll later regret. Let's take a moment to experiment with the model to see what it would take to bring the property in line with our investment parameters. Take a moment to examine Table 12.2.

Table 12.2 is identical to Table 12.1 with one exception—the purchase price has been reduced from $1.55 million in Table 12.1 to $1.3 million in Table 12.2. Now let's take a look at how the $250,000 reduction in price affects the output in the model. First of all, the average unit cost in the key ratios section was reduced by approximately $10,000 in Table 12.2. Since the purchase price was reduced in Table 12.2, the cap rate increased from 7.62 percent to 9.06 percent. Revenues and operating expenses remain unchanged, so now let's take a look at how the DSCR was affected. Recall that in Table 12.1, it was slightly less than 1.0. That compares with just under 1.19 in Table 12.2. This improved ratio would certainly be considered more favorable to lenders. Now let's shift our focus to the section on returns. The net income ROI is unfavorable in both tables, in large part due to the depreciation value considered by the model. I prefer to focus on the cash ROI and the total ROI, which in Table 12.2 are greatly improved. Although the returns are more favorable in this second scenario, they are still marginal. Let's tweak the model one more time by adjusting the interest rate to a level more in line with today's market rates. Take a moment to examine Table 12.3.

Table 12.2 Property Analysis Worksheet. The Value Play Income Analyzer

Cost and Revenue Assumptions

Land	300,000
Building	1,000,000
Improvements	0
Closing Costs	20,000
Total	1,320,000
Number of Units	24
Average Monthly Rent	720
Gross Monthly Revenues	17,280

Financing Assumptions

Total Purchase	100.00%	1,320,000
Owner's Equity	17.50%	231,000
Balance to Finc	82.50%	1,089,000
	Annual	Monthly
Interest Rate	8.000%	0.667%
Amort Period	25	300
Payment	100,861	8,405

Key Ratios

Total Square Feet	25,700.00
Avg Sq Ft/Unit	1,070.83
Avg Rent/Sq Ft	0.67
Avg Cost/Sq Ft	51.36
Avg Unit Cost	55,000.00
Capitalization Rate	9.06%
Gross Rent Multiplier	6.37
Expense/Unit	3,397.32
Expense/Foot	3.17

Rental Income Projections / Average Monthly Rent / Operating Expense Projections

	Year 1	Year 2	Year 3	Year 4	Year 5
Rental Income Projections	0.00%	3.50%	4.00%	3.00%	3.00%
Average Monthly Rent	720	745	775	798	822
Operating Expense Projections	0.00%	-2.50%	0.00%	1.50%	2.00%

Operating Revenues

		Actual Monthly	Year 1	Year 2	Projected Year 3	Year 4	Year 5
Gross Scheduled Income		17,280	207,360	214,618	223,202	229,898	236,795
Vacancy Rate	5.0%	864	10,368	10,731	11,160	11,495	11,840
Net Rental Income		16,416	196,992	203,887	212,042	218,403	224,956
Other Income		350	4,200	4,347	4,521	4,657	4,796
Gross Income	100.0%	16,766	201,192	208,234	216,563	223,060	229,752

Operating Expenses

		Actual Monthly	Year 1	Year 2	Year 3	Year 4	Year 5
Repairs and Maintenance	14.7%	2,462	29,544	28,805	28,805	29,237	29,822
Property Management Fees	4.0%	671	8,048	7,846	7,846	7,964	8,123
Taxes	12.2%	2,050	24,600	23,985	23,985	24,345	24,832
Insurance	2.8%	465	5,580	5,441	5,441	5,522	5,633
Salaries and Wages	1.5%	250	3,000	2,925	2,925	2,969	3,028
Utilities	2.2%	365	4,380	4,271	4,271	4,335	4,421
Trash Removal	0.5%	82	984	959	959	974	993
Professional Fees	0.6%	100	1,200	1,170	1,170	1,188	1,211

	%	Yr 0	Yr 1	Yr 2	Yr 3	Yr 4	Yr 5
Advertising	0.9%	150	1,800	1,755	1,755	1,781	1,817
Other	1.2%	200	2,400	2,340	2,340	2,375	2,423
Total Op. Exp.	40.5%	6,795	81,536	79,497	79,497	80,690	82,304
Net Operating Income	59.5%	9,971	119,656	128,736	137,066	142,370	147,448
Interest on Loan	43.3%	7,260	86,605	85,422	84,140	82,752	81,249
Dep. Exp. - Building		3,030	36,364	36,364	36,364	36,364	36,364
Dep. Exp. - Equip.		0	0	0	0	0	0
Net Income Before Taxes		(319)	(3,312)	6,951	16,562	23,254	29,835
Income Tax Rate	0.0%	0	0	0	0	0	0
Net Income After Taxes		(319)	(3,312)	6,951	16,562	23,254	29,835
Cash Flow From Operations							
Net Income After Taxes		(319)	(3,312)	6,951	16,562	23,254	29,835
Dep. Exp.		3,030	36,364	36,364	36,364	36,364	36,364
Total CF From Ops.		2,711	33,052	43,315	52,926	59,618	66,199
Interest on Loan		7,260	86,605	85,422	84,140	82,752	81,249
Total Cash Available for Loan Servicing		9,971	119,656	128,736	137,066	142,370	147,448
Debt Service		8,405	100,861	100,861	100,861	100,861	100,861
Remaining After Tax CF From Ops		1,566	18,795	27,875	36,205	41,509	46,587
Plus Principal Reduction		1,188	14,256	15,439	16,721	18,109	19,612
Total Return		2,754	33,052	43,315	52,926	59,618	66,199
CF/Debt Servicing Ratio		118.63%	118.63%	127.64%	135.90%	141.15%	146.19%
Net Income ROI			-1.43%	3.01%	7.17%	10.07%	12.92%
Cash ROI			8.14%	12.07%	15.67%	17.97%	20.17%
Total ROI			14.31%	18.75%	22.91%	25.81%	28.66%
Net CFs From Investment - 1 Yr Exit		(231,000)	494,052				
Net CFs From Investment - 3 Yr Exit		(231,000)	18,795	27,875	618,621		
Net CFs From Investment - 5 Yr Exit		(231,000)	18,795	27,875	36,205	41,509	791,724

	Exit Price	Gain on Sale	Cap Rate		IRR
Estimated Exit Price/Gain On Sale - 1 Yr	1,550,000	230,000	7.72%	Annualized IRR - 1 Yr	113.88%
Estimated Exit Price/Gain On Sale - 3 Yr	1,625,000	305,000	8.43%	Annualized IRR - 3 Yr	44.59%
Estimated Exit Price/Gain On Sale - 5 Yr	1,750,000	430,000	8.43%	Annualized IRR - 5 Yr	35.27%

Table 12.3 Property Analysis Worksheet. The Value Play Income Analyzer

Cost and Revenue Assumptions

Land	300,000
Building	1,000,000
Improvements	0
Closing Costs	20,000
Total	1,320,000
Number of Units	24
Average Monthly Rent	720
Gross Monthly Revenues	17,280

Financing Assumptions

Total Purchase	100.00%	1,320,000
Owner's Equity	17.50%	231,000
Balance to Finc	82.50%	1,089,000
	Annual	Monthly
Interest Rate	6.000%	0.500%
Amort Period	25	300
Payment	84,197	7,016

Key Ratios

Total Square Feet	25,700.00
Avg Sq Ft/Unit	1,070.83
Avg Rent/Sq Ft	0.67
Avg Cost/Sq Ft	51.36
Avg Unit Cost	55,000.00
Capitalization Rate	9.06%
Gross Rent Multiplier	6.37
Expense/Unit	3,397.32
Expense/Foot	3.17

	Year 1	Year 2	Year 3	Year 4	Year 5
Rental Income Projections	0.00%	3.50%	4.00%	3.00%	3.00%
Average Monthly Rent	720	745	775	798	822
Operating Expense Projections	0.00%	-2.50%	0.00%	1.50%	2.00%

		Actual Monthly	Year 1	Year 2	Projected Year 3	Year 4	Year 5
Operating Revenues							
Gross Scheduled Income		17,280	207,360	214,618	223,202	229,898	236,795
Vacancy Rate	5.0%	864	10,368	10,731	11,160	11,495	11,840
Net Rental Income		16,416	196,992	203,887	212,042	218,403	224,956
Other Income		350	4,200	4,347	4,521	4,657	4,796
Gross Income	100.0%	16,766	201,192	208,234	216,563	223,060	229,752
Operating Expenses							
Repairs and Maintenance	14.7%	2,462	29,544	28,805	28,805	29,237	29,822
Property Management Fees	4.0%	671	8,048	7,846	7,846	7,964	8,123
Taxes	12.2%	2,050	24,600	23,985	23,985	24,345	24,832
Insurance	2.8%	465	5,580	5,441	5,441	5,522	5,633
Salaries and Wages	1.5%	250	3,000	2,925	2,925	2,969	3,028
Utilities	2.2%	365	4,380	4,271	4,271	4,335	4,421
Trash Removal	0.5%	82	984	959	959	974	993
Professional Fees	0.6%	100	1,200	1,170	1,170	1,188	1,211

	%						
Advertising	0.9%	150	1,800	1,755	1,755	1,781	1,817
Other	1.2%	200	2,400	2,340	2,340	2,375	2,423
Total Op. Exp.	40.5%	6,795	81,536	79,497	79,497	80,690	82,304
Net Operating Income	59.5%	9,971	119,656	128,736	137,066	142,370	147,448
Interest on Loan	32.5%	5,445	64,813	63,617	62,348	61,000	59,569
Dep. Exp. - Building		3,030	36,364	36,364	36,364	36,364	36,364
Dep. Exp. - Equip.		0	0	0	0	0	0
Net Income Before Taxes		1,496	18,480	28,756	38,354	45,006	51,515
Income Tax Rate	0.0%	0	0	0	0	0	0
Net Income After Taxes		1,496	18,480	28,756	38,354	45,006	51,515
Cash Flow From Operations							
Net Income After Taxes		1,496	18,480	28,756	38,354	45,006	51,515
Dep. Exp.		3,030	36,364	36,364	36,364	36,364	36,364
Total CF From Ops.		4,526	54,844	65,119	74,718	81,370	87,879
Interest on Loan		5,445	64,813	63,617	62,348	61,000	59,569
Total Cash Available for Loan Servicing		9,971	119,656	128,736	137,066	142,370	147,448
Debt Service		7,016	84,197	84,197	84,197	84,197	84,197
Remaining After Tax CF From Ops		2,955	35,459	44,539	52,868	58,173	63,251
Plus Principal Reduction		1,615	19,385	20,580	21,850	23,197	24,628
Total Return		4,570	54,844	65,119	74,718	81,370	87,879
CF/Debt Servicing Ratio	142.11%	142.11%	152.90%	162.79%	169.09%	175.12%	

Net Income ROI	8.00%	12.45%	16.60%	19.48%	22.30%
Cash ROI	15.35%	19.28%	22.89%	25.18%	27.38%
Total ROI	23.74%	28.19%	32.35%	35.23%	38.04%

	Exit Price	Gain on Sale			
Net CFs From Investment - 1 Yr Exit	(231,000)	515,844			
Net CFs From Investment - 3 Yr Exit	(231,000)	35,459	650,683		
Net CFs From Investment - 5 Yr Exit	(231,000)	35,459	52,868	833,890	

	Exit Price	Gain on Sale	Cap Rate		IRR
Estimated Exit Price/Gain On Sale - 1 Yr	1,550,000	230,000	7.72%	Annualized IRR - 1 Yr	123.31%
Estimated Exit Price/Gain On Sale - 3 Yr	1,625,000	305,000	8.43%	Annualized IRR - 3 Yr	51.24%
Estimated Exit Price/Gain On Sale - 5 Yr	1,750,000	430,000	8.43%	Annualized IRR - 5 Yr	40.96%

Table 12.3 is identical to Table 12.2 with one exception—the interest rate in Table 12.3 has been adjusted downward from 8.0 percent to 6.0 percent. Let's start with the financing and assumptions section this time. Note that the annual debt service has been reduced from $100,861 to $84,197—a difference of more than $16,000. Now take a look at the key ratios section. Not a single one of these values has changed, including the cap rate. Although it may initially seem that the cap rate should increase since we are adding more than $16,000 to the bottom line, the value remains unchanged because the interest expense falls below the NOI, which is the numerator in the cap rate equation. Let's move down now to the NOI section of the model. Notice that net income has improved by almost $22,000, which is the difference in the amount of interest paid annually. This favorable difference in interest expense has a significant impact on the amount of cash left over after satisfying all debt requirements, which in turn has a favorable impact on the DSCR and the return ratios. For example, the DSCR has increased from about 1.19 in Table 12.2 to slightly over 1.42 in Table 12.3. Lenders would be much more likely to fund this investment with the higher DSCR than they would the previous model. The cash ROI and total ROI have also greatly improved and would now be considered an acceptable rate of return by most investors. Simply by reducing the interest rate, this investment has moved from a marginally acceptable position to one that is *definitely* acceptable.

In this case study, we analyzed a 24-unit multifamily project to see whether it met our investment criteria. We evaluated this investment opportunity on its ability to generate an acceptable rate of return on a stand-alone basis. We concluded that the property did not meet an investor's acceptable rate of return at the price it was being offered for sale. We also learned that reducing the price brought it closer to an acceptable rate of return, but it was still marginal at best. Finally, by reducing the interest rate a full two percentage points, the bottom line was favorably affected, as net income improved dramatically, thereby producing a positive effect on the property's cash ROI and total ROI. Using The Value Play Income Analyzer in this case study enabled us to quickly and easily make changes in the model and immediately see their effect on its output.

Chapter 13

Case Study 4: Single-Family Conversion to Commercial Office Building

In this case study, we examine the conversion of a single-family residence to one of commercial office space. We also examine the differences between the two valuation methods used for each type of property—the sales comparison method and the income capitalization method. This example will help you to further understand why it is so important to become familiar with all three of the valuation methods discussed in this book. By being familiar with the different approaches, it is possible to create value in a property simply by changing the way it is used to a higher and better use.

The single-family house in this example is one I purchased about a year ago for the sole purpose of converting it to office space. It's located in the downtown area of a small but growing community on a state highway that runs right through the middle of town. It is also located in what is considered to be a high traffic area, which gives the building great visibility and exposure by the 22,000 motorists who pass it each day. When the house was originally built back in 1903, it was probably inconceivable that the street running in front of the house would eventually become the state highway that it is today. This two-story house has approximately 2,400 square feet of space that is well suited for converting to office space. In addition, there's a large basement that is used for storage. Although the house had been fairly well maintained over the years, extensive repairs and improvements were required to successfully convert it into usable office space.

For most of the past 100 years, the house had been occupied as a residence. I did, however, recently come across an old newspaper article that highlighted the house's use as a small hospital for a brief period in the early 1900s. The current seller of the house had lived there since about 1980. From the time he and his wife bought the house, significant growth had occurred in the area. The elderly couple had been trying unsuccessfully to sell the house for close to a year with the assistance of a real estate agent. With new communities being developed in the surrounding area, not many people want to live on a busy state highway. You can rule out families with small children. Being that close to a busy road would be much too dangerous for them. You can rule out the seniors, too. They prefer quiet communities with sidewalks and streetlights. Who does that leave? No one, really, except maybe a guy like me looking for cheap office space.

The house is actually in an ideal location for an office building. The high traffic location is especially appealing in that it enables our company, Symphony Homes, to greatly increase its brand identity and name recognition in that particular community. Approximately 22,000 motorists pass by our brightly lit sign each and every day, 365 days a year, and as they do, they become more and more familiar with our name. Eventually, many of them will come to us seeking the services we offer. With 2,400 square feet of space, the building is large enough to meet our current needs. Furthermore, it is a much cheaper alternative to leasing office or retail space in the same area, and certainly much cheaper than purchasing office or retail space.

Since my partner and I need only a small office for ourselves, my idea in purchasing the building was to either form our own mortgage and title company and traditional real estate office, or to lease out the excess space to another mortgage or real estate company. The combination of those services is a perfect fit for a residential construction builder. The idea was to create a synergistic effect among the three types of services that would enable our company to grow at an accelerated rate. As prospective buyers visit one of our model homes, we can refer them to our mortgage company for financing. Having a title company in the same building provides us with a great deal of convenience. Rather than driving to another location, spending half a day in travel time and the actual closing, I can now continue to work at my desk and sign off on everything when the closing agent is ready. The real estate company provides traditional buy-and-sell services, with a broker and agents who have their own network of buyers and sellers. Since the real estate company is a Symphony Homes affiliate, we strongly encourage the agents to bring their clients to one of our new-home communities. The agents are, of course, free to sell any home to their clients, but we provide incentives for selling these clients one of our homes. The real estate agents also benefit because they are able to obtain the listings of clients who need to sell their home before buying one of ours. Under this arrangement, Symphony Homes wins, the mortgage and title company wins, the real estate company wins, and most important, the customer wins!

As previously mentioned, this is why understanding the differences of the three market valuation methods is so important. If you can grasp the underlying logic and the fundamental principles of each method, you can use them to your advantage to create value. In this case, when considering the property as a single-family house, the most appropriate valuation method was the comparable sales approach. This was the method the appraiser used when he came out to appraise the property. He examined other properties similar to the subject property and made adjustments as necessary to derive a value that was most appropriate for the property in its use as a residence. Now that the house has been converted to an income-producing office building, its use has changed from residential to commercial. The value of the building is no longer based on comparable sales of similar houses. It is instead based on the income produced from its rents. As we've already learned, the income capitalization method is the most appropriate method of valuing a property such as this.

My objective going into this transaction was as always, to apply the OPM principle—that is, to use as much of other people's money as possible and as little of my own money as possible. Being a century old, the house was in need of both repairs and capital improvements. There were also additional costs to convert the property from residential use to commercial use. The owner and I agreed on a sales price of $188,000 with a repair and/or improvement allowance of $40,000, making the effective sales price $148,000. To avoid paying costly private mortgage insurance (PMI), I obtained an 80 percent loan, leaving me with a down payment of 20 percent of the purchase price, or $37,600. At closing, I received an allowance for the necessary repairs and improvements for the agreed-upon amount of $40,000. Exhibit 13.1 shows how the deal was structured.

Structuring the transaction in this manner allowed me to limit the out-of-pocket cash to 20 percent of the total deal value at the time of closing. Since I received the credit for improvements, my actual out-of-pocket cash at closing was zero. This is a creative and effective way to pull cash out of a deal at closing, especially when you have an immediate need for the cash, such as for property improvements. To take advantage of this financing strategy, there are two caveats you should be aware of. The first one is that the house has to appraise for a high enough value in its existing condition. In this example, the house had to appraise for the sales price of $188,000 before any repairs or improvements were made. That means the appraiser had to find legitimate existing comparable sales that he could use to support the purchase price.

The second caveat is that you have to have a lender who is willing to work with you by allowing the credit at closing. While most lenders will allow the buyer to receive some type of credit, they generally limit it to anywhere from 3 to 5 percent of the sales price to help reduce the out-of-pocket expenditures for closing costs. I usually have the most success using a mortgage broker when trying to structure a deal like this rather than going directly to a lender. Many smaller community banks, however, will work with you as long as they understand what you are trying to do. In addition, they may require the funds credited at closing to be placed into an escrow account and paid out only after the improvements have been made.

Now take a moment to study Table 13.1, "Property Analysis Worksheet." The worksheet illustrated here is a proprietary model I

Exhibit 13.1

Deal structure:
Single-family to commercial office
building conversion.

1. Sales price: $188,000
2. Down payment: $37,600 (20%)
3. Term: 30 years
4. Interest rate: 6.0%
5. Cash back at closing: $40,000

have developed to quickly and easily analyze potential value play investment opportunities. I call it *The Value Play Rehab Analyzer.* Once I have gathered the necessary data, I can input the information into the model and in less than five minutes know within a reasonable degree of accuracy whether a rehab opportunity makes sense based on my investment criteria. All I have to do is key in the information and the model automatically makes all of the calculations. Although the model was designed specifically for flipping and rehab opportunities, its application is suitable here, because we know the property will require substantial improvements. The objective in using this model is to be sure that our investment will, at a minimum, break even using comparable sales to determine its value.

Under the purchase assumptions section, the basic property information is listed, including a project name, address, and pricing information. The value of the land does not really matter as long as the price of the land plus the price of the house is equal to the total purchase price. In the purchase assumptions box, I used $148,000 ($30,000 + $118,000) for the purchase price since that is the net effective sales price of the house. There are two sections for financing

Table 13.1 Property Analysis Worksheet. The Value Play Rehab Analyzer

Purchase Assumptions

Project Name:	Residential to Office	
Address:	123 South State St.	
City, State, Zip:	Anywhere, MI 48423	
Contact:	Mr. Please Buy My House	
Telephone:	(800) 555-1234	

Land	30,000
Building/House	118,000
Closing Costs	2,700
Other Related Costs	300
Total Purchase Price	151,000

Financing Assumptions - Primary

Primary Mortgage or Loan:		
Total Purchase	100.00%	151,000
Down Payment	20.00%	30,200
Balance to Finc	80.00%	120,800

	Annual	Monthly
Interest Rate	6.000%	0.500%
Amort Period	30	
Payment	8,691	724
Interest Only	7,248	604

Financing Assumptions - Secondary

Secondary Financing/Line of Credit:		
Total Imprvmnts	100.00%	40,000
Down Payment	20.00%	8,000
Balance to Finc	80.00%	32,000

	Annual	Monthly
Interest Rate	6.000%	0.500%
Amort Period	30	360
Payment	2,302	192
Interest Only	1,920	160

Estimate for Improvements

Appliances		Flooring		Lighting	750
Dishwasher	0	Carpet	2,000	Masonry	0
Disposal	0	Ceramic Tile	0	Parking Lot & Drive	8,400
Microwave	0	Hardwood	0	Other	0
Range	0	Vinyl	1,500	Other	0
Refrigerator	0	Subtotal	3,500	Painting: Exterior	1,200
Subtotal	0			Painting: Interior	2,100
		Foundation	0	Permits	250
Architectural Drawings	0	Framing	0	Subtotal	12,700
Cabinets	0	Garage	500		
Caulking	450	Gas & Electric Hookup	0	Plumbing	
Subtotal	450	Glass: Mirrors, showers	0	Commodes	0
		Gutters	0	Drain Lines	0
Cement Work		Subtotal	500	Faucets	250
Basement Floor	0			Fixtures	250
Driveway	0	HVAC		Hot Water Heater	0
Garage Floor	0	Air Conditioner	1,800	Showers	0
Porches	0	Duct Work	0	Tubs	0

Cost of Improvements

Filters	1,200
Furnace	1,200
Subtotal	**1,200**
Cleaning	1,000
Counter Tops	0
Decorating	1,500
Doors	500
Drywall	250
Electrical	500
Engineering	0
Equipment Rental	0
Excavation Work	0
Fences	2,500
Fireplace	0
Subtotal	**6,250**

Insulation	0
Insurance Premiums	525
Subtotal	**525**
Landscaping	0
Irrigation System	0
Lot Clearing	0
Mowing Services	50
Sod	0
Trees, Plants, & Shrubs	1,400
Subtotal	**1,450**

Sidewalks	25
Subtotal	**225**
Water Lines	0
Subtotal	**500**
	2,050
Roofing	7,800
Siding	0
Site Planning & Engineering	2,200
Steel	0
Trim	0
Utility: Gas & Electric	250
Utility: Water & Sewer	125
Warranty	0
Windows	500
Subtotal	**10,875**
Total Cost of Improvements	**40,000**

Comp #1

Address:	
Sales Price	179,900.00
Adjustments to Price	1,200.00
Adjusted Price	181,100.00
Square Feet	2,200.00
Price Per Square Foot	82.32

Comp #2

Address:	
Sales Price	186,500.00
Adjustments to Price	1,800.00
Adjusted Price	188,300.00
Square Footage	2,320.00
Price Per Square Foot	81.16

Comp #3

Address:	
Sales Price	189,450.00
Adjustments to Price	(2,600.00)
Adjusted Price	186,850.00
Square Feet	2,275.00
Price Per Square Foot	82.13

Comp Averages

Sales Price	185,283.33
Adjustments to Price	133.33
Adjusted Price	185,416.67
Square Feet	2,265.00
Price Per Square Foot	81.86
Turn Comps Off/On	ON
Est Price/Sq Ft If Turned OFF	80.00

Subject Property — 123 South State St.

Square Feet	2,400.00
Price/Sq Ft	62.92
Imprvmnts/Sq Ft	16.67
Total Price/Sq Ft	79.58
Estimated Time To Complete Project	4.00

Adjustments to Comps (5.00)

Description	Best Case	Most Likely	Worst Case
Est Sales Price	208,468	196,468	184,468
Purchase Price	151,000	151,000	151,000
Improvements	40,000	40,000	40,000
Interest Charges	3,056	3,056	3,056
Taxes	450	450	450
Closing Costs	1,575	1,575	1,575
Total Costs	196,081	196,081	196,081
Profit Margin	12,387	387	(11,613)
Return On Inv	32.43%	1.01%	-30.40%

assumptions—one for primary financing and another one for secondary financing. The primary financing section is used for the primary source of financing, which can be in the form of a loan from a mortgage company, bank, or private individual, as this example illustrates. The loan terms for the purchase price are reflected in the financing assumptions—primary box.

The secondary financing section is used for any additional loans secured, such as a home equity line of credit (HELOC). Home equity loans are generally easy to obtain, especially if your credit is decent. For lower-cost improvements, you may want to use all cash. On the other hand, if the cost of the improvements is greater than the amount of capital you want to use, then this is the appropriate section to use. Rates and terms are typically different for a line of credit, such as a home equity line or a credit card, than they are for a regular mortgage, so having two sections for financing allows you to more accurately determine the carrying costs, or interest charges. The total cost of improvements for this project was estimated at $40,000. This total was entered into the estimate for improvements section and is captured in financing assumptions—secondary. In this case, since the primary and secondary financing will be combined into one note, the same interest rate and term are used. To calculate the total payment, the two values are added together.

Under the estimate for improvements section, there are several categories that provide for estimating the costs for virtually everything in a house—in this case, a soon-to-be office building. The estimates for improvements section is organized alphabetically by category, with related subcategories as needed. Estimating these costs accurately is especially important for the proper analysis of making improvements on a larger scale, such as is illustrated in this example. The more experience you have as an investor, the easier it becomes to estimate costs.

The next section of the model gives investors the ability to enter information for comparable home sales. This information is needed to help make accurate projections of the estimated resale value of an investment property. Any sales agent can provide you with comparable sales data for your area. You can also check the Internet for listings in your area, which will give you a good idea of what houses are selling for.

In addition, a provision in this section allows for making adjustments to the sales price of the comps. This provision permits investors to compare apples to apples. For example, if the subject property has a two-car garage and the comparable home sale has a three-car garage, the price should be revised downward in the adjustments to price section. This is exactly how real estate agents and appraisers determine the market value of a house. They start with an average price per square foot of several similar houses and make compensating adjustments to estimate value.

In this example, comparable sale #1 had a sales price of $179,900, with an adjustment upward of $1,200, resulting in an adjusted sales price of $181,100. Since the house had 2,200 square feet, the average price per square foot after adjustments is $82.32. Comparable sale #2 had a sales price of $186,500, with an adjustment upward of $1,800, resulting in an adjusted sales price of $188,300. Since the house had 2,320 square feet, the average price per square foot after adjustments is $81.16. Comparable sale #3 had a sales price of $189,450, with a downward adjustment of $2,600, resulting in an adjusted sales price of $186,850. Since the house had 2,275 square feet, the average price per square foot after adjustments is $82.13.

The comp averages section simply takes an average of the three comps' sales prices to come up with an average sales price, which in this example is $185,283. The adjustments to the sales price are minimal, resulting in an upward adjustment of only $133, which gives us an adjusted average sales price of $185,417. Since the average square footage of the three homes is 2,265 square feet, the average price per square foot after adjustments is $81.86. The result is a weighted average price per square foot of the three homes.

The comp averages section also has a provision that allows users to turn the comps section off or on. An investor who is already familiar with values in a given area will most likely know the average sales price per square foot, so the sales comp data would not need to be entered in. Instead, the comps section can be turned off and the estimated value can then be entered.

The average sales price per square foot from the comp averages section is then fed into the subject property section. All of the information previously keyed into the rest of the model is summarized in this section. The square footage of the subject property must be known so that an accurate comparison can be made. In this example, it is 2,400 square feet. The purchase price per square foot is automatically calculated, as is the total cost of the improvements per square foot. The two numbers are then added together to provide the total cost of the project. In this example, the total cost of improvements of $40,000 was added to the total purchase price of $151,000. The resulting sum was then divided by 2,400 square feet, for a total price per square foot of $79.59. This number is the cost basis and represents the total cost of the house after all improvements have been made.

Below the total price per square foot section is a provision that allows users to estimate the total time in months for completion and resell. In other words, it calculates the carrying costs for interest, a factor that many less experienced investors do not consider. If the home is your own, however, the number should be set to zero, since you are receiving the benefit of living there while the improvements are being made. In the example here, the number of months is set to four since that is the estimated length of time needed to make the improvements, and also since there is no benefit from the house while the repairs are being made.

The adjustment to comps cell is used to create the estimated sales price if an investor were to resell the property after the repairs and improvements were made. This section provides a range of three different sales scenarios—best-case, most likely, and worst-case. In this example, $5.00 per square foot is used, but the value can be set to whatever number is desired. For the best-case sales price, the model adds $5.00 to the price per square foot cell in the comp averages section and then multiplies the sum of the two by the square feet of the subject property. Here's how it works:

Best-Case Sales Price

(Average price/square foot + adjustments to comps)

× subject property square feet = best-case sales price

($81.86 + $5.00) × 2,400 = $208,464

The most likely sales price calculation in the model neither adds nor subtracts the value of $5.00 to the price per square foot cell in the comp averages section. It is simply the product of the average price per square foot and the square feet. Take a moment to review the following calculation.

Most Likely Sales Price

Average price/square foot × subject property square feet

= most likely sales price $81.86 × 2,400 = $196,464

For the worst-case sales price, the model subtracts $5.00 from the price per square foot cell in the comp averages section, and then multiplies the difference of the two by the square feet of the subject property.

Worst-Case Sales Price

(Average price/square foot − Adjustment to comps)

× subject property square feet = worst-case sales price

($81.86 − $5.00) × 2,400 = $184,464

The purpose of creating three different scenarios in the model is to provide a range for the estimated sales price. This allows users of the model to evaluate the very minimum that might be expected on the low end of the price range, and the very most that might be expected on the high end of the price range. Take a moment to refer back to Table 13.1. The purchase price, improvements, interest charges, taxes, and closing costs remain constant among all three scenarios, since these values are not affected by the adjustment to comps variable of $5.00. The profit margin is the dollar amount that can be expected from the sale after all costs have been accounted for. The return on investment is calculated as the ratio of the profit margin divided by the total cash invested in the property. It is calculated for the most likely scenario, as follows:

Return on Investment

$$\frac{\text{Profit margin}}{\text{Primary down payment} + \text{secondary down payment}} = \text{ROI}$$

$$\frac{\$387}{\$30,200 + \$8,000} = 1.01\%$$

After factoring in transaction costs, the profit margin in the most likely scenario shows a meager gain of only $387, which gives us an anemic ROI of only 1.01 percent. At first glance, it appears that investing in this project would be a complete waste of our investment capital. Remember, however, that the value shown here is *before* any of the improvements have actually been made. Now let's take a few minutes to study Table 13.2. Although this model is similar to The Value Play Rehab Analyzer, it is really quite different. This model is known as *The Value Play Income Analyzer,* which was discussed in greater detail in Chapter 12. It is used to measure the value of an income-producing property, such as an apartment building or our soon-to-be-converted office building.

In Table 13.2, notice that we have the same sales price of $148,000, plus $40,000 in improvements, plus $3,000 in closing costs and other costs, for a total of $191,000, just as we did in Table 13.1. Notice also that the information in the financing assumptions section is exactly the same, except for the fact that it is consolidated into one section rather than two. The key ratios section in Table 13.2 captures important data relative to income-producing property. The most important number to focus on for this example is the capitalization rate. The cap rate, as you recall, is the ratio between net operating income and sales price.

$$\frac{\text{Net operating income}}{\text{Sales price}} = \text{capitalization rate}$$

or

$$\frac{\text{Net operating income}}{\text{Cap rate}} = \text{sales price}$$

The capitalization rate, or yield, on an income-producing property will vary within a given range and generally falls between 8 and 12 percent. Cap rates are driven by a variety of market conditions, including supply and demand for real estate, the current interest rate environment, the type and condition of the property, its location, and tax implications imposed by local, state, and federal authorities. Under the key ratios section in Table 13.2, note the cap rate of 14.32 percent. This number represents the yield of the property as a whole since it is based on the sales price, not the equity. Remember that return on investment (ROI) measures the relationship between equity and returns. A yield of 14.32 percent would be exceptional on a certificate of deposit. It is also considered high on real estate. This indicates the property's sales price is low relative to its ability to generate income in its newly converted state as an office. Translated, it means we are buying the property at a bargain price and that there is plenty of upside in the deal.

The average monthly rent is based on a rate of $1 per square foot per month, or $12 per square foot annually, multiplied by the square feet of the house, which gives us $2,400 of rental income per month. In the market in which the building is located, this rate is conservative. While a vacancy rate of 5 percent is used, three- to five-year lease agreements are typically the minimum lease terms. Since the lease will be a net lease, there are no expenses, as they will all be paid by the tenant. Now take a look at the bottom of Table 13.2 at the three different estimated exit prices. Based on the information we know to be true regarding market rates and capitalization rates, the property can be sold at the end of Year 1 at an exit price of $292,000, at a very conservative cap rate of 9.37 percent, which will yield an attractive gain on sale of $100,000 excluding transaction costs. The internal rate of return (IRR) is derived by measuring the rate of return over time given a series of cash flows (taken from net CFs from investment—one-year exit). In this example, the IRR is a

Table 13.2 Property Analysis Worksheet. The Value Play Income Analyzer

Cost and Revenue Assumptions

Land	30,000
Building	118,000
Improvements	40,000
Closing Costs	3,000
Total	191,000
Number of Units	1
Average Monthly Rent	2,400
Gross Monthly Revenues	2,400

Financing Assumptions

Total Purchase	100.00%	191,000
Owner's Equity	20.00%	38,200
Balance to Finc	80.00%	152,800
	Annual	Monthly
Interest Rate	6.000%	0.500%
Amort Period	30	360
Payment	10,993	916

Key Ratios

Total Square Feet	2,400.00
Avg Sq Ft/Unit	2,400.00
Avg Rent/Sq Ft	1.00
Avg Cost/Sq Ft	79.58
Avg Unit Cost	191,000.00
Capitalization Rate	14.32%
Gross Rent Multiplier	6.63
Expense/Unit	0.00
Expense/Foot	0.00

0.00%	0.00%	0.00%	0.00%	0.00%	0.00%
2,400	2,400	2,400	2,400	2,400	2,400
0.00%	0.00%	0.00%	0.00%	0.00%	0.00%

Rental Income Projections
Average Monthly Rent
Operating Expense Projections

	Actual Monthly	Year 1	Year 2	Year 3	Year 4	Year 5
				Projected		
Operating Revenues						
Gross Scheduled Income	2,400	28,800	28,800	28,800	28,800	28,800
Vacancy Rate 5.0%	120	1,440	1,440	1,440	1,440	1,440
Net Rental Income	2,280	27,360	27,360	27,360	27,360	27,360
Other Income	0	0	0	0	0	0
Gross Income 100.0%	2,280	27,360	27,360	27,360	27,360	27,360
Operating Expenses						
Repairs and Maintenance 0.0%	0	0	0	0	0	0
Property Management Fees 0.0%	0	0	0	0	0	0
Taxes 0.0%	0	0	0	0	0	0
Insurance 0.0%	0	0	0	0	0	0
Salaries and Wages 0.0%	0	0	0	0	0	0
Utilities 0.0%	0	0	0	0	0	0
Trash Removal 0.0%	0	0	0	0	0	0
Professional Fees 0.0%	0	0	0	0	0	0

Advertising	0.0%	0	0	0	0	0
Other	0.0%	0	0	0	0	0
Total Op. Exp.	0.0%	0	0	0	0	0
Net Operating Income	100.0%	2,280	27,360	27,360	27,360	27,360	27,360

Interest on Loan	33.5%	764	9,117	9,001	8,878	8,748	8,609
Dep. Exp. - Building		358	4,291	4,291	4,291	4,291	4,291
Dep. Exp. - Equip.		0	0	0	0	0	0
Net Income Before Taxes		1,158	13,952	14,068	14,191	14,321	14,460
Income Tax Rate	0.0%	0	0	0	0	0	0
Net Income After Taxes		1,158	13,952	14,068	14,191	14,321	14,460

Cash Flow From Operations

Net Income After Taxes		1,158	13,952	14,068	14,191	14,321	14,460
Dep. Exp.		358	4,291	4,291	4,291	4,291	4,291
Total CF From Ops.		1,516	18,243	18,359	18,482	18,612	18,751
Interest on Loan		764	9,117	9,001	8,878	8,748	8,609
Total Cash Available for Loan Servicing		2,280	27,360	27,360	27,360	27,360	27,360
Debt Service		916	10,993	10,993	10,993	10,993	10,993
Remaining After Tax CF From Ops		1,364	16,367	16,367	16,367	16,367	16,367
Plus Principal Reduction		156	1,876	1,992	2,115	2,245	2,384
Total Return		1,520	18,243	18,359	18,482	18,612	18,751

CF/Debt Servicing Ratio	248.88%	248.88%	248.88%	248.88%	248.88%	248.88%

Net Income ROI		36.52%	36.83%	37.15%	37.49%	37.85%
Cash ROI		42.84%	42.84%	42.84%	42.84%	42.84%
Total ROI		47.76%	48.06%	48.38%	48.72%	49.09%

Net CFs From Investment - 1 Yr Exit	(38,200)	157,443	16,367	16,367	16,367	16,367
Net CFs From Investment - 3 Yr Exit	(38,200)	16,367	16,367	169,550	16,367	16,367
Net CFs From Investment - 5 Yr Exit	(38,200)	16,367	16,367	16,367	16,367	184,180

	Exit Price	Gain on Sale	Cap Rate		IRR
Estimated Exit Price/Gain On Sale - 1 Yr	292,000	101,000	9.37%	Annualized IRR - 1 Yr	312.15%
Estimated Exit Price/Gain On Sale - 3 Yr	300,000	109,000	9.12%	Annualized IRR - 3 Yr	89.32%
Estimated Exit Price/Gain On Sale - 5 Yr	310,000	119,000	8.83%	Annualized IRR - 5 Yr	63.14%

respectable 312 percent in Year 1! For investors who think this kind of return may be wishful thinking, let me remind you that these numbers are actually conservative and are on the low end of the market based on the rate of $12 per square foot. Now take a moment to study Table 13.3, the Refinance Analyzer.

The Refinance Analyzer provides investors with an alternative to selling their income-producing property. Given a certain set of assumptions, it calculates the maximum loan amount that an investor can borrow based on the income the property generates. In Table 13.3, the maximum loan amount based on an 80 percent LTV ratio is $244,444. The Refinance Analyzer also tells us that we have to be able to get an appraisal in the amount of $305,554, which shouldn't be too difficult based on the cap rate of 8.954 percent indicated in the key ratios section of this table. Since the new loan would be a commercial loan and not a residential mortgage, we use a slightly higher interest rate of 6.75 percent and a shorter amortization period of 25 years. Now let's take a moment to review the effect of these changes.

New loan amount:	$244,444
Pay off existing loan:	<u>$152,800</u>
Cash back to investor:	$91,644

Refinancing the property based on the income capitalization method has allowed us to justify a much higher value than the one based on the comparable sales method. In this example, refinancing would put $91,644 cash back in your pocket. I'm sure you would agree with me that you can find something to do with that much money!

Let's look at one more example. We'll make a quick change in the Income Analyzer by adjusting the rental income upward, from $12 per square foot to $16 per square foot, which is at the upper end of market rates, and see how that affects the property's value. All other assumptions remain the same. Take a minute to study Table 13.4.

As you can see, by increasing the rents, we are significantly increasing the value of the property. This is similar to increasing the income generated by a certificate of deposit. Since the yield is held constant, it is the value of the certificate that must be increased. With the cap rate held constant in the Income Analyzer at about 9.5 percent, the estimated exit price increases from $292,000 in Table 13.2 to $385,000 in Table 13.4. If the property were sold at the end of Year 1, the estimated gain on sale is $194,000, which represents an increase of $93,000 over the estimated gain on sale in Table 13.2. We now have two different versions, or scenarios, of this property— one at the lower end of income per square foot and one at the higher end of income per square foot. This provides us with a broad range of values from $292,000 to $385,000. These values are a direct function of the income produced by the property; the more rental income that can be justified by local market rates, the more valuable the property becomes. Now let's examine the effect of these changes in our Refinance Analyzer in Table 13.5.

The same assumptions we used in the previous example in Table 13.4 have been applied to the model in Table 13.5. The maximum loan amount based on an 80 percent LTV ratio is $325,925. The output also tells us that we have to be able to get an appraisal in the amount of $407,406, with a cap rate of 8.954 percent, as indicated in the key ratios box. Here's how it looks.

New loan amount:	$325,925
Pay off existing loan:	<u>$152,800</u>
Cash back to investor:	$173,125

In this instance, we are able to obtain a new loan in the amount of $325,925, pay off the old loan of $152,800, and pocket the difference of $173,125. This is another powerful example of how effective the value play strategy can be. We have taken an existing property and created substantial value in it by changing its use from residential to commercial office space. The ROI on the original

Table 13.3 Refinance Analyzer

Minimum Refinance - Cash Out		
Max Refinance	80.00%	244,444
Owner's Equity @	20.00%	61,111
Required Appraisal	100.00%	305,554
	Annual	Monthly
Interest Rate	6.750%	0.563%
Amortization Period	25	300
Payment	20,267	1,689

Key Ratios	
Total Square Feet	2,400.000
Avg Sq Ft/Unit	2,400.000
Avg Rent/Sq Ft	1.000
Avg Cost/Sq Ft	127.314
Avg Unit Cost	305,554.479
Capitalization Rate	8.954%
Gross Rent Multiplier	10.610
Expense/Unit	0.000
Expense/Foot	0.000

Operating Revenues		Year 1
Gross Scheduled Income		28,800
Vacancy Rate		1,440
Net Rental Income		27,360
Other Income		0
Gross Revenues	100.0%	27,360

Operating Expenses		
Repairs and Maintenance	0.0%	0
Property Management Fees	0.0%	0
Taxes	0.0%	0
Insurance	0.0%	0

Refinance Matrix	
Max Refinance	CF/DS
329,999	100.0%
323,528	102.0%
317,307	104.0%
311,320	106.0%
305,554	108.0%
299,999	110.0%
294,642	112.0%
289,473	114.0%
284,482	116.0%
279,660	118.0%
274,999	120.0%

Salaries and Wages	0.0%	0
Utilities	0.0%	0
Trash Removal	0.0%	0
Professional Fees	0.0%	0
Advertising	0.0%	0
Other	0.0%	0
Total Op. Exp.	0.0%	0
Net Operating Income	100.0%	27,360
Dep. Exp. - Building		4,291
Dep. Exp. - Equip.		0
Net Income Before Taxes		23,069
Income Tax Rate	0.0%	0
Net Income After Taxes		23,069
Cash Flow From Operations		
Net Income After Taxes		23,069
Dep. Exp.		4,291
Total Cash Available for Loan Servicing		27,360
Debt Service		20,267
Remaining After Tax CF From Ops		7,093
Plus Principal Reduction		3,885
Total Return		10,979

122.0%	270,491
124.0%	266,128
126.0%	261,904
128.0%	257,812
130.0%	253,845
132.0%	249,999
134.0%	246,268
136.0%	242,646
138.0%	239,130
140.0%	235,713
142.0%	232,394
144.0%	229,166
146.0%	226,027
148.0%	222,972
150.0%	219,999
152.0%	217,104
154.0%	214,285
156.0%	211,538
158.0%	208,860
160.0%	206,249
162.0%	203,703
164.0%	201,219
166.0%	198,794
168.0%	196,428
170.0%	194,117
172.0%	191,860

CF/Debt Servicing Ratio	135.0%

Table 13.4 Property Analysis Worksheet. The Value Play Income Analyzer

Cost and Revenue Assumptions		Financing Assumptions			Key Ratios	
Land	30,000	Total Purchase	100.00%	191,000	Total Square Feet	2,400.00
Building	118,000	Owner's Equity	20.00%	38,200	Avg Sq Ft/Unit	2,400.00
Improvements	40,000	Balance to Finc	80.00%	152,800	Avg Rent/Sq Ft	1.33
Closing Costs	3,000				Avg Cost/Sq Ft	79.58
Total	191,000		Annual	Monthly	Avg Unit Cost	191,000.00
		Interest Rate	6.000%	0.500%	Capitalization Rate	19.10%
Number of Units	1	Amort Period	30	360	Gross Rent Multiplier	4.97
Average Monthly Rent	3,200	Payment	10,993	916	Expense/Unit	0.00
Gross Monthly Revenues	3,200				Expense/Foot	0.00

Rental Income Projections	0.00%	0.00%	0.00%
Average Monthly Rent	3,200	3,200	3,200
Operating Expense Projections	0.00%	0.00%	0.00%

	Actual Monthly	Year 1	Year 2	Year 3	Year 4	Year 5
				Projected		
Operating Revenues						
Gross Scheduled Income	3,200	38,400	38,400	38,400	38,400	38,400
Vacancy Rate 5.0%	160	1,920	1,920	1,920	1,920	1,920
Net Rental Income	3,040	36,480	36,480	36,480	36,480	36,480
Other Income	0	0	0	0	0	0
Gross Income 100.0%	3,040	36,480	36,480	36,480	36,480	36,480
Operating Expenses						
Repairs and Maintenance 0.0%	0	0	0	0	0	0
Property Management Fees 0.0%	0	0	0	0	0	0
Taxes 0.0%	0	0	0	0	0	0
Insurance 0.0%	0	0	0	0	0	0
Salaries and Wages 0.0%	0	0	0	0	0	0
Utilities 0.0%	0	0	0	0	0	0
Trash Removal 0.0%	0	0	0	0	0	0
Professional Fees 0.0%	0	0	0	0	0	0

	%	Monthly	Year 1	Year 2	Year 3	Year 4	Year 5
Advertising	0.0%		0	0	0	0	0
Other	0.0%		0	0	0	0	0
Total Op. Exp.	0.0%		0	0	0	0	0
Net Operating Income	100.0%	3,040	36,480	36,480	36,480	36,480	36,480
Interest on Loan	25.1%	764	9,117	9,001	8,878	8,748	8,609
Dep. Exp. - Building		358	4,291	4,291	4,291	4,291	4,291
Dep. Exp. - Equip.		0	0	0	0	0	0
Net Income Before Taxes		1,918	23,072	23,188	23,311	23,441	23,580
Income Tax Rate	0.0%	0	0	0	0	0	0
Net Income After Taxes		1,918	23,072	23,188	23,311	23,441	23,580

Cash Flow From Operations

	Monthly	Year 1	Year 2	Year 3	Year 4	Year 5
Net Income After Taxes	1,918	23,072	23,188	23,311	23,441	23,580
Dep. Exp.	358	4,291	4,291	4,291	4,291	4,291
Total CF From Ops.	2,276	27,363	27,479	27,602	27,732	27,871
Interest on Loan	764	9,117	9,001	8,878	8,748	8,609
Total Cash Available for Loan Servicing	3,040	36,480	36,480	36,480	36,480	36,480
Debt Service	916	10,993	10,993	10,993	10,993	10,993
Remaining After Tax CF From Ops	2,124	25,487	25,487	25,487	25,487	25,487
Plus Principal Reduction	156	1,876	1,992	2,115	2,245	2,384
Total Return	2,280	27,363	27,479	27,602	27,732	27,871

CF/Debt Servicing Ratio	331.84%	331.84%	331.84%	331.84%	331.84%	331.84%

	Year 1	Year 2	Year 3	Year 4	Year 5
Net Income ROI	60.40%	60.70%	61.02%	61.36%	61.73%
Cash ROI	66.72%	66.72%	66.72%	66.72%	66.72%
Total ROI	71.63%	71.93%	72.26%	72.60%	72.96%

	Initial	Year 1	Year 2	Year 3	Year 4	Year 5
Net CFs From Investment - 1 Yr Exit	(38,200)	259,563				
Net CFs From Investment - 3 Yr Exit	(38,200)	25,487	25,487	263,670		
Net CFs From Investment - 5 Yr Exit	(38,200)	25,487	25,487	25,487	25,487	268,300

	Exit Price	Gain on Sale	Cap Rate
Estimated Exit Price/Gain On Sale - 1 Yr	385,000	194,000	9.48%
Estimated Exit Price/Gain On Sale - 3 Yr	385,000	194,000	9.48%
Estimated Exit Price/Gain On Sale - 5 Yr	385,000	194,000	9.48%

	IRR
Annualized IRR - 1 Yr	579.48%
Annualized IRR - 3 Yr	128.33%
Annualized IRR - 5 Yr	87.76%

Table 13.5 Refinance Analyzer

Minimum Refinance - Cash Out		
Max Refinance	80.00%	325,925
Owner's Equity @	20.00%	81,481
Required Appraisal	100.00%	407,406
	Annual	**Monthly**
Interest Rate	6.750%	0.563%
Amortization Period	25	300
Payment	27,022	2,252

Operating Revenues		Year 1
Gross Scheduled Income		38,400
Vacancy Rate		1,920
Net Rental Income		36,480
Other Income		0
Gross Revenues	100.0%	36,480

Operating Expenses		
Repairs and Maintenance	0.0%	0
Property Management Fees	0.0%	0
Taxes	0.0%	0
Insurance	0.0%	0

Key Ratios	
Total Square Feet	2,400.000
Avg Sq Ft/Unit	2,400.000
Avg Rent/Sq Ft	1.333
Avg Cost/Sq Ft	169.752
Avg Unit Cost	407,405.972
Capitalization Rate	8.954%
Gross Rent Multiplier	10.610
Expense/Unit	0.000
Expense/Foot	0.000

Refinance Matrix	
Max Refinance	**CF/DS**
439,998	100.0%
431,371	102.0%
423,075	104.0%
415,093	106.0%
407,406	108.0%
399,999	110.0%
392,856	112.0%
385,964	114.0%
379,309	116.0%
372,880	118.0%
366,665	120.0%

Item	%	Amount
Salaries and Wages	0.0%	0
Utilities	0.0%	0
Trash Removal	0.0%	0
Professional Fees	0.0%	0
Advertising	0.0%	0
Other	0.0%	0
Total Op. Exp.	0.0%	0
Net Operating Income	100.0%	36,480
Dep. Exp. - Building		4,291
Dep. Exp. - Equip.		0
Net Income Before Taxes		32,189
Income Tax Rate	0.0%	0
Net Income After Taxes		32,189

Cash Flow From Operations

Item	Amount
Net Income After Taxes	32,189
Dep. Exp.	4,291
Total Cash Available for Loan Servicing	36,480
Debt Service	27,022
Remaining After Tax CF From Ops	9,458
Plus Principal Reduction	5,181
Total Return	14,638

CF/Debt Servicing Ratio	135.0%

%	Amount
122.0%	360,654
124.0%	354,837
126.0%	349,205
128.0%	343,749
130.0%	338,460
132.0%	333,332
134.0%	328,357
136.0%	323,528
138.0%	318,839
140.0%	314,285
142.0%	309,858
144.0%	305,554
146.0%	301,369
148.0%	297,296
150.0%	293,332
152.0%	289,473
154.0%	285,713
156.0%	282,050
158.0%	278,480
160.0%	274,999
162.0%	271,604
164.0%	268,292
166.0%	265,059
168.0%	261,904
170.0%	258,823
172.0%	255,813

investment of $38,200, if sold using the assumptions in Table 13.4, is 508 percent.

Return on Investment

$$\frac{\text{Profit margin}}{\text{Primary down payment} + \text{secondary down payment}} = \text{ROI}$$

$$\frac{\$194,000}{\$38,200} = 507.85\%$$

I'm sure you'll agree with me that there is great value in using dynamic models such as those illustrated in this case study. By keying in the basic assumptions, the user can very easily change a few variables to quickly see the corresponding changes and to identify any upside potential that may exist in a property. Appendix A provides additional information regarding the availability of the models used in this example.

In summary, *The Complete Guide to Real Estate Finance for Investment Properties* has covered a number of key financial topics. This body of knowledge will enable individuals and businesses who are actively investing in income-producing properties, as well as those who desire to invest in them, to more accurately assess the inherent value within each property. We have taken the theories of real estate finance discussed in other books and demonstrated how they can be used in real-world situations by exploring their practical application. The thorough analysis of four different case studies has provided the learning platform necessary to make the transition from the theory of real estate finance to its useful and appropriate application. Investor comprehension has been further augmented by demonstrating several proprietary financial models designed for the sole purpose of making sound investment decisions.

A comprehensive understanding of the concepts presented herein will furthermore provide a sound basis for making all real estate investment decisions. Whether an investor is buying, holding, or selling income-producing property, the basis for all decisions must be founded on the fundamental principles of finance as they apply to real estate valuations. The failure to understand these key principles will almost certainly result in the failure of the individual investor. At a minimum, it will place him or her at a competitive disadvantage compared to those who do understand them. Recall from Chapter 1 the millions of investors who purchased stocks for no other reason than because they received a hot tip from a friend or coworker. As the equities bubble quickly deflated, many of those investors stood by helplessly as their life savings evaporated into thin air. A similar outcome is almost certain for those individuals investing in real estate who fail to exercise sound valuation principles and who act on nothing more than the advice of someone who has no business giving advice, such as a broker with a hot tip. You now have within your hands the proper tools to help you avoid the costly mistakes made by other real estate investors. I encourage you to use these tools to the fullest extent possible. Implementing the body of knowledge contained herein will enable you to achieve your fullest potential and master the world of real estate finance.

Part 3

Epilogue and Appendixes

Chapter 14

Epilogue:
Destined for Greatness

PRIOR WORKS

In Chapter 14, the final chapter of *The Complete Guide to Buying and Selling Apartment Buildings*, I wrote about the five keys to success. Following is an excerpt taken from Chapter 14.

The central focus of this book is on arming you with the specific tools necessary to identify potential acquisition candidates, to acquire and manage those properties once identified, to implement sound techniques for creating value, and finally, to capture all of that value, or as much of it as possible, through various exit strategies. The process by which all of this can be accomplished rests, I believe, on six keys that are crucial to success. These keys do not deal with the mechanical processes involved in buying and selling apartment buildings, but are grounded in principles fundamental to life itself. These laws deal with the human psyche. They govern our thoughts, which in turn direct our actions. The failure to understand these keys—which can provide the foundation of happiness, and ultimately of success—will almost certainly guarantee your defeat.

The Six Keys to Success

1. Understanding risk
2. Overcoming fear of failure
3. Mastering courage
4. Accepting responsibility
5. Willingness to persevere
6. Defining your sense of purpose

After completing the book on buying and selling apartments, I wrote *The Complete Guide to Flipping Properties.* In Chapter 11, the concluding chapter, I wrote about the three principles of power. Following is an excerpt taken from Chapter 11.

In this chapter, I will discuss what I refer to as the three principles of power. These three principles have absolutely nothing to do with real estate in particular, yet everything to do with your success in it. For that matter, the three principles of power can be applied to any business or profession and are not just limited to real estate. Furthermore, these laws can be used in your personal life and, when properly applied, can be a source of great joy and happiness to you and to those with whom you associate.

Although I have a passion for investing in real estate, the things that I write in this chapter are far more important to me than finding the next house to buy or sell. These principles lie at the very core of my belief system. They are an integral part of who I am. They are what compel me each and every day to strive for a perfection that I know I will never achieve in this life. It is my hope to inspire you to incorporate these three principles of power into your belief system. Doing so will enable you to reach the highest level of achievement of which you are truly capable. You will be empowered to fulfill the measure of your creation, to reach your potential, and to enjoy the abundant gifts life has to offer.

The Three Principles of Power

1. The Principle of Vision
2. The Principle of Passion
3. The Principle of Autonomy

By now you are probably beginning to get the idea. The first 13 chapters of this book have been devoted to the topic of real estate finance and, more specifically, how to analyze single-family, multi-family, and commercial investment properties. In Chapter 14, it is my desire to provide you with something more than just the how-tos of real estate finance, just as I did in the concluding chapters of previous books. It is my heartfelt belief that each of us needs to understand a body of knowledge outside of our chosen profession that deals more specifically with various factors that can help prepare us to become successful. If I can offer even one bit of advice that will help you to achieve your goals, whatever they may be, then the time I have taken to write this chapter will have been worth every minute of it.

DESTINED FOR GREATNESS

Upon graduating from college, my lovely wife, Nancy, presented me with a gift that I still use and cherish to this day. It is a handsome gold and silver wristwatch bearing the academic seal of Rice University on its face. Inscribed on the back of the watch are the inspiring words of a wife's faith and confidence in her husband—*SHB, Class of '94, Destined for Greatness.* In a concerted effort to live up to her expectations of me, I have often thought about what exactly the phrase "destined for greatness" means. One might presuppose the phrase refers to attaining a high station or position in life: an executive of a Fortune 500 company, perhaps a congressional leader such as a representative or senator, maybe even a cabinet member or personal aide to the president. Over the years, however, I have come to conclude that greatness is not found in the high positions of the world—except in the eyes of man—but rather that it lies within a person's heart. Greatness lies in the small acts of kindness we demonstrate for our fellow man on a daily basis. Greatness lies in the humility, compassion, and charity we exhibit toward our friends and neighbors. Greatness lies within each of us.

Although investing in real estate is a wonderful thing, in reality it has very little to do with achieving greatness or discovering our true purpose in life. It seems that most of the real estate books and courses available from late-night TV gurus promote the notion of getting rich as a means of achieving true happiness in life. Proponents of this theory are largely mistaken. While real estate is one of the most effective vehicles you can use to accumulate wealth, have you ever stopped to really think about why you want to become wealthy in the first place? Is it because you are dreaming of a new car, perhaps a new boat, or even a larger house? Although these are worthwhile goals, there is far more to life than accumulating material goods.

I am confident that many of you have already determined where in life you want to go, that is, you have established well-defined goals and have a plan of action for your journey in life. While it is important that you have determined *where* in life you want to go, what is even more important is *why* you want to go there. If you have not yet set a course for yourself in life, I encourage you to do so. With no clear direction, you will find yourself wandering aimlessly from day to day, being tossed to and fro across life's waters as the wind and rain descend unmercifully upon you. If you have already set your course of action and have determined *where* your journey in life will take you, then I encourage you to establish *why* you have chosen your particular course, if you have not already done so. What compels you each and every day to pursue your life's dream? Why have you chosen this particular course? What do you really want to accomplish? Without truly understanding your own underlying motives, chances are the first storm that comes along will dash your hopes and dreams, just as a ship traveling across the ocean can be dashed by torrential rains.

Please allow me to be so bold as to suggest a worthy and noble cause for seeking wealth. Each one of us has been blessed with a unique set of gifts and talents. For each one of us who has been granted the ability to accumulate wealth, there are at least a thousand others who have not. With the blessing of wealth also comes the burden of responsibility. Each one of us has the capacity to bless the lives of those around us who are perhaps less fortunate than we are. Through our own generosity, we have the ability to show forth an increase in love to many who are in need. Religious leader Gordon B. Hinckley relates the following story in the December 2000 issue of a magazine called *The Ensign*. It is a powerfully moving story of love and compassion, a fine example of our ability to reach out to others who are in need.

Years ago there was a little one-room schoolhouse in the mountains of Virginia where the boys were so rough that no teacher had been able to handle them. A young, inexperienced teacher applied, and the old director scanned him and asked, "Young fellow, do you know that you are asking for an awful beating? Every teacher that we have had here for years has had to take one." "I will risk it," he replied

The first day of school came, and the teacher appeared for duty. One big fellow named Tom whispered, "I won't need any help with this one. I can lick him myself." The teacher said, "Good morning, boys, we have come to conduct school." They yelled and made fun at the top of their voices. "Now, I want a good school, but I confess that I do not know how unless you help me. Suppose we have a few rules. You tell me, and I will write them on the blackboard." One fellow yelled, "No stealing!" Another yelled, "On time." Finally, ten rules appeared on the blackboard. "Now," said the teacher, "a law is not good unless there is a penalty attached. What shall we do with one who breaks the rules?" "Beat him across the back ten times without his coat on," came the response from the class. "That is pretty severe, boys. Are you sure that you are ready to stand by it?" Another yelled, "I second the motion," and the teacher said, "All right, we will live by them! Class, come to order!"

In a day or so, "Big Tom" found that his lunch had been stolen. The thief was located—a little hungry fellow, about ten years old. "We have found the thief and he must be punished according to your rule—ten stripes across the back. Jim, come up here!" the teacher said. The little fellow, trembling, came up slowly with a big coat fastened up to his neck and pleaded, "Teacher, you can lick me as hard as you like, but please, don't take my coat off!" "Take your coat off," the teacher said. "You helped make the rules!" "Oh, teacher, don't make me!" He began to unbutton, and what did the teacher see? The boy had no shirt on, and revealed a bony little crippled body. "How can I whip this child?" he thought. "But I must, I must do something if I am to keep this school."

Everything was quiet as death. "How come you aren't wearing a shirt, Jim?" He replied, "My father died and my mother is very poor. I have only one shirt and she is washing it today, and I wore my brother's big coat to keep me warm." The teacher, with rod in hand, hesitated. Just then "Big Tom" jumped to his feet and said, "Teacher, if you don't object, I will take Jim's licking for him." "Very well, there is a certain law that one can become a substitute for another. Are you all agreed?" Off came Tom's coat, and after five strokes the rod broke! The teacher bowed his head in his hands and thought, "How can I finish this awful task?" Then he heard the class sobbing, and what did he see? Little Jim had reached up and caught Tom with both arms around his neck. "Tom, I'm sorry that I stole your lunch, but I was awful hungry. Tom, I will love you till I die for taking my licking for me! Yes, I will love you forever!"

What a tremendous example of love Big Tom is to us. His heart was full of compassion for his frail little friend named Jim. Who would have thought that even one of these rough-and-tumble boys was capable of demonstrating such charity for another person? So it is with each of us. We have the capacity to "take Little Jim's licking for him" by simply reaching out to embrace those around us. It is not necessary that our acts of kindness be on a large and grandiose scale. It is the simple acts of kindness toward others each and every day that make a difference. It is tying your child's shoelace, or helping your spouse with the dishes, or shoveling the snow for the little old widow across the street. Surely greatness lies within these simple acts of benevolence.

The law of love centers around our capacity to extend charity and compassion toward one another. This includes our family, friends, and business associates. When we demonstrate our love toward others through our actions, it is almost certain to be returned to us in one form or another. The law of love implies that some form of action be required of us. The following principle is fundamental to a proper understanding of what it means to love someone: *Love is a verb that requires action.* What you *feel* inside is the fruit of that love. This principle is so important, it bears repeating: *Love is a verb that requires action.* What you *feel* inside is the fruit of that love. So many people maintain the mistaken notion that to love someone is to really like them a great deal. While this is a good start, there is much more to love than that. According to the principle, we must demonstrate our love for others through our actions.

To love our children, for example, means to show that love by providing some level of service in their behalf. From the time our children are born, we are continuously in their service. We feed them, change their diapers, bathe them, clothe them, teach them, and play with them. We care for them when they are sick, we comfort them, and we pray for them. Through these many daily acts of service, we are *loving* them. The good feelings we have inside are the fruit of that love. For those of you who are parents, take a minute to seriously reflect on this truly remarkable and profound principle of love. Of all the people you know and care for, my guess is that your feelings of love are probably the strongest for your children. Of course you have feelings of love for your parents and of course you have feelings of love for your spouse, but if you are like me, the feelings of love you have for your children are unlike any that you have ever before experienced.

Children are the essence of life. They are the hope of the future. Greatness lies within each of them. I have three wonderful children myself. I have been blessed with three fine sons. They are Philip who is age seven, Samuel who is age five, and my little Benjamin who is age one. These boys have added a whole new dimension to the meaning of love for me and my wife Nancy. I am especially impressed with feelings of love for Ben, who is fresh from the presence of our Heavenly Father. When I gaze into my little Ben's beautiful, blue eyes, it is like peering directly into the windows of heaven, through which I can see clear through to eternity. He is completely pure and innocent, undefiled by the stains of the world. I often lie awake at night after he has gone to sleep and look with awe and wonderment at this beautiful child God has entrusted into my care. I marvel at the purity and virtue that radiates from his countenance. I marvel at his complete and total trust in me. As he reaches up to me with his tiny hands, he looks to me for strength, for guidance, and for love. And when he is especially happy, his squeals of delight and laughter fill my soul with indescribable joy.

These overwhelming feelings of intense love I have for him, as well as for my other sons, stem from my service to them each and every day. These daily acts of service are simplistic in nature and include small things such as helping them get dressed in the morning, reading with them during the day, and kneeling with them in prayer at night. It is the small and consistent acts of kindness and love that your children will remember the most about you. I encourage you to take time for them each and every day. Greatness lies in the gift of love and service to your children. Best of all, this gift of love costs you nothing but your time. Showering your children with material things such as toys and bikes is not the way to their hearts. Shower them instead with your love.

In *The Complete Guide to Buying and Selling Apartment Buildings,* I wrote the following words:

Albert Einstein provides some insight into man's purpose in life. He states, "The most important human endeavor is the striving for morality in our actions. Our inner balance and even our very existence depend on it. Only morality in our actions can give beauty and dignity to life." This beauty and dignity in life Mr. Einstein refers to can provide us with a sense of peace and happiness. I believe ultimately that is exactly what each of us is striving for. I know I am. I am seeking a higher quality of life, not only for me, but for those closest to me. The process of wealth accumulation challenges us to grow in ways we never thought possible. It provides a conduit to a higher plane in life by empowering us to reach our full potential. It is simply a means to an end. Wealth enables us to enrich the lives of those around us who may not be as fortunate as we are for any number of reasons. Our purpose is much greater than to amass riches for the sake of serving only ourselves. I am not suggesting that we work hard all of our lives to accumulate wealth only to turn around and give it all away. What I am suggesting, however, is that once we are fortunate enough to have achieved our objectives, that much happiness lies in the giving of ourselves and of that which we have attained through our labors.

Embodied within this sense of purpose is the underlying catalyst which can propel us to unimaginable heights. It gives us a reason to reach far beyond what we may otherwise be capable of. As we seek to bless the lives of others, doors are opened for us from which shine bright shafts of light illuminating the way. We learn to selflessly reach beyond the scope of our own needs so that we might lift up those around us. This sense of purpose gives us hope—hope for a higher quality of life, and hope to ease the burdens of those around us who are heavy laden.

Just a few weeks ago, I had a rather unusual opportunity to "ease the burdens of those around us." While driving down the freeway, I saw a van parked on the side of the road. About a half mile past the van I saw a man and a young boy walking down the shoulder of the freeway. As soon as I saw them, I thought to myself that they were probably out of gas. I don't know why, but I felt compelled to pull over and ask them if they needed help. This impression was strong and it was almost as if I could not pass them by, so I stopped to see if they needed help. Sure enough, they had run out of gas. I took the man, whose name was Kevin, and his son, who was about six years old or so, to the gas station at the next exit. They bought a small gas can, filled it up, and afterward I took them back to their van. We had a nice visit while driving. They were very grateful for the help. I left the man and his son wondering to myself why I had bothered to stop and help. That's the first time in more than 10 years that I've stopped to assist someone on the side of the road like that, I suppose primarily out of concern for the safety of my family as well as myself. You hear stories on the news about kooks and begin not to trust anyone. I sincerely believe that most people are basically good inside, and maybe sometimes we just need to be more trusting of them. I am thankful that I had the opportunity to help this man and his son. You never know. Next time it might be me and one of my young sons stranded on the roadside hoping that a kind stranger will stop to lend a helping hand.

For many years now, I have felt an overwhelming need within my own life to give something of myself back, to be an influence for good, to repay a debt of gratitude to my Creator for all that He has given me. I wondered for almost as long how I might go about doing that. I have discovered over the years that the more I seek to align my actions with the will of my Creator, the greater is my joy and happiness. In these recent years, He has granted me the opportunity to express myself through my writings to each of you. I hope that in some small way you will have learned something that will be of value to you, something that will change your life for the better.

It is with all the energy of my heart that I hope and pray that each of us seek to find ways to lend a helping hand to our families, to our friends and neighbors, and to all those with whom we associate. I know that as we do so our own lives will be greatly blessed and that we will experience the joy and inner peace that comes with giving of ourselves. There is enough war and bloodshed throughout the world today to last a hundred lifetimes. Let us not contribute to the hatred that so violently consumes this earth. Let us instead stand up and be counted for those noble and honorable causes we know to be true and just and ever worthy of the handiwork of our Creator. As we each commit to being ambassadors of goodness and virtue, I know that together our efforts will be greatly magnified and will surely make a difference in the lives of those around us, for we are each *destined for greatness.*

The family has always been the cornerstone of American society. Our families nurture, preserve and pass on to each succeeding generation the values we share and cherish, values that are the foundation of our freedoms. In the family, we learn our first lessons of God and man, love and discipline, rights and responsibilities, human dignity and human frailty.

Our families give us daily examples of these lessons being put into practice. In raising and instructing our children, in providing personal and compassionate care for the elderly, in maintaining the spiritual strength of religious commitment among our people—in these and many other ways, America's families make immeasurable contributions to America's well-being.

Today more than ever, it is essential that these contributions not be taken for granted and that each of us remember that the strength of our families is vital to the strength of the nation.

—President Ronald Reagan

APPENDIX A

WWW.THEVALUEPLAY.COM

Current ordering information for The Value Play Rental House Analyzer, Rehab Analyzer, Income Analyzer, Refi Analyzer, and other real estate products can be found at www.thevalueplay.com.

APPENDIX B

WWW.SYMPHONY-HOMES.COM

Symphony Homes is one of Michigan's premier builders of high-quality new homes. We maintain a tradition of excellence by ensuring that each and every home we build meets our strict standards of quality. Symphony Homes is built on a foundation of three principals—quality, value, and service. From start to finish, we take care to ensure that only the best materials and the finest craftsmanship are used throughout the construction process. By partnering with key suppliers and efficiently managing our resources, we can effectively create value for home buyers by offering superior homes at competitive prices. Offering personal service to home buyers and fulfilling commitments to them allows us to provide each and every customer with an enjoyable building experience.

As a custom builder, Symphony Homes builds on home sites owned by individuals or those owned by the company. We offer new-home construction services in all of Genesee County, Lapeer County, and North Oakland County. For information regarding Symphony Homes, one of Michigan's premier builders, please log on to www.symphony-homes.com.

Catch the Symphony Homes Vision!
Log on to www.symphony-homes.com!

GLOSSARY

Real estate investors will find the Glossary helpful for understanding words and terms used in real estate transactions. However, some factors may affect these definitions. Terms are defined as they are commonly understood in the mortgage and real estate industry. The same terms may have different meanings in other contexts. The definitions are intentionally general, nontechnical, and short. They do not encompass all possible meanings or nuances that a term may acquire in legal use. State laws, as well as custom and use in various states or regions of the country, may in fact modify or completely change the meanings of certain terms. Before signing any documents or depositing any money preparatory to entering into a real estate contract, purchasers should consult with an attorney to ensure that their rights are properly protected.

Abstract of title   A summary of the public records relating to the title to a particular piece of land. An attorney or title insurance company reviews an abstract of title to determine whether there are any title defects that must be cleared before a buyer can purchase clear, marketable, and insurable title.

Acceleration clause   Condition in a mortgage that may require the balance of the loan to become due immediately in the event regular mortgage payments are not made or other conditions of the mortgage are not met.

Accounts payable   Money a business owes to its suppliers.

Accounts receivable   Money owed to a business by its customers.

Accrued interest   Interest earned but not yet paid.

Adjustable rate mortgage (ARM) loans   Loans with interest rates that are adjusted periodically based on changes in a preselected index. As a result, the interest rate on your loan and the monthly payment will rise and fall with increases and decreases in overall interest rates. These mortgage loans must specify how their interest rate changes, usually in terms of a relation to a national index such as (but not always) Treasury bill rates. If interest rates rise, your monthly payments will rise. An interest rate cap limits the amount by which the interest rate can change; look for this feature when you consider an ARM loan.

Amortization   A payment plan that enables the borrower to reduce a debt gradually through monthly payments of principal, thereby liquidating or extinguishing the obligation through a series of installments.

Amortization schedule   A table showing precisely how a loan will be repaid. It gives the required payment on each payment date and a breakdown of the payment, showing how much is interest and how much is repayment of principal.

Amortized loan   A loan that is repaid in equal payments over its life.

Annual compounding   The arithmetic process of determining the final value of a cash flow or series of cash flows when interest is added once a year

Annual percentage rate (APR)   The cost of credit expressed as a yearly rate. The annual percentage rate is often not the same as the interest rate. It is a percentage that results from an equation considering the amount financed, the finance charges, and the term of the loan.

Annuity   A stream of equal payments that lasts for a specific period of time.

Annuity in advance   An annuity that has an immediate payment, such as the day the annuity begins.

Annuity in arrears   An annuity that has the first payment due one full period from its date of commencement, such as one month from the day the annuity begins.

Application   An initial statement of personal and financial information required to apply for a loan.

Application fee   Fee charged by a lender to cover the initial costs of processing a loan application. The fee may include the cost of obtaining a property appraisal, a credit report, and a lock-in fee or other closing costs incurred during the process, or the fee may be in addition to these charges.

Appraisal   An expert judgment or estimate of the quality or value of real estate as of a given date. The process through which conclusions of property value are obtained. It is also refers to the formalized report that sets forth the estimate and conclusion of value.

Assessed value   An official valuation of property most often used for tax purposes.

Asset   Anything a business or firm owns, such as land, buildings, or equipment.

Assumption of mortgage   An obligation undertaken by the purchaser of property to be personally liable for payment of an existing mortgage. In an assumption, the purchaser is substituted for the original mortgagor in the mortgage instrument and the original mortgagor is released from further liability. In an assumption, the mortgagee's consent is usually required. The original mortgagor should always obtain a written release from further liability if he or she desires to be fully released under the assumption. Failure to obtain such a release renders the original mortgagor liable if the person assuming the mortgage fails to make the monthly payments. An assumption of mortgage is often confused with "purchasing subject to a mortgage." When one purchases subject to a mortgage, the purchaser agrees to make the monthly mortgage payments on an existing mortgage, but the original mortgagor remains personally liable if the purchaser fails to make the monthly payments. Since the original mortgagor remains liable in the event of default, the mortgagee's consent is not required on a sale subject to a mortgage. Both assumption of mortgage and purchasing subject to a mortgage are used to finance the sale of property. They may also be used when a mortgagor is in financial difficulty and desires to sell the property to avoid foreclosure.

Balance statement   A statement of the firm's financial position at a specific point in time.

Balloon mortgage   Balloon mortgage loans are short-term fixed-rate loans with fixed monthly payments for a set number of years followed by one large final balloon payment (the *balloon*) for all of the remainder of the principal. Typically, the balloon payment may be due at the end of 5, 7, or 10 years. Borrowers with balloon loans may have the right to refinance the loan when the balloon payment is due, but the right to refinance is not guaranteed.

Bankruptcy   A proceeding in a federal court to relieve certain debts of a person or a business unable to pay its debts.

Beneficiary   A person for whose benefit property or funds are placed in trust; also the recipient of funds from an insurance fund or annuity contract.

Beta coefficient   A measure of the degree of sensitivity of a security's returns to the movements in an underlying factor, such as a broad basket of stocks.

Bill of sale   A written document or instrument that provides evidence of the transfer of right, title, and interest in personal property from one person to another.

Black-Scholes pricing model   A formula used to calculate the price of an option.

Bond   Any obligation under seal. A real estate bond is a written obligation, usually issued on security of a mortgage or deed of trust.

Breach   The breaking of a law or failure of a duty, either by omission or commission; the failure to perform, without legal excuse, any promise that forms a part or the whole of a contract.

Break-even analysis   The analysis of the level of sales required for a business to exactly break even, resulting in zero profit.

Brokers   Those who engage on behalf of others in negotiations for contacts relative to property in which they have no custodial concern.

Broker, real estate   Any person, partnership, association, or corporation who, for compensation or valuable consideration, sells or offers for sale, buys or offers to buy, or negotiates the purchase or sale or exchange of real estate, or rents or offers to rent, any real estate or the improvements thereon for others.

Capital   Accumulated wealth; a portion of wealth set aside for the production of additional wealth; specifically, the funds belonging to the partners or shareholders of a business, invested with the express purpose and intent of remaining in the business to generate profits.

Capital asset pricing model (CAPM)   A model based on the proposition that any stock's required rate of return is equal to the risk-free rate of return plus a risk premium that reflects only the risk remaining after diversification.

Capital budgeting   The process of planning expenditures on assets whose cash flows are expected to extend beyond one year.

Capital expenditures   Investments of cash or other property, or the creation of a liability in exchange for property to remain permanently in the business—usually pertaining to land, buildings, machinery, and equipment.

Capitalization   The act or process of converting or obtaining the present value of future incomes into current equivalent capital value; also the amount so determined; commonly refers to the capital structure of a corporation or other such legal entity.

Capital structure   The blend of both debt and equity capital maintained by an entity.

Carrying costs   Costs that increase with increases in the level of assets such as interest, taxes, and insurance.

Cash flow   Cash generated by a business and paid to creditors and shareholders. It can be classified as (1) cash flow from operations, (2) cash flow from changes in fixed assets, and (3) cash flow from changes in net working capital.

Cash out   Any cash received when you get a new loan that is larger than the remaining balance of your current mortgage, based on the equity you have already built up in the house. The cash-out amount is calculated by subtracting the sum of the old loan and fees from the new mortgage loan.

Certificate of title   A certificate issued by a title company or a written opinion rendered by an attorney that the seller has good marketable and insurable title to the property that he or she is offering for sale. A certificate of title offers no protection against any hidden defects in the title that an examination of the records could not reveal. The issuer of a certificate of title is liable only for damages due to negligence. The protection offered a home-owner under a certificate of title is not as great as that offered in a title insurance policy.

Chain of title   A history of conveyances and encumbrances affecting the title to a particular real property.

Compounding   The arithmetic process of determining the final value of a cash flow or series of cash flows when compound interest is applied.

Compound interest   Interest paid on the original principal of an indebtedness and also on the accrued and unpaid interest that has accumulated over time.

Condominium   Individual ownership of a dwelling unit and an individual interest in the common areas and facilities that serve the multiunit project.

Consideration   Something of value, usually money, that is the inducement of a contract. Any right, interest, property, or benefit accruing to one party; any forbearance, detriment, loss or responsibility given, suffered or undertaken, may constitute a consideration that will sustain a contract.

Conventional mortgage   A mortgage loan not insured by HUD or guaranteed by the Veterans Administration. It is subject to conditions established by the lending institution and state statutes. The mortgage rates may vary with different institutions and between states. (States have various interest limits.)

Corporation   A form of business organization that is created as a separate legal entity consisting of one or more actual individuals or other entities.

Conversion clause   A provision in some **adjustable rate mortgages** (**ARMs**) that allows you to change an ARM to a fixed-rate loan, usually after the first adjustment period. The new fixed rate will be set at current rates, and there may be a charge for the conversion feature.

Covenant   An agreement between two or more persons entered into by deed whereby one of the parties promises the performance of certain acts or promises that a given state does or shall, or does not or shall not, exist.

Convertible ARMs   A type of **ARM loan** with the option to convert to a fixed-rate loan during a given time period.

Conveyance   The document used to effect a transfer, such as a deed, or mortgage.

Cost-of-funds index (COFI)   An index of the weighted average interest rate paid by savings institutions for sources of funds, usually set by members of the 11th Federal Home Loan Bank District.

Current assets   Those assets in the form of cash or that are expected to be converted to cash within the next 12-month period, such as **accounts receivable.**

Current liabilities   Those financial obligations that are expected to require cash payments within the next 12-month period to satisfy them, such as **accounts payable.**

Current ratio   A ratio used to measure the short-term solvency of a business, calculated as total current assets divided by total current liabilities.

Credit report   A report detailing the credit history of a prospective borrower that's used to help determine borrower creditworthiness.

Debt   An obligation to repay a specified amount at a specified time.

Debt service   The portion of funds required to repay a financial obligation, such as a mortgage, which includes interest and principal payments.

Deed   A formal written instrument by which title to real property is transferred from one owner to another. The deed should contain an accurate description of the property being conveyed, should be signed and witnessed according to the laws of the state where the property is located, and should be delivered to the purchaser on the day of closing. There are two parties to a deed—the grantor and the grantee.

Deed of trust   Like a mortgage, a security instrument whereby real property is given as security for a debt; however, in a deed of trust there are three parties to the instrument—the borrower, the trustee, and the lender (or beneficiary). In such a transaction, the borrower transfers the legal title for the property to the trustee, who holds the property in trust as security for the payment of the debt to the lender or beneficiary. If the borrower pays the debt as agreed, the deed of trust becomes void. If, however, the borrower defaults in the payment of the debt, the trustee may sell the property at a public sale under the terms of the deed of trust. In most jurisdictions where the deed of trust is in force, the borrower is subject to having his or her property sold without benefit of legal proceedings. A few states have begun in recent years to treat the deed of trust like a mortgage.

Default   Failure to make mortgage payments as agreed to in a commitment based on the terms and at the designated time set forth in the mortgage or deed of trust. It is the mortgagor's responsibility to remember the due date and to remit the payment prior to the due date, not after. Generally, if payment is not received 30 days after the due date, the mortgage is in default. In the event of default, the mortgage may give the lender the right to accelerate payments, take possession and receive rents, and start foreclosure. Defaults may also come about by the failure to observe other conditions in the mortgage or deed of trust.

Depreciation   Decline in value of a house due to wear and tear, adverse changes in the neighborhood, or any other reason. The term is most often applied for tax purposes.

Discount points (or points)   An up-front fee paid to the lender at the time that you get your loan. Each point equals 1 percent of your total loan amount. Points and interest rates are inherently connected: In general, the more points you pay, the lower the interest rate. However, the more points you pay, the more cash you need up front, because points are paid in cash at closing.

Down payment   The amount of money to be paid by the purchaser to the seller on the signing of the agreement of sale. The agreement of sale will refer to the down payment amount and will acknowledge receipt of the down payment. Down payment is the difference between the sales price and maximum mortgage amount. The down payment may not be refundable if the purchaser fails to buy the property without good cause. If purchasers want the down payment to be refundable, they should insert a clause in the agreement of sale specifying the conditions under which the deposit will be refunded (if the agreement does not already contain such clause). If the seller cannot deliver good title, the agreement of sale usually requires the seller to return the down payment and to pay interest and expenses incurred by the purchaser.

Earnest money   The deposit money given to sellers or their agents by potential buyers on signing the agreement of sale to show that they are serious about buying a house or any other type or real property. If the sale goes through, the earnest money is applied against the down payment. If the sale does not go through, the earnest money will be forfeited or lost unless the binder or offer to purchase expressly provides that it is refundable.

Economic life   The period over which a property may be profitably used or the period over which a property will yield a return on the investment over and above the economic or ground rent due to its land.

Economic obsolescence   Impairment of desirability or useful life arising from economic forces, such as changes in optimum land use, legislative enactments that restrict or impair property rights, and changes in supply and demand relationships.

Equity   The value of a homeowner's unencumbered interest in real estate. Equity is computed by subtracting from the property's fair market value the total of the unpaid mortgage balance and any outstanding liens or other debts against the property. A homeowner's equity increases as he or she pays off the mortgage or as the property appreciates in value. When the mortgage and all other debts against the property are paid in full the homeowner has 100 percent equity in that property.

Escrow   Funds paid by one party to another (the escrow agent) to hold until the occurrence of a specified event, after which the funds are released to a designated individual. In FHA mortgage transactions an escrow account usually refers to the funds a mortgagor pays the lender at the time of the periodic mortgage payments. The money is held in a trust fund provided by the lender for the buyer. Such funds should be adequate to cover yearly anticipated expenditures for mortgage insurance premiums, taxes, hazard insurance premiums, and special assessments.

Execute   To perform what is required to give validity to a legal document. To execute a document, for example, means to sign it so that it becomes fully enforceable by law.

Expected return   The average of possible returns weighted by their corresponding probability.

Fiduciary   A person to whom property is entrusted; a trustee who holds, controls, or manages for another. A real estate agent is said to have a fiduciary responsibility and relationship with a client.

Financial Accounting Standards Board (FASB)   The governing body in accounting.

Financial distress   The events that lead to the declaration of bankruptcy by a business.

Fixed rate   An interest rate that is fixed for the term of the loan.

Fixed-rate loans   Fixed-rate loans have interest rates that do not change over the life of the loan. As a result, monthly payments for principal and interest are also fixed for the life of the loan. Fixed-rate loans typically have 15- or 30-year terms. With a fixed-rate loan, you will have predictable monthly mortgage payments for as long as you have the loan.

Foreclosure   A legal term applied to any of the various methods of enforcing payment of the debt secured by a mortgage or deed of trust by taking and selling the mortgaged property and depriving the mortgagor of possession.

Functional obsolescence   An impairment of desirability of a property arising from its being out-of-date with respect to design and style, capacity, and utility in relation to site, lack of modern facilities, and the like.

Future value (FV)   The amount to which a cash flow or series of cash flows will grow over a given period of time when compounded at a given interest rate.

Generally accepted accounting principles (GAAP)   A standardized set of accounting principles and concepts by which financial statements are prepared.

General warranty deed   A deed that conveys not only all the grantor's interests in and title to the property to the grantee, but also warrants that if the title is defective or has a "cloud" on it (such as mortgage claims, tax liens, title claims, judgments, or mechanic's liens) the grantee may hold the grantor liable.

Good faith estimate   Written estimate of the settlement costs the borrower will likely have to pay at closing. Under the Real Estate Settlement Procedures Act (RESPA), the lender is required to provide this disclosure to the borrower within three days of receiving a loan application.

Grace period   Period of time during which a loan payment may be made after its due date without incurring a late penalty. The grace period is specified as part of the terms of the loan in the note.

Grantee   That party in the deed who is the buyer or recipient; the person to whom the real estate is conveyed.

Grantor   That party in the deed who is the seller or giver; the person who conveys the real estate.

Gross income   Total income before taxes or expenses are deducted.

HUD   U.S. Department of Housing and Urban Development. Office of Housing and Federal Housing Administration within HUD insures home mortgage loans made by lenders and sets minimum standards for such homes.

Income statement   The financial report that summarizes a business's performance over a specific period of time.

Interest   A charge paid for borrowing money, which is calculated as the remaining loan balance.

Interest rate   The annual rate of interest on the loan, expressed as a percentage of 100.

Interest rate cap   Consumer safeguards that limit the amount the interest rate on an ARM loan can change in an adjustment interval and/or over the life of the loan. For example, if the per-period cap is 1 percent and the current rate is 5 percent, then the newly adjusted rate must fall between 4 and 6 percent regardless of actual changes in the index.

Internal rate of return (IRR) method   A method of ranking investment proposals using the rate of return on an investment, calculated by finding the discount rate that equates the present value of future cash inflows to the project's cost.

Lease   A species of contract, written or oral, between the owner of real estate, the landlord, and another person, the tenant, covering the conditions on which the tenant may possess, occupy, and use the real estate.

Lessee   A person who leases property from another person, usually the landlord.

Lessor   The owner who rents or leases property to a tenant or lessee; the landlord.

Liabilities   The debts of a business or entity that are in the form of financial claims on its assets.

LIBOR (London Interbank Offered Rate)   The interest rate charged among banks in the foreign market for short-term loans to one another. A common index for ARM loans.

Lien   A claim by one person on the property of another as security for money owed. Such claims may include obligations not met or satisfied, judgments, unpaid taxes, materials, or labor.

Limited liability partnership (limited liability company)   A hybrid form of organization in which all partners enjoy limited liability for the business's debts. It combines the limited liability advantage of a corporation with the tax advantages of a partnership.

Limited partnership   A hybrid form of organization consisting of general partners, who have unlimited liability for the partnership's debts, and limited partners, whose liability is limited to the amount of their investment.

Line of credit   An informal arrangement in which a bank agrees to lend up to a specified maximum amount of funds during a designated period.

Liquid asset   An asset that can be converted to cash quickly without having to reduce the asset's price very much.

Loan application   An initial statement of personal and financial information required to apply for a loan.

Loan application fee   Fee charged by a lender to cover the initial costs of processing a loan application. The fee may include the cost of obtaining a property appraisal, a credit report, and a lock-in fee or other closing costs incurred during the process, or the fee may be in addition to these charges.

Loan-origination fee   Fee charged by a lender to cover administrative costs of processing a loan.

Loan-to-value ratio (LTV)   The percentage of the loan amount to the appraised value (or the sales price, whichever is less) of the property.

Lock or lock-in   A lender's guarantee of a given interest rate for a set period of time. The time period is usually that between loan application approval and loan closing. The lock-in protects you against rate increases during that time.

Marketable title   A title that is free and clear of objectionable liens, clouds, or other title defects. A title that enables owners to sell their property freely to others and that others will accept without objection.

Market value   The amount for which a property would sell if put on the open market and sold in the manner in which property is ordinarily sold in the community where the property is situated. The highest price estimated in terms of money that a buyer would be warranted in paying and that a seller would be justified in accepting, provided both parties were fully informed, acted intelligently and voluntarily, and furthermore that all the rights and benefits inherent in or attributable to the property were included in the transfer.

Meeting of minds   A mutual intention of two persons to enter into a contract affecting their legal status based on agreed-upon terms.

Modified IRR (MIRR)   The discount rate at which the present value of a project's cost is equal to the present value of its terminal value, where the terminal value is found as the sum of the future values of the cash inflows, compounded at the firm's cost of capital.

Mortgage   A lien or claim against real property given by the buyer to the lender as security for money borrowed. Under government-insured or loan guarantee provisions, the payments may include escrow amounts covering taxes, hazard insurance, water charges, and special assessments. Mortgages generally run from 10 to 30 years, during which the loan is to be paid off.

Mortgage insurance premium   The payment made by a borrower to the lender for transmittal to HUD to help defray the cost of the FHA mortgage insurance program and to provide a reserve fund to protect lenders against loss in insured mortgage transactions. In FHA-insured mortgages, this represents an annual rate of one-half of 1 percent paid by the mortgagor on a monthly basis.

Mortgage note   A written agreement to repay a loan. The agreement is secured by a mortgage, serves as proof of an indebtedness, and states the manner in which it shall be paid. The note states the actual amount of the debt that the mortgage secures and renders the mortgagor personally responsible for repayment.

Mortgage (open end)   A mortgage with a provision that permits borrowing additional money in the future without refinancing the loan or paying additional financing charges. Open-end provisions often limit such borrowing to no more than would raise the balance to the original loan figure.

Mortgagee   The lender in a mortgage agreement.

Mortgagor   The borrower in a mortgage agreement.

Negative amortization   A loan payment schedule in which the outstanding principal balance of a loan goes up rather than down because the payments do not cover the full amount of interest due. The monthly shortfall in payment is added to the unpaid principal balance of the loan.

Net cash flow   The actual net cash, as opposed to accounting net income, that a firm generates during some specified period.

Net float   The difference between our checkbook balance and the balance shown on the bank's books.

Net income   In general, synonymous with net earnings, but considered a broader and better term; the balance remaining after deducting from the gross income all expenses, maintenance, taxes, and losses pertaining to operating properties except for interest or other financial charges on borrowed or other forms of capital.

Net present value (NPV) method A method of ranking investment proposals using the NPV, which is equal to the present value of future net cash flows discounted at the marginal cost of capital.

Net present value profile A graph showing the relationship between a project's NPV and the firm's cost of capital.

Net working capital Current assets minus current liabilities.

Nominal (quoted, or stated) interest rate The contracted, or quoted, or stated, interest rate.

Nominal (quoted) risk-free rate (kRF) The rate of interest on a security that is free of all risk: kRF is proxied by the T-bill rate or the T-bond rate. kRF includes an inflation premium.

Nonassumption clause A statement in a mortgage contract forbidding the assumption of the mortgage by another borrower without the prior approval of the lender.

Normal (constant) growth Growth that is expected to continue into the foreseeable future at about the same rate as that of the economy as a whole (i.e., g is a constant).

Note An instrument of credit given to attest a debt; a written promise to pay money which may or may not accompany a mortgage or other security agreement.

Offer A proposal, oral or written, to buy a piece of property at a specified price with specified terms and conditions.

Option The exclusive right to purchase or lease a property at a stipulated price or rent within a specified period of time.

Partnership A form of business organization in which two or more people form a business.

Payment cap Consumer safeguards that limit the amount that monthly payments on an adjustable rate mortgage may change.

Since they do not limit the amount of interest the lender is earning, they may cause negative amortization.

Per diem interest   Interest calculated per day. (Depending on the day of the month on which closing takes place, you will have to pay interest from the date of closing to the end of the month. Your first mortgage payment will probably be due the first day of the following month.)

PITI   Acronym for *principal, interest, taxes, and insurance,* the components of a monthly mortgage payment.

Points   Sometimes referred to as *discount points.* A point is equal to 1 percent of the amount of the mortgage loan. For example, if a loan is for $250,000, one point is $2,500. Points are charged by a lender to raise the yield on a loan at a time when money is tight, when interest rates are high, and when a legal limit caps the interest rate that can be charged on a mortgage. Buyers are prohibited from paying points on HUD or Veterans Administration guaranteed loans (sellers can pay them, however). On a conventional mortgage, points may be paid by either buyer or seller or split between them.

Portfolio   The combined holdings of more than one stock, bond, real estate asset, or other assets owned by an investor.

Prepayment   Payment of mortgage loan, or part of it, before due date. Mortgage agreements often restrict the right of prepayment, either by limiting the amount that can be prepaid in any one year or by charging a penalty for prepayment. The Federal Housing Administration does not permit such restrictions on FHA-insured mortgages.

Prepayment penalty   Fee charged by a lender for a loan paid off in advance of the contractual due date.

Present value (PV)   The value today of a future cash flow or series of cash flows.

Prime rate   A published interest rate charged by commercial banks to large, strong borrowers.

Principal   The basic element of the loan, as distinguished from interest and mortgage insurance premium. In other words, principal is the amount on which interest is paid. The word also means one who appoints an agent to act for and in behalf of; the person bound by an agent's authorized contract.

Property   The term used to describe the rights and interests a person has in lands, chattels, and other determinate things.

Purchase agreement   An offer to purchase that has been accepted by the seller and has become a binding contract.

Real estate investment trust (REIT)   An entity that allows a very large number of investors to participate in the purchase of real estate, but as passive investors. The investors do not buy directly, but instead purchase shares in the REIT that owns the real estate investment. REITs are fairly common with the advent of mutual funds and can be purchased for as little as $10 per share and sometimes less.

Real property   Land and buildings and anything that may be permanently attached to them.

Recording   The placing of a copy of a document in the proper books in the office of the register of deeds to make a public record of it.

Redemption   The right of owner-mortgagors, or those claiming under them, after execution of a mortgage, to recover title to the mortgaged property by paying the mortgage debt, plus interest and any other costs or penalties imposed, prior to the occurrence of a valid foreclosure. The payment discharges the mortgage and places the title as it was at the time the mortgage was executed.

Refinancing   The process of paying off one loan with the proceeds from another loan.

Rescission of contract   The abrogating or annulling of a contract; the revocation or repealing of contract by mutual consent of the parties to the contract or for other causes as recognized by law.

Retained earnings That portion of the firm's earnings saved rather than paid out as dividends.

Return on assets (ROA) The ratio of net income to total assets.

Return on equity (ROE) The ratio of net income to equity; measures the rate of return on common stockholders' investment.

Revocation The recall of a power of authority conferred, or the vacating of an instrument previously made.

Special warranty deed A deed in which the grantor conveys title to the grantee and agrees to protect the grantee against title defects or claims asserted by the grantor and those persons whose right to assert a claim against the title arose during the period the grantor held title to the property. In a special warranty deed, grantors guarantee to a grantee that they have done nothing during the time they held title to the property that has impaired, or that might in the future impair, the grantee's title.

Statement of cash flows A statement reporting the impact of a firm's operating, investing, and financing activities on cash flows over an accounting period.

Statement of retained earnings A statement reporting how much of the firm's earnings were retained in the business rather than paid out in dividends. The figure for retained earnings that appears here is the sum of the annual retained earnings for each year of the firm's history.

Statute A law established by the act of the legislative powers; an act of the legislature; the written will of the legislature solemnly expressed according to the forms necessary to constitute it as the law provides.

Subordination clause A clause in a mortgage or lease whereby one who has a prior claim or interest agrees that his or her interest or claim shall be secondary or subordinate to a subsequent claim, encumbrance, or interest.

Survivorship The distinguishing feature of a tenancy by the entirety whereby, on the death of one spouse, the surviving spouse acquires full ownership.

Tax As applied to real estate, an enforced charge imposed on persons, property, or income to be used to support the state. The governing body in turn uses the funds in the best interests of the general public.

Time is of the essence A phrase meaning that time is of crucial value and vital importance and that failure to fulfill time deadlines will be considered a failure to perform the contract.

Title As generally used, the rights of ownership and possession of particular property. In real estate usage, title may refer to the instruments or documents by which a right of ownership is established (title documents), or it may refer to the ownership interest one has in the real estate.

Title insurance Protects lenders or homeowners against loss of their interest in property due to legal defects in the title. Title insurance may be issued to a mortgagee's title policy. Insurance benefits will be paid only to the "named insured" in the title policy, so it is important that an owner purchase an "owner's title policy" if he or she desires the protection of title insurance.

Title search or examination A check of the title records, generally at the local courthouse, to make sure that the buyer is purchasing a house from the legal owner and that there are no liens, overdue special assessments, or other claims or outstanding restrictive covenants filed in the record that would adversely affect the marketability or value of title.

Trust A relationship under which one person, the trustee, holds legal title to property for the benefit of another person, the trust beneficiary.

Trustee A party who is given legal responsibility to hold property in the best interest of, or for the benefit of, another. The trustee is one who is placed in a position of responsibility for another, a responsibility enforceable in a court of law.

Truth-in-Lending Act   Federal law requiring written disclosure of the terms of a mortgage (including the APR and other charges) by a lender to a borrower after application. Also requires a right-to-rescission period.

Underwriting   In mortgage lending, the process of determining the risks involved in a particular loan and establishing suitable terms and conditions for the loan.

Unimproved   As relating to land, vacant or lacking in essential appurtenant improvements required to serve a useful purpose.

Useful life   The period of time over which a commercial property can be depreciated for tax purposes. A property's useful life is also referred to as its *economic life*.

Usury   Charging a higher rate of interest on a loan than allowed by law.

Valid   Having force, or binding forces; legally sufficient and authorized by law.

Valuation   The act or process of estimating value; the amount of estimated value.

Value   Ability to command goods, including money, in exchange; the quantity of goods, including money, that should be commanded or received in exchange for the item valued. As applied to real estate, value is the present worth of all the rights to future benefits arising from ownership.

Void   That which is unenforceable; having no force or effect.

Waiver   Renunciation, disclaiming, or surrender of some claim, right, or prerogative.

Warranty deed   A deed that transfers ownership of real property and in which the grantor guarantees that the title is free and clear of any and all encumbrances.

Weighted average cost of capital (WACC)   A weighted average of the component costs of debt, preferred stock, and common equity of a business's existing projects and activities.

White knight   A company that is acceptable to the management of a firm under threat of a hostile takeover.

Working capital   A firm's investment in short-term assets—cash, marketable securities, inventory, and accounts receivable.

Working capital policy   Basic policy decision regarding (1) target levels for each category of current assets and (2) how current assets will be financed.

Worst-case scenario   An analysis in which all the input variables are set at their worst reasonably forecasted values.

INDEX

9 780471 647126